Recent Research in Psychology

Charles H. Russell   Inger Megaard

The General Social Survey, 1972–1986

The State of the American People

Springer-Verlag
New York Berlin Heidelberg
London Paris Tokyo

Charles H. Russell, Ph.D.
Inger Megaard, RN, Dipo. Hosp. Admin.
Gerentology Associates
Bethlehem, CT 06751
USA

Library of Congress Cataloging-in-Publication Data
Russell, Charles H.
  The general social survey, 1972–1986 : the state of the American
people / Charles H. Russell and Inger Megaard.
    p.   cm.—(Recent research in psychology)
  Bibliography: p.
  Includes index.
    1. United States—Social conditions—1960–1980—Public opinion.
2. United States—Social conditions—1980–   —Public opinion.
3. United States—Politics and government—20th century—Public
opinion.   4. Public opinion—United States.   5. Social surveys—
—United States.   I. Megaard, Inger.   II. Title.   III. Series.
HN59.R88 1988
306′.0973—dc19   88–4939

Camera-ready text prepared by the authors using Appleworks and Multimate.
Printed and bound by Edwards Brothers, Inc., Ann Arbor, Michigan.
Printed in the United States of America.

9 8 7 6 5 4 3 2 1

ISBN 0-387-96746-X Springer-Verlag New York Berlin Heidelberg
ISBN 3-540-96746-X Springer-Verlag Berlin Heidelberg New York

In appreciation to Professors Tom Smith of the National Opinion Research Center, University of Chicago, and Jim Davis, Harvard University, and the survey staff who have made the General Social Survey a reality with the help of the National Science Foundation.

With thanks to Professors Myra Marx Ferree, Kenneth Hadden, and Jerold Heiss of the University of Connecticut for training in contemporary research methods in the social sciences; and in acknowledgement for the support of Amjad Mahmood and Lois Timms of the Roper Center, University of Connecticut.

This project was made possible by President Richard Sanders of Mattatuck Community College and the Trustees of Connecticut Regional Community Colleges, who recognized the role of community college faculty in performing research and writing by granting the leave necessary to accomplish the work reported here.

CONTENTS

INTRODUCTION AND GUIDE TO THE TABLES

Scientific observation, it has been said, is a quest conducted with deliberateness and forethought. It has also been said that scientific research is a circular process that ends with data analysis but that must often begin with it. These two observations have motivated the publication of this introductory reference book on the results of the General Social Survey from 1972 to 1986.

In his opening essay for the 1987 Annual Review of Sociology Robert Merton expressed an idea that applies well to the current volume. No small part of inquiry in the social realm, he said, "is given over to establishing of social facts before proceeding to explain how they come to be." (Merton, 1987, p.3) The purpose of this book is to contribute to that effort.

Begun as a compilation for inductive teaching in undergraduate sociology courses, it soon became evident that the GSS data would be useful in other subjects and graduate level explorations of the social, psychological, and political experiences of the American people. Further, the general public, including journalists, policy makers, market researchers - in fact anyone interested in following indicators of trends, tastes, attitudes, and affective states of our people - will find this an invaluable basic reference work on these phenomena.

The enormous value of the General Social Survey goes far beyond its usefulness to researchers who apply sophisticated statistical techniques to the data to explore relationships and causes. More, it lies in the wide variety of topics covered, which range over poltical behavior recorded in voting in presidential elections, attitudes on public policy issues, standards regarding acceptable sexual behavior, states of inner feeling, health indicators, and religious attitudes and behavior – to mention only a few. The availabilty of these data over a period of years not only documents the present and exposes trends, but offers possibilities for studying changes in particular age groups, or cohorts, over the long term.

Why is the General Social Survey such an invaluable tool? Designed principally by Professors James Davis of Harvard University and Tom Smith of the University of Chicago and sponsored by the National Science Foundation, it has been executed annually (excepting 1979 and 1981) since 1972. The total number of completed interviews was 20,056 by 1986, with annual samples ranging from 1468 to 1713. The interviews for the survey have been carried out face-to-face, one-on-one by the staff of the National Opinion Research Center (NORC) at the University of Chicago using a standard questionnaire, including some questions originally asked in the 1930s that can be explored back to that decade. The GSS national probability sample of respondents to the survey represents high quality data on the American public residing in households and outside institutions. A recent count showed that over 1600 articles and books have drawn on GSS data, and that users have included major business corporations as well as scholars and researchers.

THE PRESENT VOLUME

The present volume is an introductory compilation of responses to 170 questions asked from the start of the survey in 1972 through 1986, and selected according to two criteria: 1) wide general interest to social scientists and to the public; 2) frequency of inclusion in the survey. GSS studies carried out for special purposes, such as the 1986 inquiry into social networks and the 1982 oversample of the black population, provided too few cases to be included in the present reference work. The data were derived from a computer tape supplied by the Roper Center at the University of Connecticut, which serves as the repository for the General Social Survey and other national polls. The Statistical Package for the Social Sciences (SPSSx) was used to process the data into tables.

The data are generally arranged and reported for all years (1972-1986), representing 13 annual surveys, for all variables. In some cases, such as the topic on income, a change of 5% or more has occurred between the early and later years of the survey. A footnote designates any table where the results changed by this or a greater percentage, and a breakdown by year groups (1972-1976, 1977-1981, 1982-1986) will be supplied at cost on request to the authors at 108 Main St. North, Bethlehem, Ct. 06751.

The age groupings used in this volume are by decades, from mid-decade to mid-decade (e.g. 25-34, 35-44, 45-54, etc.) - a method chosen because it is widely used in reporting age data. The groupings break at the fourth year (25-34) rather than at a fifth year (25-35) to avoid counting respondents twice - a 25-35 and a 35-45 grouping, for instance, would cause 35 year old respondents to be counted twice. Public opinion surveys of the GSS type usually poll only adults from age 18 and up, with the

consequence that the 18-24 year old age cluster represents
an age span of seven years rather than the ten years usual
in the other age brackets.

   While most of the questions reported in this volume
have been asked in all, or nearly all years, some have been
asked less frequently. Table headings indicate the general
range of years in which a question was asked, and a check of
the total number of cases given at the top of the right hand
column (see Legend p. xxi) of each table is desirable. This
is especially necessary when a question has been asked in
four years or less, a situation which may result in a small
number of cases in the oldest age group (e.g. table B2.10
has only 15 respondents age 85 or more because the question
involved was asked in 1986 only). Readers who wish to know
the precise years in which a question was asked may refer to
the GSS codebook described below.

   It will be noted that the figures given in the body of
the tables represent percentages. To convert these
percentages to numbers of respondents all one needs to do is
multiply the percentage in a cell times the total number of
cases given at the end of the row. The example given on the
Legend (p. 13) is for females age 45-54 who said they did
not vote in 1972 - 25.8% multiplied times the row total of
651 shows that 168 women in this age group reported not
voting.

   Occasionally specific features of the tables require
explanation. Such is the case with tables that report
levels of social activity, where the responses to
sub-elements were totalled to derive a social activity

scale. The technical procedure used in this and other such cases appears in Appendix B.

Every year the National Opinion Research Center publishes a GSS Code Book, distributed by the Roper Center, that contains annual and cumulative results of the surveys. This volume explains the sampling design, interviewer and coding instructions, changes in question wording or numbering, and other technical information. Persons interested in such matters may contact the Roper Center for Public Opinion Research, P.O. Box 440, University of Connecticut, Storrs, Ct. 06268 (ph. 203 486-4440) to obtain a copy of the code book.

In the present volume the topical structure of each chapter of tables is similar to one suggested in the General Social Survey Codebook for 1986 (readers who want information on a specific subject without using the topical structure may refer to the Index). In this structure standard types of demographic data appear with related sets of variables concerning the respondent's experience, attitudes, affective states, and views on public policy issues relevant to the topic at hand - an arrangement that provides a coherent organization of topics. Although not every subtopic appears within each topic, the general structure, along with an example from the area of COMMUNITY, appears on the next page.

TYPE OF DATA	TOPICS AND SUBTOPICS
1. TITLE OF TOPIC	– Community
2. AT BIRTH	– (no data relating to birth date reported in this topic)
3. AT AGE 16	– Size of respondent's place of residence at age 16
4. BETWEEN AGE 16 AND INTERVIEW	– Respondent experience in moving from place to place
5. STATUS, OR EXPOSURE, OR KNOWLEDGE	– Size of place and region of present residence
6. ATTITUDES OR AFFECTIVE STATES	– Satisfaction with community
7. PUBLIC POLICY	– Government spending on big cities and environment

INTERPRETATION OF DATA

This initial volume reports the data by age and gender (sex) because a more detailed breakdown (by income, education, race, religion, region) would result in a multi-volume work too cumbersome to make a reference tool for general use. If the response to the present work warrants it, further volumes with the other types of breakdowns may follow.

Reporting of the GSS data by age and gender permits comparison of the men and women at various ages of life. The noticeable differences in marital happiness reported by the two groups at different ages offers one illustration (see p. 21). Women start married life (the 18-24 age bracket) with a slightly higher percentage (71.3%) reporting a "very happy" married life than men (69.5% "very happy"). For the age 25-34 group the percentage reporting "very happy" marriages is lower for both men and women; however, the percentage for women (62.6%) is considerably less than in the 18-24 year age cluster, and is now below that for men (65.1%). Thereafter the proportion of males reporting "very happy" marriages is nearly always greater than the proportion of females.

Marital happiness also illustrates the differing features of the respective age groups. Following the drop in the proportion reporting "very happy" marriages in the first sets of age groups there is a reversal of the pattern. The proportion of both men and women reporting "very happy" marriages increases constantly until the very last set of years. For men the low is 62.6% at 45-54 years of age and the high 75.7% at age 75-84. For women the low is 60% at age 35-44 and the high 68.5% at age 75-84.

Having noted these differences by gender and age it is important to caution against hasty generalizations that attribute differences directly to either one or both of these characteristics. It is obvious that other factors than age or gender may enter the picture in explaining differences. Social scientists, in fact, point out that there are many "spurious correlations" found in data. In one such instance a high rate of alcohol consumption was immediately attributed to school teachers when a study showed that more alcohol was consumed in communities with many teachers. The actual explanation related to community income - high income communities could hire more teachers and consume more alcohol as well. This finding showed that the early conclusion attributing heavy alcohol consumtion to teachers was quite unwarranted, or spurious.

In spite of the need for caution, attempting to interpret the data can lead to one of the more pleasurable adventures in working with the General Social Survey. Often the data are quite unexpected and arresting. They easily draw one into speculations about what may be the real explanation for the statistics at hand. To engage in this kind of "research," all one has to do is think of the factors that may actually influence or cause the observed results. Having thought of what these may be, one can simply turn to tables that provide information on the other factors and see what they show. The ramifications of this sort of process are vast, and they provide deep insight if not final answers in every case.

The performance of the respective age groups on the GSS word test (p. 208) offers an example of one such search. The younger age groups generally achieve a higher score than the older ages. This type of finding has led some researchers to believe that I.Q. falls with age - as one grows older one's intelligence drops. But does it? One can begin to address this question by looking at the table that deals with levels of education (p. 83). Here one learns that the younger age groups have obtained far more years of education than their senior fellows. Levels of education, then, very likely enter the picture in explaining performance on the word test, and they may be more important than I.Q..

A final technical note on the data concerns the total number of cases for questions that have been asked in all years of the survey (1972-86, excepting 1979 and 1981). The number in this volume, 19,614, is less than the total of 20,056 given in the GSS codebook because the black oversample (354 cases) had to be excluded along with individuals (88 cases) who did not give their ages.

THE STATE OF THE AMERICAN PEOPLE

As a general rule the authors have refrained from efforts to explain the survey findings, choosing for the most part merely to describe them in the opening commentaries for each chapter. Explanatory approaches require the use of advanced statistical procedures, such as multivariate log-linear models, that are outside the purpose of a basic reference work of data like this one. It is hoped, however, that publication of this volume will make available a set of data that researchers will use for explanatory studies.

In addition, it is hazardous to attempt to generalize about the state of the American people. Obvious differences appear between the age groups, and though the sexes at each age level are quite alike there are differences in some areas. Nor does the data present findings on sub-populations, such as racial and ethnic groups, religious denominations, social classes, regions, income, educational levels, and other factors. The present volume addresses the overall picture.

Consequently, the summary of findings at this point includes only topics where a clear majority of each age and gender group has given a like response or exhibits a similar characteristic. The general areas of findings include: personal background and circumstances; attitudes on sexuality; activities; experience with crime; affective states; attitudes on public policy; and reaction to the interview. The reader will be aware that a summary based on a majority of the respondents addresses only a portion of the topics reported in this volume. In the view of the authors, however, these topics offer significant information on the American public, and its typical, enduring attitudes and feelings.

Personal Background and Circumstances (the persons who make up the majorities of respondents report as follows): respondent and respondent parents born in the U.S.; European ancestry; Protestant religious preference; reside in a place under 100,000 persons; lived with both parents until age 16; live in an average home with a telephone; married between 20 and 30; happily married, never divorced, greatly satisfied with family life; agree that children sometimes need spanking; had no military service; worked for at least a year (except age 18-24); hold or held a lower prestige job; never been on welfare or received unemployment insurance; have an income that they consider average (except men 35-54); satisfied with income; did not experience hospitalization last year; feel in good to excellent health; oppose suicide except in cases of incurable disease (less than half of the 75+ respondents approve of suicide even for this reason); believe in life after death.

Sexual Attitudes: consider sexual relations between persons 14 to 16 always wrong; sex outside of marriage is always wrong; consider homosexuality wrong; have never seen an X-rated movie; acknowledge that sexual materials (e.g. pornography) provide an outlet for bottled up impulses (less than half the women age 85 or more accept this).

Activities: hold membership in at least one organization; spend a social evening with relatives (except at age 85 or more) and friends at least once a month; get a great deal of satisfaction from friendships; watch TV 2 to 4 hours per day; get a great deal of satisfaction from hobbies; don't smoke.

Experience with Violence and Crime: have never been punched, beaten, threatened with a gun, or shot at; have not been mugged or experienced a burglary; feel safe at home.

Positive Affective States: are very happy or pretty happy; feel people are helpful and fair (less than half the 18-24 year olds share these feelings); don't feel left out of things; don't think that money, next to health, is the most important thing in life; believe there are right ways and wrong ways to make money; feel that hard work is what accounts for getting ahead in life; believe it's fair to bring a child into the world.

Negative Affective States: think that their opinion doesn't count much any more; don't know whom one can count on; feel that people don't care about others; believe that the lot of the average man is getting worse; think that officials are not interested in the lot of the average man.

Public Policy: claim to have voted in the last presidential election; think that the income tax is too high; feel that too much is being spent on foreign aid; affirm that the U.S. should be active in world affairs (except women of 65 or more); support more government expenditures for health; endorse present efforts to improve the condition of black persons; favor Social Security; believe laws requiring gun permits are necessary and support the death penalty; think that the courts are not harsh enough with criminals; oppose the legalization of marijuana; want to spend more to halt crime and drug addiction.

Response to the GSS Interview: friendly and cooperative.

Whatever the reader's motivation in resorting to this book, the authors believe that the data will prove stimulating, edifying, and meaningful. The creators of the General Social Survey have performed a major service in conceiving it, and carrying it out through NORC with the help of the National Science Foundation over so many years. This survey work, which has now spread to Europe and may become world wide, can have profound significance for the future. In a sense it is the equivalent to turning the Mt. Palomar telescope on the heavens - except in this case the phenomena being observed are people and society. The Roper Center is to be commended for its part, as is the Springer-Verlag publishing company for publishing this compilation. We can look forward to continuing good results from the outstanding work of the General Social Survey.

TABLE   LEGEND

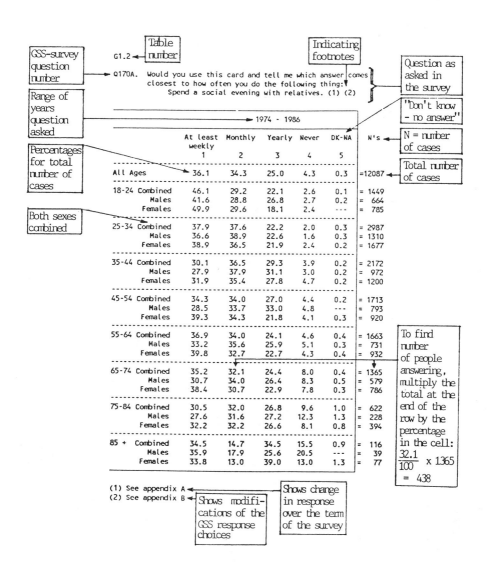

GSS-survey question number

Table number

Indicating footnotes

Question as asked in the survey

G1.2

Q170A.   Would you use this card and tell me which answer comes
closest to how often you do the following thing:
Spend a social evening with relatives. (1) (2)

Range of years question asked

"Don't know - no answer"

1974 - 1986

N = number of cases

	At least weekly 1	Monthly 2	Yearly 3	Never 4	DK-NA 5	N's	
All Ages	36.1	34.3	25.0	4.3	0.3	=12087	
18-24 Combined	46.1	29.2	22.1	2.6	0.1	= 1449	
Males	41.6	28.8	26.8	2.7	0.2	= 664	
Females	49.9	29.6	18.1	2.4	---	= 785	
25-34 Combined	37.9	37.6	22.2	2.0	0.3	= 2987	
Males	36.6	38.9	22.6	1.6	0.3	= 1310	
Females	38.9	36.5	21.9	2.4	0.2	= 1677	
35-44 Combined	30.1	36.5	29.3	3.9	0.2	= 2172	
Males	27.9	37.9	31.1	3.0	0.2	= 972	
Females	31.9	35.4	27.8	4.7	0.2	= 1200	
45-54 Combined	34.3	34.0	27.0	4.4	0.2	= 1713	
Males	28.5	33.7	33.0	4.8	---	= 793	
Females	39.3	34.3	21.8	4.1	0.3	= 920	
55-64 Combined	36.9	34.0	24.1	4.6	0.4	= 1663	
Males	33.2	35.6	25.9	5.1	0.3	= 731	
Females	39.8	32.7	22.7	4.3	0.4	= 932	
65-74 Combined	35.2	32.1	24.4	8.0	0.4	= 1365	
Males	30.7	34.0	26.4	8.3	0.5	= 579	
Females	38.4	30.7	22.9	7.8	0.3	= 786	
75-84 Combined	30.5	32.0	26.8	9.6	1.0	= 622	
Males	27.6	31.6	27.2	12.3	1.3	= 228	
Females	32.2	32.2	26.6	8.1	0.8	= 394	
85 + Combined	34.5	14.7	34.5	15.5	0.9	= 116	
Males	35.9	17.9	25.6	20.5	---	= 39	
Females	33.8	13.0	39.0	13.0	1.3	= 77	

Percentages for total number of cases

Total number of cases

Both sexes combined

To find number of people answering, multiply the total at the end of the row by the percentage in the cell:
$$\frac{32.1}{100} \times 1365 = 438$$

(1) See appendix A
(2) See appendix B

Shows modifications of the GSS response choices

Shows change in response over the term of the survey

LIST OF TABLES

COMMUNITY

Size of place statistics in the General Social Survey show an interesting difference between women and men - as age increases the proportion of men living in rural areas increases relative to the proportion of women. There is little difference between the sexes in the level of suburban dwelling, but the highest ratio of suburbanites is in the 35 to 54 age range. Overall about 25 percent of the GSS respondents live in the suburbs. Generational change appears in the comparatively high proportion of older age groups who have lived on farms in their early lives.

Regional distribution of the survey population shows the trend toward residence in the west. The high rate of mobility of the American population is evident in the comparatively large proportions of older age groups who have changed their state or city of residence at some time since age 16 (tables A1.3 and A2.2). Men report slightly higher rates of mobility than women. The GSS provides a useful contrast with the U.S. census in regard to population mobility - the census reports current changes of residence whereas the GSS reports on past changes. (U.S. Bureau of the Census, 1987, p.25)

Older respondents express greater satisfaction with their place of residence than others - a worthy subject of investigation might be to determine whether deliberate choice of place of residence on the part of the older age groups accounts for this difference, or whether greater life satisfaction in general explains it.

Comparison of the responses on improving the environment with those on solving the problems of big cities shows greater support for the environment than the cities. Women and men differ little on these issues, but the younger age groups are more willing to commit themselves to government action in both areas.

3

A1.1

Q52. NORC size of place. (1) (2)

	City GT 250K 1	City 50K- 250K 2	Suburb 3	City Section 4	City LT 50K 5	Town or Village 6	Rural 7	N's
All Ages	19.1	10.1	24.4	15.3	6.5	5.7	18.8	=19614
18-24 Combined	22.3	11.5	23.8	13.9	6.6	5.3	16.6	= 2468
Males	20.9	10.7	25.1	14.2	6.3	5.4	17.4	= 1162
Females	23.5	12.3	22.7	13.7	6.8	5.2	15.8	= 1306
25-34 Combined	20.7	10.2	24.8	16.0	6.8	5.0	16.5	= 4696
Males	20.2	10.1	24.2	15.7	7.1	5.0	17.7	= 2070
Females	21.0	10.3	25.2	16.3	6.5	5.0	15.6	= 2626
35-44 Combined	18.3	8.9	26.2	18.0	5.7	4.5	18.5	= 3451
Males	18.8	7.7	26.6	17.8	5.3	4.5	19.3	= 1552
Females	17.9	9.8	25.8	18.2	6.0	4.5	17.8	= 1899
45-54 Combined	16.7	10.2	26.7	16.1	6.0	5.9	18.4	= 2877
Males	17.1	9.6	25.0	16.6	6.2	5.9	19.5	= 1330
Females	16.4	10.7	28.1	15.7	5.9	5.9	17.3	= 1547
55-64 Combined	17.9	9.3	24.1	15.3	6.4	6.0	21.0	= 2775
Males	18.2	9.8	24.8	15.5	5.4	5.5	20.8	= 1245
Females	17.6	8.8	23.6	15.2	7.3	6.3	21.2	= 1530
65-74 Combined	17.5	11.0	20.8	12.2	7.5	8.0	23.1	= 2181
Males	17.9	9.3	19.9	12.9	6.6	8.4	25.2	= 946
Females	17.2	12.2	21.5	11.7	8.2	7.7	21.0	= 1235
75-84 Combined	19.4	10.2	20.9	12.2	7.6	8.0	21.6	= 984
Males	19.2	7.6	24.9	10.5	9.0	5.9	22.9	= 354
Females	19.5	11.6	18.7	13.2	6.8	9.2	21.0	= 630
85 + Combined	22.0	9.3	23.1	8.8	8.2	8.8	19.8	= 182
Males	16.2	11.8	22.1	5.9	10.3	7.4	26.5	= 68
Females	25.4	7.9	23.7	10.5	7.0	9.6	15.8	= 114

1973 - 1986

(1) See appendix A
(2) See appendix B

A1.2

Q54. Actual size of place of interview.

	Less than 9,999 1	10,000 - 99,999 2	100,000 - 999,999 3	One million or more 4	N's
	1972 - 1986				
All Ages	36.8	36.8	19.3	7.1	=19614
18-24 Combined	34.6	34.8	22.4	8.2	= 2468
Males	35.8	35.5	21.3	7.4	= 1162
Females	33.5	34.1	23.5	8.9	= 1306
25-34 Combined	35.0	36.4	21.1	7.6	= 4696
Males	36.2	35.3	21.1	7.4	= 2070
Females	34.1	37.2	21.0	7.7	= 2626
35-44 Combined	35.9	39.7	17.1	7.3	= 3451
Males	37.7	38.0	17.3	7.0	= 1552
Females	34.5	41.0	16.9	7.6	= 1899
45-54 Combined	36.7	39.3	16.8	7.2	= 2877
Males	37.5	38.6	16.6	7.2	= 1330
Females	36.1	39.9	16.9	7.2	= 1547
55-64 Combined	39.4	36.2	18.1	6.4	= 2775
Males	39.1	35.7	18.3	6.9	= 1245
Females	39.5	36.6	17.9	5.9	= 1530
65-74 Combined	39.8	35.4	19.0	5.8	= 2181
Males	42.0	34.1	17.4	6.4	= 946
Females	38.2	36.4	20.2	5.3	= 1235
75-84 Combined	40.0	32.4	21.0	6.5	= 984
Males	39.0	35.0	17.5	8.5	= 354
Females	40.6	31.0	23.0	5.4	= 630
85 + Combined	40.7	27.5	25.8	6.0	= 182
Males	48.5	26.5	22.1	2.9	= 68
Females	36.0	28.1	28.1	7.9	= 114

A1.3

Q51. Region of interview. (2)

	Northeast 1	Central 2	Southeast 3	West 4	N's
1972 - 1986					
All Ages	21.4	28.5	24.2	25.8	=19614
18-24 Combined	19.8	28.7	24.1	27.4	= 2468
Males	19.4	28.7	25.0	26.8	= 1162
Females	20.1	28.7	23.3	27.9	= 1306
25-34 Combined	21.2	28.1	23.0	27.7	= 4696
Males	19.9	29.7	23.5	26.9	= 2070
Females	22.2	26.8	22.7	28.4	= 2626
35-44 Combined	23.4	26.3	23.3	27.1	= 3451
Males	23.1	25.8	22.8	28.3	= 1552
Females	23.5	26.7	23.6	26.1	= 1899
45-54 Combined	22.4	28.5	23.1	26.0	= 2877
Males	21.6	29.5	22.7	26.2	= 1330
Females	23.1	27.7	23.5	25.7	= 1547
55-64 Combined	23.1	29.5	25.2	22.2	= 2775
Males	24.9	30.0	22.4	22.7	= 1245
Females	21.6	29.1	27.5	21.8	= 1530
65-74 Combined	19.1	28.9	28.0	24.0	= 2181
Males	19.2	28.0	27.4	25.4	= 946
Females	18.9	29.6	28.5	23.0	= 1235
75-84 Combined	17.8	33.2	25.6	23.4	= 984
Males	18.4	35.0	20.3	26.3	= 354
Females	17.5	32.2	28.6	21.7	= 630
85 + Combined	19.2	34.6	23.6	22.5	= 182
Males	17.6	32.4	27.9	22.1	= 68
Females	20.2	36.0	21.1	22.8	= 114

(2) See appendix B

A2.1

Q22. Which of the categories on this card comes closest to the type of place
you were living in when you were 16 years old? (1)

				1972 - 1986				
	Country, Non-Farm 1	Farm 2	Town LT 50000 3	50000 to 250000 4	Big-City Suburb 5	City GT 250000 6	DK 7	N's
All Ages	10.3	21.0	31.6	13.4	8.1	15.4	0.2	=19614
18-24 Combined	12.8	9.3	32.4	16.1	13.5	15.6	0.4	= 2468
Males	13.3	9.6	32.8	14.1	14.7	15.2	0.2	= 1162
Females	12.3	9.0	32.1	17.8	12.3	15.9	0.6	= 1306
25-34 Combined	12.2	11.6	31.9	15.7	12.3	16.2	0.2	= 4696
Males	12.3	13.5	31.2	15.4	12.9	14.6	0.1	= 2070
Females	12.1	10.1	32.4	16.0	11.9	17.4	0.2	= 2626
35-44 Combined	10.8	17.5	32.4	14.1	9.3	15.8	0.1	= 3451
Males	11.6	19.1	31.4	13.6	9.4	14.7	0.2	= 1552
Females	10.1	16.2	33.1	14.5	9.3	16.7	0.1	= 1899
45-54 Combined	10.1	23.2	31.6	12.1	6.0	17.0	---	= 2877
Males	9.8	25.4	31.4	12.0	5.0	16.4	0.1	= 1330
Females	10.3	21.3	31.8	12.2	6.9	17.6	---	= 1547
55-64 Combined	8.3	29.6	31.5	11.7	3.4	15.2	0.2	= 2775
Males	8.7	30.1	30.4	12.0	2.9	15.7	0.2	= 1245
Females	8.0	29.2	32.4	11.4	3.9	14.8	0.3	= 1530
65-74 Combined	7.2	35.4	30.3	10.7	2.9	13.2	0.2	= 2181
Males	7.1	36.6	30.5	9.1	2.2	14.2	0.3	= 946
Females	7.4	34.6	30.1	11.9	3.5	12.4	0.2	= 1235
75-84 Combined	6.6	40.3	29.6	9.6	2.7	11.0	0.2	= 984
Males	7.3	40.7	29.9	7.6	2.5	11.3	0.6	= 354
Females	6.2	40.2	29.4	10.6	2.9	10.8	---	= 630
85 + Combined	6.6	45.1	24.2	6.0	2.7	14.3	1.1	= 182
Males	11.8	52.9	19.1	5.9	---	10.3	---	= 68
Females	3.5	40.4	27.2	6.1	4.4	16.7	1.8	= 114

(1) See appendix A

A2.2

Q23. In what state or foreign country were you living when you were
      16 years old? (2)

	1972 - 1986					
	Northeast 1	Central 2	Southeast 3	West 4	Foreign 5	N's
All Ages	21.4	30.0	23.9	20.5	4.2	=19614
18-24 Combined	20.0	29.9	23.1	25.0	1.9	= 2468
Males	19.4	29.7	24.6	24.6	1.7	= 1162
Females	20.5	30.2	21.8	25.3	2.1	= 1306
25-34 Combined	21.4	28.7	22.4	23.4	4.0	= 4696
Males	21.3	29.8	22.4	22.9	3.6	= 2070
Females	21.6	27.9	22.5	23.8	4.2	= 2626
35-44 Combined	22.8	27.0	23.2	21.7	5.4	= 3451
Males	23.3	27.4	22.4	21.9	5.0	= 1552
Females	22.4	26.6	23.9	21.5	5.6	= 1899
45-54 Combined	21.7	29.1	24.6	20.0	4.6	= 2877
Males	21.4	30.4	24.2	20.2	3.8	= 1330
Females	21.9	28.1	24.9	19.9	5.2	= 1547
55-64 Combined	23.1	32.8	24.8	15.8	3.5	= 2775
Males	26.1	33.3	22.4	15.3	2.9	= 1245
Females	20.7	32.4	26.7	16.2	4.0	= 1530
65-74 Combined	19.9	31.9	27.1	17.0	4.1	= 2181
Males	20.2	31.7	26.5	16.2	5.4	= 946
Females	19.7	32.1	27.5	17.7	3.1	= 1235
75-84 Combined	17.7	36.1	23.8	15.7	6.8	= 984
Males	18.6	37.0	17.8	16.7	9.9	= 354
Females	17.1	35.6	27.1	15.1	5.1	= 630
85 + Combined	17.0	37.9	22.0	11.5	11.5	= 182
Males	19.1	33.8	22.1	10.3	14.7	= 68
Females	15.8	40.4	21.9	12.3	9.6	= 114

(2) See appendix B

A2.3

Q23A. When you were 16 years old, were you living
in this same (city/town/county)? (1)

	1972 - 1986			
	Same city 1	Same state Diff. city 2	Diff. state 3	N's
All Ages	42.1	25.1	32.8	=19614
18-24 Combined	60.4	19.4	20.1	= 2468
Males	64.2	18.3	17.5	= 1162
Females	57.0	20.4	22.5	= 1306
25-34 Combined	44.2	25.8	30.0	= 4696
Males	45.7	24.9	29.4	= 2070
Females	43.0	26.5	30.5	= 2626
35-44 Combined	38.5	27.0	34.5	= 3451
Males	38.5	25.8	35.7	= 1552
Females	38.4	28.1	33.5	= 1899
45-54 Combined	36.7	26.0	37.3	= 2877
Males	37.4	25.3	37.3	= 1330
Females	36.1	26.6	37.2	= 1547
55-64 Combined	38.4	25.1	36.5	= 2775
Males	40.3	23.9	35.7	= 1245
Females	36.8	26.0	37.2	= 1530
65-74 Combined	38.0	25.6	36.4	= 2181
Males	37.0	24.4	38.6	= 946
Females	38.8	26.6	34.7	= 1235
75-84 Combined	36.5	24.8	38.7	= 984
Males	34.2	25.1	40.7	= 354
Females	37.8	24.6	37.6	= 630
85 + Combined	30.2	25.3	44.5	= 182
Males	27.9	29.4	42.6	= 68
Females	31.6	22.8	45.6	= 114

(1) See appendix A

A3.1

Q161A. For each area of life I am going to name, tell me how much
satisfaction you get from that area.
The city or place you live in. (2)

	1973 - 1986					
	A great deal 1	A fair amount 2	Some or little 3	None 4	DK-NA 5	N's
All Ages	47.4	38.3	11.6	2.2	0.4	=16479
18-24 Combined	31.6	45.1	18.9	4.0	0.3	= 2111
Males	30.7	45.4	21.0	2.9	0.1	= 978
Females	32.5	44.9	17.1	5.0	0.4	= 1133
25-34 Combined	36.8	45.0	15.3	2.7	0.3	= 3965
Males	34.4	46.9	15.7	2.7	0.3	= 1716
Females	38.6	43.5	15.0	2.7	0.2	= 2249
35-44 Combined	45.3	40.9	11.7	2.0	0.2	= 2930
Males	43.9	41.1	12.8	1.9	0.3	= 1322
Females	46.4	40.6	10.8	2.2	0.1	= 1608
45-54 Combined	52.6	36.4	9.4	1.3	0.4	= 2351
Males	49.9	37.9	9.9	1.9	0.5	= 1051
Females	54.8	35.2	8.9	0.8	0.3	= 1300
55-64 Combined	58.2	32.5	7.3	1.3	0.7	= 2302
Males	56.0	33.9	7.7	1.6	0.8	= 1010
Females	59.9	31.4	7.0	1.0	0.7	= 1292
65-74 Combined	63.4	27.4	6.8	1.6	0.8	= 1851
Males	63.7	27.4	6.9	1.2	0.7	= 807
Females	63.2	27.5	6.7	1.8	0.8	= 1044
75-84 Combined	63.4	29.2	5.3	1.3	0.9	= 816
Males	61.1	32.6	4.4	1.3	0.7	= 298
Females	64.7	27.2	5.8	1.4	1.0	= 518
85 + Combined	63.4	22.9	8.5	2.0	3.3	= 153
Males	61.1	31.5	5.6	1.9	---	= 54
Females	64.6	18.2	10.1	2.0	5.1	= 99

(2) See appendix B

10

A4.1

Q69B. We are faced with many problems in this country, none of
which can be solved easily or inexpensively. I'm going
to name some of these problems, and for each one I'd
like you to tell me whether you think we're spending too
much money on it, too little money, or about the right
amount.

Improving and protecting the environment

	1973 - 1986				
	Too little 1	About right 2	Too much 3	DK-NA 4	N's
All Ages	54.3	30.4	9.2	6.1	=18006
18-24 Combined	73.4	20.5	3.2	2.9	= 2268
Males	74.7	19.5	3.7	2.0	= 1049
Females	72.2	21.3	2.8	3.7	= 1219
25-34 Combined	65.6	25.7	5.5	3.3	= 4338
Males	66.7	23.7	6.8	2.7	= 1888
Females	64.8	27.1	4.4	3.7	= 2450
35-44 Combined	57.1	29.5	8.9	4.6	= 3211
Males	56.2	28.3	11.7	3.8	= 1444
Females	57.8	30.4	6.6	5.2	= 1767
45-54 Combined	48.7	33.3	12.1	5.9	= 2561
Males	47.9	31.7	15.8	4.7	= 1161
Females	49.4	34.6	9.1	6.9	= 1400
55-64 Combined	42.6	37.0	13.2	7.3	= 2523
Males	44.1	34.3	16.0	5.5	= 1119
Females	41.3	39.1	10.9	8.7	= 1404
65-74 Combined	38.0	37.1	13.5	11.4	= 2023
Males	37.5	35.8	18.0	8.7	= 872
Females	38.3	38.1	10.2	13.4	= 1151
75-84 Combined	33.6	37.2	13.1	16.2	= 909
Males	33.1	36.2	19.9	10.7	= 326
Females	33.8	37.7	9.3	19.2	= 583
85 + Combined	27.2	40.5	14.5	17.9	= 173
Males	27.0	39.7	14.3	19.0	= 63
Females	27.3	40.9	14.5	17.3	= 110

A4.2

Q69D. We are faced with many problems in this country, none of
which can be solved easily or inexpensively. I'm going
to name some of these problems, and for each one I'd
like you to tell me whether you think we're spending too
much money on it, too little money, or about the right
amount.

Solving the problems of the big cities.

	Too little 1	About right 2	Too much 3	DK-NA 4	N's
1973 - 1986					
All Ages	40.2	28.0	18.2	13.5	=18006
18-24 Combined	50.8	28.3	12.0	8.9	= 2268
Males	51.8	26.9	13.5	7.8	= 1049
Females	50.0	29.5	10.7	9.8	= 1219
25-34 Combined	45.2	29.4	15.5	10.0	= 4338
Males	43.4	30.8	18.3	7.5	= 1888
Females	46.5	28.3	13.3	11.9	= 2450
35-44 Combined	40.3	29.3	19.9	10.5	= 3211
Males	38.6	28.1	24.9	8.4	= 1444
Females	41.7	30.2	15.8	12.2	= 1767
45-54 Combined	39.4	28.6	18.9	13.1	= 2561
Males	38.6	27.0	23.9	10.5	= 1161
Females	40.0	30.0	14.7	15.3	= 1400
55-64 Combined	35.8	26.1	21.8	16.3	= 2523
Males	35.5	24.3	26.5	13.7	= 1119
Females	36.0	27.5	18.0	18.4	= 1404
65-74 Combined	31.6	26.3	21.5	20.5	= 2023
Males	32.0	25.0	27.1	15.9	= 872
Females	31.4	27.4	17.3	24.0	= 1151
75-84 Combined	26.7	25.2	20.5	27.6	= 909
Males	27.0	24.5	25.8	22.7	= 326
Females	26.6	25.6	17.5	30.4	= 583
85 + Combined	23.1	21.4	26.0	29.5	= 173
Males	22.2	20.6	28.6	28.6	= 63
Females	23.6	21.8	24.5	30.0	= 110

FAMILY AND LIFE COURSE

AGE AND SEX DISTRIBUTION; BIRTH MONTH; EARLY RESIDENCE WITH
PARENTS

The data in this volume represent the total number of
cases in all the surveys from 1972-1986 combined, and can be
compared to the U.S. census only for the entire survey
period. When this comparison is made, the age and sex
distributions closely parallel the census. (U.S. Bureau of
the Census, 1987, p.14)

The record of birth months shows that the highest rates
of birth occur in August, September, October, and March.
The matching months of conception are December, January,
February, and July.

The data on residence in early life shows that
habitation with both parents has persisted at about 75
percent for all age groups in spite of the differences in
divorce rates among the generations. For the older age
groups the reason given for not living with both father and
mother is primarily the death of a parent, whereas for the
younger ages the reason is mainly divorce or separation of
parents.

MARITAL STATUS, HAPPINESS, AND DIVORCE

The reports of marital status parallel census patterns.
(U.S. Bureau of the Census, 1987, p. 38,39) For instance,
women report earlier age of marriage than men, and the 20s
have been and remain the most common years of first
marriage. After age 65 far higher proportions of men than
women report being married. This is undoubtedly due to the
younger ages of women at time of marriage and to their

14

greater longevity. Widowhood is common for the women respondents after age 65.

In nearly every age group the percentage of men describing their marriages as "very happy" is greater than the percentage of women, which may come as a surprise to some. The pattern for both sexes is one of an initially high rate of happiness followed by a decline, and then an increase as age advances. Women start with a higher proportion reporting "very happy" marriages but then decline below men and remain below them in every age group but 45-54. The lower level of women's marital happiness after age 85 could be due to a statistically unrepresenatative, small number of cases, as well as to such other factors as ill-health on the part of one or both marital partners.

The highest rate of divorce appears in the 35-44 age group, with this group also showing the highest rate of multiple divorces. Although the young are the most favorable to easier divorce, the greatest proportion of each age group feels that divorces should be more difficult to obtain.

BIRTHRATE, FAMILY DISCIPLINE, AND FAMILY LIFE SATISFACTION

The data on siblings and the number of children the respondent has had reveals the higher birth rates and larger family sizes of past times. Attitudes on family size show a change by generation – the older age groups consider a larger number of children "ideal" than the younger age groups do. Still, contrary to what one might expect, it is the younger age groups in the child rearing years who are most inclined to agree that "a good hard spanking" is

sometimes necessary.   Women and men differ little on   this
issue.

The   figures on family life satisfaction reverse   the
position of the sexes when compared to the earlier table   on
marital happiness.   A higher percentage of women than   men
express a   great   deal   of   satisfaction   with   family   life
(except in two of the older age groups when widowhood   or
other life conditions may be factors).   When the two sets
of tables are examined together, higher ratios of both sexes
express satisfaction with family life than they express
happiness with their marriages. However, in most age groups
the   difference   between   marital   happiness   and   family
satisfaction for women is greater than it is for men,   which
suggests that family life may be more important for women
and marital happiness more important for men.

HOUSEHOLD COMPOSITION

More young persons than old live in homes with higher
numbers of residents. The peak household sizes are two and
four persons, but men are more likely than women to   live
alone in the early years of life whereas women are more
likely to live alone late in life. The vast majority of
nearly all age groups reside with related persons - living
with unrelated persons appears to be a rarity in spite of
the publicity given to alternative family life styles.

Young and old differ considerably on the question of
parents sharing homes with   grown children -   sizable
proportions of younger persons favor the idea but a majority
of the older (55+) groups do not. The presence of minors in
homes declines sharply after age 54.

DIFFICULTIES IN LIFE

The experience of diffulties in life - unemployment,
divorce, illness, and death - follows varied patterns
related to age. Unemployment and divorce are phenoma of the
earlier years of life, while deaths increase with years.
The death of a child or child's spouse is experienced by 30
percent by age 75-84 and more than 40 percent at age 85+.
Death of a spouse is consistently higher for women than for
men.

Studies have shown that death of family members and
divorce are the most traumatic experiences of life, but when
all four difficulties are combined the proportions reporting
difficulties are quite similar among all age groups.
(Holmes and Rahe, 1967, p. 216) No age is trouble free, and
the ratios of the sexes reporting difficulties are quite
alike. The most trouble free ages for individuals are
18-44, but when family members are taken into account the
most advanced years show the least experience of traumatic
events.

B1.1

Q9. Respondent's age?

| | 1972 - 1986 | | |
	Male 1	Female 2	N's
All Ages	44.5	55.5	=19614
18-24 yrs. old	47.1	52.9	= 2468
25-34 yrs. old	44.1	55.9	= 4696
35-44 yrs. old	45.0	55.0	= 3451
45-54 yrs. old	46.2	53.8	= 2877
55-64 yrs. old	44.9	55.1	= 2775
65-74 yrs. old	43.4	56.6	= 2181
75-84 yrs. old	36.0	64.0	= 984
85 & OVER	37.4	62.6	= 182

B1.2

Q10. Which month were you born in?

		Jan 1	Feb 2	Mar 3	Apr 4	May 5	Jun 6	Jul 7	Aug 8	Sep 9	Oct 10	Nov 11	Dec 12	DK-NA 13	N's
1976 - 1986														
All Ages		8.2	7.9	8.5	7.8	7.8	8.1	8.3	8.8	9.0	8.7	8.2	8.3	0.3	=13543
18-24	C	8.9	8.6	7.7	7.6	7.6	6.9	7.6	9.6	10.1	8.1	8.9	8.3	0.1	= 1637
	M	10.3	7.2	8.5	7.8	8.0	7.0	7.0	10.1	8.4	7.8	9.1	8.5	0.1	= 739
	F	7.7	9.8	7.0	7.3	7.2	6.8	8.1	9.1	11.6	8.4	8.7	8.1	0.1	= 898
25-34	C	8.5	7.9	8.6	6.9	7.0	8.5	8.8	8.8	8.9	9.2	8.0	8.6	0.3	= 3369
	M	8.4	7.5	8.6	7.2	7.2	7.6	8.7	9.0	9.5	8.9	7.6	9.3	0.3	= 1478
	F	8.5	8.2	8.6	6.6	6.9	9.1	8.8	8.7	8.5	9.4	8.3	8.1	0.4	= 1891
35-44	C	8.0	7.4	8.2	8.0	8.3	7.7	8.7	8.5	9.1	8.5	8.7	8.7	0.2	= 2424
	M	8.0	7.3	9.1	9.4	7.6	7.2	8.7	6.9	8.9	8.9	8.5	9.4	0.1	= 1090
	F	8.0	7.4	7.5	6.8	8.9	8.2	8.7	9.9	9.2	8.1	8.8	8.1	0.3	= 1334
45-54	C	8.7	8.3	9.0	8.6	8.1	8.5	8.3	8.5	7.1	8.5	8.0	8.3	0.2	= 1828
	M	8.8	7.1	9.7	8.5	9.6	8.0	7.1	7.8	7.4	9.7	8.0	8.3	---	= 834
	F	8.7	9.3	8.5	8.7	6.8	9.0	9.3	9.1	6.8	7.5	7.9	8.2	0.3	= 994
55-64	C	7.8	7.2	9.2	8.6	8.1	9.2	7.2	8.4	9.4	8.1	8.2	8.2	0.5	= 1900
	M	7.6	7.1	8.9	8.2	8.3	9.5	7.7	9.3	10.9	7.1	7.5	7.3	0.5	= 817
	F	8.0	7.3	9.3	9.0	7.8	8.9	6.8	7.7	8.3	8.9	8.7	8.8	0.6	= 1083
65-74	C	6.9	8.0	8.4	8.2	8.2	7.8	8.8	8.8	9.6	9.7	8.4	6.6	0.5	= 1505
	M	7.0	9.1	8.0	8.5	8.6	7.2	9.6	8.3	9.6	8.5	9.0	6.2	0.3	= 613
	F	6.8	7.2	8.7	8.0	7.8	8.3	8.3	9.2	9.6	10.5	8.0	7.0	0.6	= 892
75-84	C	8.7	8.3	8.9	7.4	8.6	7.9	7.6	9.4	9.0	8.6	6.4	8.4	0.8	= 734
	M	8.7	11.6	8.3	8.7	5.4	8.3	9.1	7.1	10.8	5.8	8.3	7.5	0.4	= 241
	F	8.7	6.7	9.1	6.7	10.1	7.7	6.9	10.5	8.1	9.9	5.5	8.9	1.0	= 493
85 +	C	7.5	6.8	8.2	10.3	4.8	2.1	9.6	11.6	9.6	7.5	6.8	13.0	2.1	= 146
	M	10.0	4.0	14.0	14.0	4.0	4.0	4.0	14.0	4.0	6.0	4.0	16.0	2.0	= 50
	F	6.3	8.3	5.2	8.3	5.2	1.0	12.5	10.4	12.5	8.3	8.3	11.5	2.1	= 96

B2.1.1

Q24. Were you living with both your own mother and father around the time you
      were 16? (IF NO: With whom were you living around that time?) (IF R.
      MARRIED OR LEFT HOME BY AGE 16, PROBE "BEFORE THAT.") (2)

				1972 - 1986				
	Own parents 1	One step -parent 2	Father only 3	Mother only 4	Other relative 5	Other 6	DK-NA 7	N's
All Ages	75.4	5.7	2.3	10.5	4.2	1.8	0.1	=19614
18-24 Combined	73.5	7.6	1.9	12.6	2.9	1.5	---	= 2468
Males	77.1	6.5	1.9	10.6	2.6	1.3	0.1	= 1162
Females	70.2	8.7	1.8	14.3	3.2	1.8	---	= 1306
25-34 Combined	76.6	6.0	1.9	10.9	3.2	1.3	0.1	= 4696
Males	78.2	5.5	1.7	10.0	3.0	1.5	0.1	= 2070
Females	75.4	6.3	2.0	11.6	3.4	1.2	---	= 2626
35-44 Combined	76.0	6.1	1.2	11.0	3.9	1.8	---	= 3451
Males	76.6	6.1	1.2	10.4	3.6	2.1	---	= 1552
Females	75.5	6.2	1.3	11.4	4.2	1.5	0.1	= 1899
45-54 Combined	75.4	4.8	2.3	10.8	4.8	1.9	0.1	= 2877
Males	75.9	4.6	2.3	10.3	4.9	2.0	---	= 1330
Females	74.9	5.0	2.3	11.3	4.7	1.7	0.1	= 1547
55-64 Combined	76.5	5.0	2.6	8.6	4.8	2.5	---	= 2775
Males	76.4	5.4	2.8	8.1	4.4	2.9	---	= 1245
Females	76.7	4.6	2.5	9.0	5.2	2.1	---	= 1530
65-74 Combined	73.4	5.6	4.1	9.0	5.6	2.1	0.1	= 2181
Males	74.9	5.1	4.3	7.3	5.8	2.4	0.1	= 946
Females	72.2	6.0	4.0	10.4	5.5	1.9	0.1	= 1235
75-84 Combined	73.2	4.1	4.2	10.0	6.5	2.0	0.1	= 984
Males	74.3	5.1	2.8	9.9	5.4	2.3	0.3	= 354
Females	72.5	3.5	4.9	10.0	7.1	1.9	---	= 630
85 + Combined	74.7	4.9	4.4	8.8	5.5	1.6	---	= 182
Males	73.5	5.9	4.4	7.4	4.4	4.4	---	= 68
Females	75.4	4.4	4.4	9.6	6.1	---	---	= 114

(2) See appendix B

B2.1.2

Q24A. IF NOT LIVING WITH BOTH OWN MOTHER AND FATHER: What happened? (1)

	Parent Died 1	Divorce, Separated 2	Armed Forces 3	Insti- tution 4	Other 5	DK-NA 6	N's
All Ages	51.9	37.2	0.2	0.4	8.0	2.3	= 4415
18-24 Combined	31.0	58.9	0.2	0.2	7.0	2.8	= 613
Males	31.3	57.8	0.4	---	6.4	4.0	= 249
Females	30.8	59.6	---	0.3	7.4	1.9	= 364
25-34 Combined	34.1	58.9	0.2	0.4	9.7	2.7	= 1010
Males	34.7	49.6	---	0.5	10.5	4.6	= 409
Females	33.6	55.2	0.3	0.3	9.2	1.3	= 601
35-44 Combined	46.3	42.4	0.3	0.4	7.7	2.9	= 766
Males	49.9	39.7	0.3	---	7.9	2.3	= 343
Females	43.5	44.7	0.2	0.7	7.6	3.3	= 423
45-54 Combined	60.4	30.2	0.2	0.3	7.5	1.4	= 626
Males	62.3	29.7	---	0.4	6.6	1.1	= 273
Females	58.9	30.6	0.3	0.3	8.2	1.7	= 353
55-64 Combined	69.2	20.3	---	0.9	7.9	1.7	= 581
Males	64.8	24.1	---	0.8	8.8	1.5	= 261
Females	72.8	17.2	---	0.9	7.2	1.9	= 320
65-74 Combined	73.2	16.5	0.2	0.4	7.5	2.3	= 533
Males	71.9	16.3	0.5	0.5	7.2	3.6	= 221
Females	74.0	16.7	---	0.3	7.7	1.3	= 312
75-84 Combined	79.8	10.7	---	0.4	7.8	1.2	= 243
Males	81.5	6.2	---	---	12.3	---	= 81
Females	79.0	13.0	---	0.6	5.6	1.9	= 162
85 + Combined	86.0	4.7	---	---	7.0	2.3	= 43
Males	88.9	---	---	---	11.1	---	= 18
Females	84.0	8.0	---	---	4.0	4.0	= 25

1973 - 1986

(1) See appendix A

B2.2

Q3A. IF EVER MARRIED:
      How old were you when you first married? (1)

| | 1972 - 1986 | | | | | |
	10-19 yrs 1	20-29 yrs 2	30-39 yrs 3	40 yrs & over 4	DK-NA 5	N's
All Ages	32.3	60.8	5.5	0.8	0.5	=16570
18-24 Combined	60.9	38.2	---	---	0.9	= 1003
Males	42.9	55.4	---	---	1.7	= 354
Females	70.7	28.8	---	---	0.5	= 649
25-34 Combined	36.2	62.3	1.1	---	0.3	= 3794
Males	19.5	78.6	1.8	---	0.1	= 1567
Females	48.0	50.9	0.7	---	0.5	= 2227
35-44 Combined	31.4	62.7	5.5	0.1	0.4	= 3216
Males	15.3	75.7	8.6	0.1	0.3	= 1427
Females	44.2	52.3	3.1	---	0.4	= 1789
45-54 Combined	32.2	61.0	5.6	0.9	0.3	= 2749
Males	15.0	73.8	9.1	1.8	0.4	= 1247
Females	46.5	50.3	2.7	0.2	0.3	= 1502
55-64 Combined	24.5	65.2	7.7	1.9	0.6	= 2644
Males	9.9	76.4	11.0	2.2	0.4	= 1170
Females	36.2	56.4	5.1	1.7	0.7	= 1474
65-74 Combined	27.0	59.9	10.2	2.3	0.6	= 2055
Males	9.7	71.1	14.5	4.1	0.6	= 901
Females	40.5	51.1	6.8	0.9	0.7	= 1154
75-84 Combined	24.6	60.1	11.5	2.7	1.1	= 939
Males	6.8	70.1	17.5	4.8	0.9	= 338
Females	34.6	54.4	8.2	1.6	1.2	= 601
85 + Combined	19.4	68.2	8.2	2.9	1.2	= 170
Males	9.2	75.4	4.6	7.7	3.1	= 65
Females	25.7	63.8	10.5	---	---	= 105

(1) See appendix A

B2.3

Q3. Are you currently -- married, widowed, divorced, separated, or have
you never been married? (1)

	Married	Widowed	Divorced	Separated	Never married	N's
	1	2	3	4	5	
All Ages	63.3	10.0	7.9	3.3	15.5	=19613
18-24 Combined	36.1	0.2	2.4	1.9	59.4	= 2468
Males	27.6	0.1	1.6	1.1	69.5	= 1162
Females	43.6	0.2	3.1	2.7	50.3	= 1306
25-34 Combined	67.3	0.7	8.6	4.2	19.2	= 4696
Males	66.5	0.3	6.3	2.6	24.3	= 2070
Females	68.0	0.9	10.4	5.5	15.2	= 2626
35-44 Combined	74.9	1.8	12.2	4.3	6.8	= 3450
Males	78.9	0.3	9.5	3.2	8.1	= 1552
Females	71.6	2.9	14.4	5.2	5.8	= 1898
45-54 Combined	76.2	5.1	10.7	3.5	4.4	= 2877
Males	79.8	1.9	8.6	3.5	6.2	= 1330
Females	73.1	7.8	12.6	3.6	2.9	= 1547
55-64 Combined	71.0	13.4	7.7	3.1	4.7	= 2775
Males	79.9	4.7	6.3	3.0	6.0	= 1245
Females	63.8	20.4	8.9	3.3	3.7	= 1530
65-74 Combined	56.6	30.4	4.8	2.4	5.8	= 2181
Males	76.4	12.8	3.5	2.5	4.8	= 946
Females	41.4	43.9	5.8	2.3	6.6	= 1235
75-84 Combined	35.0	56.3	2.8	1.3	4.6	= 984
Males	63.6	27.7	2.8	1.4	4.5	= 354
Females	18.9	72.4	2.9	1.3	4.6	= 630
85 + Combined	18.7	73.6	0.5	0.5	6.6	= 182
Males	39.7	52.9	1.5	1.5	4.4	= 68
Females	6.1	86.0	---	---	7.9	= 114

Column span header: 1972 - 1986

(1) See appendix A

23

B2.4

Q155. IF CURRENTLY MARRIED:
        Taking things all together, how would you describe
        your marriage? Would you say that your marriage is
        very happy, pretty happy, or not too happy? (1)

	1973 - 1986				
	Very happy 1	Pretty happy 2	Not too happy 3	DK-NA 4	N's
All Ages	65.0	31.4	3.0	0.6	=11257
18-24 Combined	70.7	26.4	2.5	0.5	= 812
Males	69.5	28.0	2.1	0.4	= 282
Females	71.3	25.5	2.6	0.6	= 530
25-34 Combined	63.7	33.1	2.7	0.6	= 2881
Males	65.1	32.4	1.9	0.6	= 1235
Females	62.6	33.6	3.3	0.5	= 1646
35-44 Combined	61.4	33.9	3.9	0.8	= 2380
Males	62.9	33.4	3.0	0.7	= 1126
Females	60.1	34.4	4.6	0.8	= 1254
45-54 Combined	63.3	32.8	3.3	0.7	= 1925
Males	62.6	34.1	2.6	0.7	= 907
Females	63.9	31.6	3.8	0.7	= 1018
55-64 Combined	67.1	29.6	2.7	0.7	= 1776
Males	68.5	29.0	1.8	0.7	= 883
Females	65.6	30.1	3.6	0.7	= 893
65-74 Combined	69.2	27.9	2.6	0.4	= 1136
Males	72.7	25.3	1.9	---	= 667
Females	64.2	31.6	3.4	0.9	= 469
75-84 Combined	73.2	24.2	1.9	0.6	= 314
Males	75.7	21.4	1.9	1.0	= 206
Females	68.5	29.6	1.9	---	= 108
85 + Combined	63.6	33.3	---	3.0	= 33
Males	65.4	30.8	---	3.8	= 26
Females	57.1	42.9	---	---	= 7

See appendix A

B2.5.1

Q3B. IF CURRENTLY MARRIED OR WIDOWED:
Have you ever been divorced or legally
separated? (1)

| | 1972 - 1986 | | | |
	Yes 1	No 2	DK-NA 3	N's
All Ages	15.7	83.5	0.8	=14378
18-24 Combined	5.1	93.9	1.0	= 895
Males	2.8	96.3	0.9	= 322
Females	6.5	92.5	1.0	= 573
25-34 Combined	13.2	85.9	0.8	= 3192
Males	11.4	87.7	0.9	= 1383
Females	14.6	84.6	0.8	= 1809
35-44 Combined	20.7	78.5	0.8	= 2647
Males	22.1	77.0	0.9	= 1230
Females	19.5	79.8	0.7	= 1417
45-54 Combined	18.6	80.6	0.8	= 2339
Males	19.5	79.4	1.1	= 1087
Females	17.7	81.7	0.6	= 1252
55-64 Combined	16.3	83.1	0.6	= 2342
Males	16.7	82.8	0.5	= 1054
Females	15.9	83.3	0.8	= 1288
65-74 Combined	15.5	83.6	0.9	= 1897
Males	14.3	84.8	0.8	= 844
Females	16.4	82.6	0.9	= 1053
75-84 Combined	13.8	85.4	0.8	= 898
Males	14.9	84.2	0.9	= 323
Females	13.2	86.1	0.7	= 575
85 + Combined	8.3	91.1	0.6	= 168
Males	9.5	88.9	1.6	= 63
Females	7.6	92.4	---	= 105

(1) See appendix A

B2.5.2

Q268. Divorces during last five years.

	None	Prior 4 years	Last year	Both	NA	
	1	2	3	4	5	N's
All Ages	89.2	6.5	2.2	0.7	1.4	= 7506
18-24 Combined	94.3	2.8	1.8	0.6	0.7	= 906
Males	97.5	1.0	1.0	0.3	0.3	= 396
Females	91.8	4.1	2.4	0.8	1.0	= 510
25-34 Combined	83.4	10.1	4.0	1.1	1.4	= 1924
Males	87.6	8.6	2.7	0.2	0.9	= 821
Females	80.3	11.2	5.0	1.7	1.7	= 1103
35-44 Combined	81.8	11.6	3.6	1.4	1.7	= 1392
Males	83.6	11.7	2.0	1.1	1.6	= 639
Females	80.3	11.4	4.9	1.6	1.7	= 753
45-54 Combined	89.0	7.1	1.1	0.4	2.4	= 970
Males	86.9	8.9	1.4	0.7	2.1	= 427
Females	90.6	5.7	0.9	0.2	2.6	= 543
55-64 Combined	95.3	2.6	0.5	0.2	1.4	= 990
Males	96.0	2.1	0.2	0.2	1.4	= 421
Females	94.7	3.0	0.7	0.2	1.4	= 569
65-74 Combined	97.0	1.2	0.2	---	1.5	= 842
Males	97.3	0.9	0.3	---	1.5	= 334
Females	96.9	1.4	0.2	---	1.6	= 508
75-84 Combined	98.5	0.7	0.2	---	0.5	= 409
Males	98.4	1.6	---	---	---	= 128
Females	98.6	0.4	0.4	---	0.7	= 281
85 + Combined	100.0	---	---	---	---	= 73
Males	100.0	---	---	---	---	= 20
Females	100.0	---	---	---	---	= 53

1978 - 1986

B2.6

Q215A. Should divorce in this country be easier or more
difficult to obtain than it is now? (1)

	1974 - 1986				
	Easier 1	More difficult 2	Stay as is 3	DK-NA 4	N's
All Ages	26.5	48.4	20.0	5.0	=13580
18-24 Combined	37.5	40.1	18.5	3.9	= 1652
Males	39.2	38.1	18.3	4.5	= 761
Females	36.0	41.8	18.7	3.5	= 891
25-34 Combined	35.2	40.8	20.1	3.9	= 3335
Males	37.1	39.4	19.7	3.8	= 1469
Females	33.7	41.9	20.5	3.9	= 1866
35-44 Combined	28.0	45.0	22.2	4.8	= 2404
Males	32.3	41.2	21.6	4.9	= 1071
Females	24.5	48.1	22.7	4.7	= 1333
45-54 Combined	21.4	51.7	22.3	4.6	= 1927
Males	24.4	50.8	19.6	5.2	= 887
Females	18.9	52.4	24.6	4.0	= 1040
55-64 Combined	19.5	56.5	18.7	5.4	= 1892
Males	21.5	54.3	18.7	5.5	= 831
Females	17.8	58.2	18.7	5.3	= 1061
65-74 Combined	16.3	58.3	18.4	7.0	= 1520
Males	18.3	57.3	17.3	7.0	= 654
Females	14.7	59.0	19.3	7.0	= 866
75-84 Combined	13.5	60.1	17.7	8.7	= 711
Males	19.2	50.8	21.9	8.1	= 260
Females	10.2	65.4	15.3	9.1	= 451
85 + Combined	11.5	61.2	15.8	11.5	= 139
Males	14.0	66.0	10.0	10.0	= 50
Females	10.1	58.4	19.1	12.4	= 89

(1) See appendix A

27

B2.7

Q7. How many brothers and sisters did you have? Please count those born
alive, but no longer living, as well as those alive now. Also include
stepbrothers and stepsisters, and children adopted by your parents. (1)

				1972 - 1986					
	None	One	Two	Three	Four	Five	Six & over	DK-NA	N's
	1	2	3	4	5	6	7	8	
All Ages	5.5	14.5	16.2	14.4	11.3	9.1	28.8	0.2	=19614
18-24 Combined	3.7	14.9	18.4	18.4	13.9	9.5	21.1	0.2	= 2468
Males	4.0	16.9	19.8	18.2	12.5	9.7	18.9	0.1	= 1162
Females	3.5	13.1	17.1	18.6	15.2	9.3	23.0	0.3	= 1306
25-34 Combined	4.8	16.6	19.6	16.1	12.1	8.6	22.0	0.1	= 4696
Males	4.6	17.3	21.2	16.6	11.8	7.5	20.9	0.1	= 2070
Females	5.0	16.1	18.4	15.7	12.3	9.6	22.8	0.1	= 2626
35-44 Combined	7.1	17.9	18.2	15.0	10.2	7.2	24.1	0.3	= 3451
Males	7.5	18.9	17.4	15.7	9.9	7.6	22.7	0.3	= 1552
Females	6.8	17.1	18.8	14.5	10.4	6.8	25.2	0.3	= 1899
45-54 Combined	6.9	15.6	15.3	12.3	11.1	9.0	29.8	0.2	= 2877
Males	7.4	15.5	15.6	12.4	10.4	9.2	29.2	0.2	= 1330
Females	6.4	15.6	15.0	12.2	11.6	8.8	30.2	0.2	= 1547
55-64 Combined	5.6	11.4	14.1	12.9	9.8	9.8	36.3	0.2	= 2775
Males	5.5	11.5	16.5	13.1	9.6	10.4	33.5	---	= 1245
Females	5.7	11.2	12.1	12.7	9.9	9.4	38.6	0.4	= 1530
65-74 Combined	4.9	9.9	10.5	11.3	11.2	11.4	40.6	0.2	= 2181
Males	5.3	9.8	10.0	11.8	10.5	11.4	40.7	0.4	= 946
Females	4.6	10.0	10.8	10.9	11.7	11.3	40.5	0.1	= 1235
75-84 Combined	4.7	8.3	11.2	11.6	10.2	9.5	44.2	0.4	= 984
Males	5.1	6.2	11.3	12.7	13.6	9.0	41.0	1.1	= 354
Females	4.4	9.5	11.1	11.0	8.3	9.7	46.0	---	= 630
85 + Combined	2.2	7.1	7.1	11.0	15.4	13.7	43.4	---	= 182
Males	4.4	7.4	4.4	8.8	11.8	16.2	47.1	---	= 68
Females	0.9	7.0	8.8	12.3	17.5	12.3	41.2	---	= 114

(1) See appendix A

B2.8

Q8.   How many children have you ever had? Please count all that were born
      alive at any time (including any you had from a previous marriage). (1)

	None	One	Two	Three	Four	Five & Over	DK-NA	N's
	1	2	3	4	5	6	7	
All Ages	26.2	15.6	23.0	15.4	8.8	10.6	0.4	=19614
18-24 Combined	70.9	18.6	7.2	1.9	0.4	----	0.9	= 2468
Males	80.2	12.0	5.1	1.2	0.2	----	1.3	= 1162
Females	62.7	24.5	9.0	2.5	0.6	0.1	0.5	= 1306
25-34 Combined	32.4	20.8	27.0	12.5	4.4	2.6	0.3	= 4696
Males	40.7	21.6	22.4	10.1	3.1	1.5	0.6	= 2070
Females	25.8	20.1	30.6	14.4	5.4	3.4	0.2	= 2626
35-44 Combined	12.5	12.7	27.6	22.8	12.1	12.1	0.2	= 3451
Males	15.4	14.2	28.9	22.0	10.2	9.2	0.1	= 1552
Females	10.1	11.4	26.6	23.5	13.7	14.4	0.3	= 1899
45-54 Combined	10.8	9.7	24.3	20.1	14.3	20.6	0.2	= 2877
Males	13.2	9.7	24.5	19.4	15.2	17.9	0.1	= 1330
Females	8.7	9.7	24.0	20.7	13.5	22.9	0.3	= 1547
55-64 Combined	16.1	13.2	23.6	18.4	12.1	16.1	0.4	= 2775
Males	16.1	11.1	23.9	19.6	13.1	16.0	0.3	= 1245
Females	16.1	14.9	23.5	17.5	11.4	16.2	0.5	= 1530
65-74 Combined	19.3	16.0	23.7	15.5	10.4	14.7	0.4	= 2181
Males	18.0	15.2	25.6	15.9	11.6	13.0	0.7	= 946
Females	20.4	16.6	22.3	15.1	9.4	16.0	0.2	= 1235
75-84 Combined	20.7	16.2	20.6	14.6	10.7	16.8	0.4	= 984
Males	20.6	15.0	20.3	18.6	11.3	13.6	0.6	= 354
Females	20.8	16.8	20.8	12.4	10.3	18.6	0.3	= 630
85 + Combined	25.8	17.0	20.3	13.2	11.0	12.6	---	= 182
Males	25.0	20.6	16.2	17.6	11.8	8.8	---	= 68
Females	26.3	14.9	22.8	10.5	10.5	14.9	---	= 114

1972 - 1986

(1) See appendix A

B3.1

Q34. Number of household members. (1)

	One	Two	Three	Four or more	NA	N's
	1	2	3	4	5	
All Ages	17.1	30.9	18.5	33.5	---	=19614
18-24 Combined	9.0	28.9	25.2	36.8	0.1	= 2468
Males	11.4	25.9	22.5	40.2	0.1	= 1162
Females	6.9	31.5	27.6	33.8	0.1	= 1306
25-34 Combined	11.7	21.2	23.2	43.8	---	= 4696
Males	16.4	23.2	22.9	37.5	---	= 2070
Females	8.1	19.7	23.5	48.7	0.1	= 2626
35-44 Combined	9.1	13.3	16.5	61.1	---	= 3451
Males	12.5	12.4	16.4	58.7	---	= 1552
Females	6.3	14.1	16.5	63.1	0.1	= 1899
45-54 Combined	11.7	29.2	23.1	35.9	---	= 2877
Males	13.1	24.8	21.5	40.6	---	= 1330
Females	10.6	33.0	24.6	31.8	---	= 1547
55-64 Combined	19.2	53.3	15.8	11.6	---	= 2775
Males	14.3	53.0	17.3	15.4	---	= 1245
Females	23.3	53.6	14.6	8.6	---	= 1530
65-74 Combined	33.7	52.7	8.2	5.5	---	= 2181
Males	18.5	64.8	10.6	6.1	---	= 946
Females	45.3	43.5	6.3	4.9	---	= 1235
75-84 Combined	54.8	37.7	4.9	2.6	---	= 984
Males	31.9	59.0	6.2	2.8	---	= 354
Females	67.6	25.7	4.1	2.5	---	= 630
85 + Combined	62.6	28.0	7.7	1.6	---	= 182
Males	51.5	45.6	2.9	----	---	= 68
Females	69.3	17.5	10.5	2.6	---	= 114

(1) See appendix A

B2.9

Q211. What do you think is the ideal number of children for a family to have? (1)

	None	One	Two	Three	Four	5 +	AMA you want	NA	N's
	1	2	3	4	5	6	7	8	
All Ages	1.2	2.0	48.9	22.4	13.6	3.5	5.6	2.7	=15188
18-24 Combined	1.1	3.0	51.9	24.6	11.5	3.0	3.6	1.3	= 1852
Males	1.3	3.0	52.1	23.7	11.4	3.1	4.0	1.5	= 874
Females	0.9	3.0	51.8	25.4	11.6	3.0	3.3	1.1	= 978
25-34 Combined	0.9	2.9	57.8	21.0	9.5	2.1	4.2	1.5	= 3693
Males	0.8	2.8	56.0	23.3	8.7	2.6	4.2	1.6	= 1651
Females	0.9	3.0	59.3	19.2	10.2	1.6	4.3	1.5	= 2042
35-44 Combined	1.6	2.3	52.6	19.7	12.1	3.3	5.9	2.5	= 2644
Males	1.9	2.5	51.7	20.9	10.0	3.2	6.8	2.9	= 1179
Females	1.4	2.0	53.4	18.8	13.8	3.4	5.1	2.1	= 1465
45-54 Combined	1.5	1.6	46.4	22.1	15.6	3.7	6.3	2.9	= 2243
Males	2.2	2.0	46.3	22.6	12.9	3.8	6.9	3.3	= 1056
Females	0.8	1.3	46.4	21.6	17.9	3.6	5.8	2.4	= 1187
55-64 Combined	1.4	1.0	44.1	24.8	14.8	4.3	6.4	3.1	= 2144
Males	1.3	1.0	43.7	25.2	13.7	4.6	6.9	3.7	= 957
Females	1.5	1.0	44.4	24.5	15.7	4.1	6.1	2.7	= 1187
65-74 Combined	1.0	1.0	38.5	23.6	19.5	5.2	7.2	3.9	= 1678
Males	1.0	1.2	39.7	23.8	16.3	6.7	6.9	4.4	= 728
Females	1.1	0.8	37.6	23.5	22.0	4.1	7.4	3.6	= 950
75-84 Combined	1.3	0.8	33.3	24.8	20.4	5.3	8.3	5.9	= 786
Males	2.1	0.7	35.8	24.0	18.1	4.9	7.3	7.3	= 288
Females	0.8	0.8	31.9	25.3	21.7	5.6	8.8	5.0	= 498
85 + Combined	0.7	0.7	28.4	22.3	22.3	5.4	10.1	10.1	= 148
Males	---	---	27.3	25.5	21.8	1.8	10.9	12.7	= 55
Females	1.1	1.1	29.0	20.4	22.6	7.5	9.7	8.6	= 93

(1) See appendix A

B2.10

Q226. Do you strongly agree, agree, disagree, or strongly disagree
       that it is sometimes necessary to discipline a child with a
       good, hard spanking?

	1986					
	Strongly agree 1	Agree 2	Disagree 3	Strongly disagree 4	DK-NA 5	N's
All Ages	27.4	55.5	13.3	3.1	0.7	= 1463
18-24 Combined	22.1	61.8	13.2	2.2	0.7	= 136
Males	19.3	63.2	14.0	3.5	---	= 57
Females	24.1	60.8	12.7	1.3	1.3	= 79
25-34 Combined	29.3	53.8	14.2	2.4	0.3	= 379
Males	29.2	53.9	14.0	2.2	0.6	= 178
Females	29.4	53.7	14.4	2.5	---	= 201
35-44 Combined	27.6	55.5	13.3	3.0	0.7	= 301
Males	23.1	63.1	9.2	3.1	1.5	= 130
Females	31.0	49.7	16.4	2.9	---	= 171
45-54 Combined	31.4	51.1	11.2	4.8	1.6	= 188
Males	36.9	46.4	8.3	4.8	3.6	= 84
Females	26.9	54.8	13.5	4.8	---	= 104
55-64 Combined	22.4	63.8	9.8	3.4	0.6	= 174
Males	25.3	65.3	6.7	1.3	1.3	= 75
Females	20.2	62.6	12.1	5.1	---	= 99
65-74 Combined	28.8	52.5	13.6	4.0	1.1	= 177
Males	21.2	62.1	12.1	3.0	1.5	= 66
Females	33.3	46.8	14.4	4.5	0.9	= 111
75-84 Combined	26.9	48.4	22.6	2.2	---	= 93
Males	14.3	53.6	25.0	7.1	---	= 28
Females	32.3	46.2	21.5	---	---	= 65
85 + Combined	20.0	80.0	----	---	---	= 15
Males	----	100.0	----	---	---	= 1
Females	21.4	78.6	----	---	---	= 14

B2.11

Q161C. For each area of life I am going to name, tell me h
        satisfaction you get from that area.
        Your family life. (2)

	1973 - 1986				
	A great deal 1	A fair amount 2	Some or little 3	None 4	DK-l 5
All Ages	75.0	17.8	4.8	1.7	0.
18-24 Combined	69.4	23.3	5.9	0.9	0.
Males	64.2	27.0	7.3	1.3	0.
Females	74.0	20.1	4.8	0.6	0.
25-34 Combined	77.4	16.9	4.1	1.2	0.
Males	74.0	18.1	5.2	2.0	0.
Females	80.0	16.0	3.2	0.6	0.
35-44 Combined	77.8	17.1	3.8	1.0	0
Males	76.3	16.8	4.7	1.8	0
Females	79.0	17.4	3.1	0.4	0
45-54 Combined	76.5	16.6	4.7	1.7	0
Males	74.0	16.7	6.2	2.4	0
Females	78.5	16.5	3.5	1.1	0
55-64 Combined	75.9	16.3	4.3	2.5	1
Males	75.2	15.0	5.1	3.0	1
Females	76.4	17.3	3.6	2.1	0
65-74 Combined	72.7	17.5	5.6	2.6	
Males	75.6	14.9	5.2	2.6	
Females	70.5	19.5	5.8	2.7	
75-84 Combined	68.3	19.4	6.6	3.9	
Males	71.1	16.8	5.0	4.4	
Females	66.6	20.8	7.5	3.7	
85 + Combined	60.8	16.3	12.4	5.2	
Males	59.3	24.1	11.1	5.6	
Females	61.6	12.1	13.1	5.1	

(2) See appendix B

B3.2

Q34A. Number of members under 6. (1)

	1972 - 1986						
	None 1	One 2	Two 3	Three 4	4 - 5 5	NA 6	N's
All Ages	79.3	13.7	5.5	1.1	0.2	0.3	=19614
18-24 Combined	72.6	18.9	6.6	1.4	0.3	0.3	= 2468
Males	82.5	11.8	4.5	0.9	0.1	0.2	= 1162
Females	63.7	25.2	8.4	1.8	0.5	0.4	= 1306
25-34 Combined	52.0	29.1	15.0	2.9	0.4	0.6	= 4696
Males	55.5	26.5	13.9	3.2	0.3	0.5	= 2070
Females	49.2	31.1	15.9	2.6	0.6	0.7	= 2626
35-44 Combined	75.6	18.2	4.5	1.0	0.2	0.5	= 3451
Males	73.2	18.7	6.1	1.4	0.3	0.4	= 1552
Females	77.6	17.8	3.2	0.7	0.1	0.6	= 1899
45-54 Combined	93.4	5.1	1.1	0.2	0.1	0.1	= 2877
Males	92.3	6.5	0.9	0.2	0.1	0.1	= 1330
Females	94.4	3.8	1.4	0.2	0.1	0.1	= 1547
55-64 Combined	97.8	1.6	0.5	---	---	0.1	= 2775
Males	97.9	1.4	0.5	---	---	0.2	= 1245
Females	97.6	1.8	0.5	0.1	---	0.1	= 1530
65-74 Combined	98.6	1.0	0.3	---	---	---	= 2181
Males	98.5	1.1	0.4	---	---	---	= 946
Females	98.6	1.0	0.2	0.1	---	0.1	= 1235
75-84 Combined	99.3	0.6	---	---	---	0.1	= 984
Males	99.4	0.6	---	---	---	---	= 354
Females	99.2	0.6	---	---	---	0.2	= 630
85 + Combined	100.0	---	---	---	---	---	= 182
Males	100.0	---	---	---	---	---	= 68
Females	100.0	---	---	---	---	---	= 114

(1) See appendix A

B3.3

Q34B. Number of members 6 through 12 years old. (1)

		1972 - 1986					
	None 1	One 2	Two 3	Three 4	4 - 6 5	DK-NA 6	N's
All Ages	76.5	13.8	7.0	1.8	0.5	0.3	=19614
18-24 Combined	87.0	9.1	2.8	0.6	0.2	0.3	= 2468
Males	86.6	9.6	2.6	0.9	0.2	0.2	= 1162
Females	87.4	8.7	2.9	0.4	0.2	0.4	= 1306
25-34 Combined	64.1	19.7	11.9	3.0	0.6	0.6	= 4696
Males	76.2	14.1	7.2	1.8	0.2	0.5	= 2070
Females	54.6	24.1	15.6	4.0	1.0	0.7	= 2626
35-44 Combined	47.5	28.7	16.6	4.9	1.7	0.6	= 3451
Males	49.9	26.1	16.9	4.8	1.7	0.5	= 1552
Females	45.5	30.9	16.3	5.0	1.7	0.6	= 1899
45-54 Combined	79.6	14.4	4.8	0.9	0.2	0.1	= 2877
Males	77.5	15.3	5.6	1.0	0.5	0.1	= 1330
Females	81.4	13.5	4.0	0.8	0.1	0.2	= 1547
55-64 Combined	94.9	4.0	0.6	0.2	0.1	0.1	= 2775
Males	93.4	5.5	0.6	0.3	---	0.2	= 1245
Females	96.1	2.8	0.7	0.1	0.1	0.1	= 1530
65-74 Combined	97.5	1.6	0.8	---	0.1	---	= 2181
Males	97.7	1.7	0.5	---	0.1	---	= 946
Females	97.3	1.5	1.1	---	0.1	0.1	= 1235
75-84 Combined	99.0	0.9	---	---	---	0.1	= 984
Males	98.6	1.4	---	---	---	---	= 354
Females	99.2	0.6	---	---	---	0.2	= 630
85 + Combined	99.5	0.5	---	---	---	---	= 182
Males	100.0	---	---	---	---	---	= 68
Females	99.1	0.9	---	---	---	---	= 114

(1) See appendix A

B3.4

Q34C. Number of members 13 to 17 years old. (1)

	None 1	One 2	Two 3	Three 4	4 - 8 5	NA 6	N's
1972 - 1986							
All Ages	79.5	12.9	5.7	1.4	0.3	0.2	=19614
18-24 Combined	78.8	13.9	5.3	1.5	0.3	0.2	= 2468
Males	73.2	17.8	6.5	1.9	0.3	0.2	= 1162
Females	83.8	10.4	4.3	1.1	0.2	0.2	= 1306
25-34 Combined	92.0	5.9	1.5	0.3	---	0.3	= 4696
Males	95.4	3.4	0.8	0.1	---	0.2	= 2070
Females	89.3	8.0	2.1	0.3	---	0.3	= 2626
35-44 Combined	51.3	26.7	16.3	4.3	0.9	0.5	= 3451
Males	61.7	21.5	12.7	3.2	0.5	0.3	= 1552
Females	42.8	31.0	19.2	5.2	1.3	0.6	= 1899
45-54 Combined	63.9	23.1	9.8	2.4	0.5	0.2	= 2877
Males	60.8	23.7	11.9	2.9	0.6	0.2	= 1330
Females	66.6	22.7	8.1	1.9	0.5	0.3	= 1547
55-64 Combined	89.0	8.6	1.9	0.3	---	0.1	= 2775
Males	86.0	10.6	2.7	0.6	---	0.2	= 1245
Females	91.5	6.9	1.2	0.1	0.1	0.1	= 1530
65-74 Combined	95.9	3.6	0.4	---	---	0.1	= 2181
Males	95.9	3.5	0.4	0.1	---	0.1	= 946
Females	95.9	3.6	0.3	---	---	0.2	= 1235
75-84 Combined	98.5	1.0	0.2	0.2	---	0.1	= 984
Males	99.7	---	---	0.3	---	---	= 354
Females	97.8	1.6	0.3	0.2	---	0.2	= 630
85 + Combined	99.5	---	0.5	---	---	---	= 182
Males	100.0	---	---	---	---	---	= 68
Females	99.1	---	0.9	---	---	---	= 114

(1) See appendix A

B3.5

Q34D. Number of members over 17 years old. (1)

		One 1	Two 2	Three 3	4 - 8 4	NA 5	N's
\multicolumn{7}{c}{1972 - 1986}							
All Ages		21.8	59.5	12.9	5.6	0.1	=19614
18-24	Combined	13.3	48.7	23.2	14.7	0.1	= 2468
	Males	13.3	40.5	28.7	17.4	0.1	= 1162
	Females	13.3	56.0	18.2	12.3	0.2	= 1306
25-34	Combined	19.7	71.6	6.3	2.4	0.1	= 4696
	Males	17.2	72.4	7.1	3.3	---	= 2070
	Females	21.6	71.0	5.6	1.6	0.1	= 2626
35-44	Combined	17.6	67.1	11.9	3.1	0.2	= 3451
	Males	14.9	72.9	9.6	2.4	0.1	= 1552
	Females	19.7	62.5	13.8	3.7	0.3	= 1899
45-54	Combined	15.4	52.2	21.5	10.7	0.1	= 2877
	Males	14.5	54.4	20.3	10.8	---	= 1330
	Females	16.2	50.4	22.6	10.7	0.2	= 1547
55-64	Combined	20.6	59.5	14.5	5.3	0.1	= 2775
	Males	14.9	61.1	17.0	6.8	0.1	= 1245
	Females	25.3	58.2	12.4	4.0	0.1	= 1530
65-74	Combined	34.4	55.1	7.7	2.6	0.1	= 2181
	Males	18.8	67.8	10.3	3.1	0.1	= 946
	Females	46.4	45.4	5.7	2.3	0.2	= 1235
75-84	Combined	55.2	38.3	5.4	1.1	---	= 984
	Males	32.2	59.3	6.5	2.0	---	= 354
	Females	68.1	26.5	4.8	0.6	---	= 630
85 +	Combined	62.6	28.0	8.2	1.1	---	= 182
	Males	51.5	45.6	2.9	---	---	= 68
	Females	69.3	17.5	11.4	1.8	---	= 114

(1) See appendix A

B3.6

Q35A. How many persons in the household are not related to you
in any way? (1)

	1972 - 1986						
	None 1	One 2	Two 3	Three 4	4 - 8 5	NA 6	N's
All Ages	93.3	4.6	1.0	0.4	0.3	0.6	=16271
18-24 Combined	84.4	10.5	2.9	0.9	0.7	0.6	= 2246
Males	83.6	10.3	3.9	0.7	1.0	0.6	= 1030
Females	85.1	10.7	2.1	1.1	0.4	0.7	= 1216
25-34 Combined	91.4	5.9	1.2	0.4	0.3	0.8	= 4146
Males	89.2	7.5	1.6	0.7	0.5	0.5	= 1732
Females	93.0	4.8	0.9	0.2	0.2	1.0	= 2414
35-44 Combined	95.0	3.3	0.4	0.3	0.3	0.6	= 3138
Males	94.3	3.8	0.6	0.5	0.3	0.6	= 1358
Females	95.6	3.0	0.3	0.2	0.2	0.7	= 1780
45-54 Combined	96.4	2.4	0.6	0.2	0.1	0.4	= 2539
Males	95.8	2.9	0.5	0.3	0.2	0.3	= 1156
Females	96.9	1.9	0.7	0.1	0.1	0.4	= 1383
55-64 Combined	96.7	2.2	0.5	0.2	0.1	0.3	= 2241
Males	97.3	1.9	0.6	---	0.1	0.2	= 1067
Females	96.2	2.5	0.5	0.3	0.2	0.3	= 1174
65-74 Combined	96.5	2.3	0.5	0.2	0.1	0.4	= 1448
Males	97.0	1.9	0.4	0.1	---	0.5	= 771
Females	95.9	2.7	0.6	0.3	0.3	0.3	= 677
75-84 Combined	96.6	2.5	0.4	---	---	0.4	= 445
Males	97.5	1.2	0.4	---	---	0.8	= 241
Females	95.6	3.9	0.5	---	---	---	= 204
85 + Combined	95.6	4.4	---	---	---	---	= 68
Males	97.0	3.0	---	---	---	---	= 33
Females	94.3	5.7	---	---	---	---	= 35

(1) See appendix A

38

B3.7

Q171. As you know, many older people share a home with
their grown children. Do you think this is generally
a good idea or a bad idea? (1)

			1973 - 1986		
	A good idea 1	A bad idea 2	Depends 3	DK-NA 4	N's
All Ages	38.3	47.0	14.0	0.3	=11984
18-24 Combined	51.2	35.8	12.2	0.8	= 1538
Males	54.0	34.1	10.9	1.0	= 698
Females	48.8	37.3	13.2	0.7	= 840
25-34 Combined	44.5	41.3	13.7	0.6	= 2914
Males	45.4	41.6	12.4	0.6	= 1263
Females	43.7	41.1	14.7	0.5	= 1651
35-44 Combined	43.1	41.4	14.8	0.7	= 2149
Males	43.7	42.0	13.8	0.5	= 981
Females	42.6	40.9	15.7	0.8	= 1168
45-54 Combined	37.2	49.0	13.2	0.6	= 1678
Males	38.9	48.0	12.1	1.0	= 735
Females	35.8	49.7	14.1	0.3	= 943
55-64 Combined	29.5	55.4	14.3	0.8	= 1646
Males	31.3	55.0	12.7	1.0	= 722
Females	28.0	55.7	15.6	0.6	= 924
65-74 Combined	23.0	62.0	14.2	0.8	= 1336
Males	25.9	60.3	13.1	0.7	= 572
Females	20.8	63.2	15.1	0.9	= 764
75-84 Combined	21.6	59.6	18.0	0.8	= 612
Males	28.5	54.2	16.4	0.9	= 214
Females	17.8	62.6	18.8	0.8	= 398
85 + Combined	26.1	51.4	18.9	3.6	= 111
Males	17.9	66.7	15.4	---	= 39
Females	30.6	43.1	20.8	5.6	= 72

(1) See appendix A

B2.9

Q211. What do you think is the ideal number of children for a family to have? (1)

		None	One	Two	Three	Four	5 +	AMA you want	NA	N's
		1	2	3	4	5	6	7	8	
All Ages		1.2	2.0	48.9	22.4	13.6	3.5	5.6	2.7	=15188
18-24	Combined	1.1	3.0	51.9	24.6	11.5	3.0	3.6	1.3	= 1852
	Males	1.3	3.0	52.1	23.7	11.4	3.1	4.0	1.5	= 874
	Females	0.9	3.0	51.8	25.4	11.6	3.0	3.3	1.1	= 978
25-34	Combined	0.9	2.9	57.8	21.0	9.5	2.1	4.2	1.5	= 3693
	Males	0.8	2.8	56.0	23.3	8.7	2.6	4.2	1.6	= 1651
	Females	0.9	3.0	59.3	19.2	10.2	1.6	4.3	1.5	= 2042
35-44	Combined	1.6	2.3	52.6	19.7	12.1	3.3	5.9	2.5	= 2644
	Males	1.9	2.5	51.7	20.9	10.0	3.2	6.8	2.9	= 1179
	Females	1.4	2.0	53.4	18.8	13.8	3.4	5.1	2.1	= 1465
45-54	Combined	1.5	1.6	46.4	22.1	15.6	3.7	6.3	2.9	= 2243
	Males	2.2	2.0	46.3	22.6	12.9	3.8	6.9	3.3	= 1056
	Females	0.8	1.3	46.4	21.6	17.9	3.6	5.8	2.4	= 1187
55-64	Combined	1.4	1.0	44.1	24.8	14.8	4.3	6.4	3.1	= 2144
	Males	1.3	1.0	43.7	25.2	13.7	4.6	6.9	3.7	= 957
	Females	1.5	1.0	44.4	24.5	15.7	4.1	6.1	2.7	= 1187
65-74	Combined	1.0	1.0	38.5	23.6	19.5	5.2	7.2	3.9	= 1678
	Males	1.0	1.2	39.7	23.8	16.3	6.7	6.9	4.4	= 728
	Females	1.1	0.8	37.6	23.5	22.0	4.1	7.4	3.6	= 950
75-84	Combined	1.3	0.8	33.3	24.8	20.4	5.3	8.3	5.9	= 786
	Males	2.1	0.7	35.8	24.0	18.1	4.9	7.3	7.3	= 288
	Females	0.8	0.8	31.9	25.3	21.7	5.6	8.8	5.0	= 498
85 +	Combined	0.7	0.7	28.4	22.3	22.3	5.4	10.1	10.1	= 148
	Males	---	---	27.3	25.5	21.8	1.8	10.9	12.7	= 55
	Females	1.1	1.1	29.0	20.4	22.6	7.5	9.7	8.6	= 93

1972 - 1986

(1) See appendix A

B2.10

Q226. Do you strongly agree, agree, disagree, or strongly disagree
that it is sometimes necessary to discipline a child with a
good, hard spanking?

	1986						
	Strongly agree 1	Agree 2	Disagree 3	Strongly disagree 4	DK-NA 5		N's
All Ages	27.4	55.5	13.3	3.1	0.7	=	1463
18-24 Combined	22.1	61.8	13.2	2.2	0.7	=	136
Males	19.3	63.2	14.0	3.5	---	=	57
Females	24.1	60.8	12.7	1.3	1.3	=	79
25-34 Combined	29.3	53.8	14.2	2.4	0.3	=	379
Males	29.2	53.9	14.0	2.2	0.6	=	178
Females	29.4	53.7	14.4	2.5	---	=	201
35-44 Combined	27.6	55.5	13.3	3.0	0.7	=	301
Males	23.1	63.1	9.2	3.1	1.5	=	130
Females	31.0	49.7	16.4	2.9	---	=	171
45-54 Combined	31.4	51.1	11.2	4.8	1.6	=	188
Males	36.9	46.4	8.3	4.8	3.6	=	84
Females	26.9	54.8	13.5	4.8	---	=	104
55-64 Combined	22.4	63.8	9.8	3.4	0.6	=	174
Males	25.3	65.3	6.7	1.3	1.3	=	75
Females	20.2	62.6	12.1	5.1	---	=	99
65-74 Combined	28.8	52.5	13.6	4.0	1.1	=	177
Males	21.2	62.1	12.1	3.0	1.5	=	66
Females	33.3	46.8	14.4	4.5	0.9	=	111
75-84 Combined	26.9	48.4	22.6	2.2	---	=	93
Males	14.3	53.6	25.0	7.1	---	=	28
Females	32.3	46.2	21.5	---	---	=	65
85 + Combined	20.0	80.0	----	---	---	=	15
Males	----	100.0	----	---	---	=	1
Females	21.4	78.6	----	---	---	=	14

B2.11

Q161C. For each area of life I am going to name, tell me how much
satisfaction you get from that area.
Your family life. (2)

| | 1973 - 1986 | | | | | |
	A great deal 1	A fair amount 2	Some or little 3	None 4	DK-NA 5	N's
All Ages	75.0	17.8	4.8	1.7	0.7	=16479
18-24 Combined	69.4	23.3	5.9	0.9	0.4	= 2111
Males	64.2	27.0	7.3	1.3	0.2	= 978
Females	74.0	20.1	4.8	0.6	0.5	= 1133
25-34 Combined	77.4	16.9	4.1	1.2	0.3	= 3965
Males	74.0	18.1	5.2	2.0	0.6	= 1716
Females	80.0	16.0	3.2	0.6	0.1	= 2249
35-44 Combined	77.8	17.1	3.8	1.0	0.2	= 2930
Males	76.3	16.8	4.7	1.8	0.4	= 1322
Females	79.0	17.4	3.1	0.4	0.1	= 1608
45-54 Combined	76.5	16.6	4.7	1.7	0.6	= 2351
Males	74.0	16.7	6.2	2.4	0.7	= 1051
Females	78.5	16.5	3.5	1.1	0.5	= 1300
55-64 Combined	75.9	16.3	4.3	2.5	1.1	= 2302
Males	75.2	15.0	5.1	3.0	1.7	= 1010
Females	76.4	17.3	3.6	2.1	0.6	= 1292
65-74 Combined	72.7	17.5	5.6	2.6	1.6	= 1851
Males	75.6	14.9	5.2	2.6	1.7	= 807
Females	70.5	19.5	5.8	2.7	1.4	= 1044
75-84 Combined	68.3	19.4	6.6	3.9	1.8	= 816
Males	71.1	16.8	5.0	4.4	2.7	= 298
Females	66.6	20.8	7.5	3.7	1.4	= 518
85 + Combined	60.8	16.3	12.4	5.2	5.2	= 153
Males	59.3	24.1	11.1	5.6	---	= 54
Females	61.6	12.1	13.1	5.1	8.1	= 99

(2) See appendix B

B3.1

Q34. Number of household members. (1)

	1972 - 1986					
	One	Two	Three	Four or more	NA	N's
	1	2	3	4	5	
All Ages	17.1	30.9	18.5	33.5	---	=19614
18-24 Combined	9.0	28.9	25.2	36.8	0.1	= 2468
Males	11.4	25.9	22.5	40.2	0.1	= 1162
Females	6.9	31.5	27.6	33.8	0.1	= 1306
25-34 Combined	11.7	21.2	23.2	43.8	---	= 4696
Males	16.4	23.2	22.9	37.5	---	= 2070
Females	8.1	19.7	23.5	48.7	0.1	= 2626
35-44 Combined	9.1	13.3	16.5	61.1	---	= 3451
Males	12.5	12.4	16.4	58.7	---	= 1552
Females	6.3	14.1	16.5	63.1	0.1	= 1899
45-54 Combined	11.7	29.2	23.1	35.9	---	= 2877
Males	13.1	24.8	21.5	40.6	---	= 1330
Females	10.6	33.0	24.6	31.8	---	= 1547
55-64 Combined	19.2	53.3	15.8	11.6	---	= 2775
Males	14.3	53.0	17.3	15.4	---	= 1245
Females	23.3	53.6	14.6	8.6	---	= 1530
65-74 Combined	33.7	52.7	8.2	5.5	---	= 2181
Males	18.5	64.8	10.6	6.1	---	= 946
Females	45.3	43.5	6.3	4.9	---	= 1235
75-84 Combined	54.8	37.7	4.9	2.6	---	= 984
Males	31.9	59.0	6.2	2.8	---	= 354
Females	67.6	25.7	4.1	2.5	---	= 630
85 + Combined	62.6	28.0	7.7	1.6	---	= 182
Males	51.5	45.6	2.9	----	---	= 68
Females	69.3	17.5	10.5	2.6	---	= 114

(1) See appendix A

B3.2

Q34A. Number of members under 6. (1)

	1972 - 1986						
	None 1	One 2	Two 3	Three 4	4 - 5 5	NA 6	N's
All Ages	79.3	13.7	5.5	1.1	0.2	0.3	=19614
18-24 Combined	72.6	18.9	6.6	1.4	0.3	0.3	= 2468
Males	82.5	11.8	4.5	0.9	0.1	0.2	= 1162
Females	63.7	25.2	8.4	1.8	0.5	0.4	= 1306
25-34 Combined	52.0	29.1	15.0	2.9	0.4	0.6	= 4696
Males	55.5	26.5	13.9	3.2	0.3	0.5	= 2070
Females	49.2	31.1	15.9	2.6	0.6	0.7	= 2626
35-44 Combined	75.6	18.2	4.5	1.0	0.2	0.5	= 3451
Males	73.2	18.7	6.1	1.4	0.3	0.4	= 1552
Females	77.6	17.8	3.2	0.7	0.1	0.6	= 1899
45-54 Combined	93.4	5.1	1.1	0.2	0.1	0.1	= 2877
Males	92.3	6.5	0.9	0.2	0.1	0.1	= 1330
Females	94.4	3.8	1.4	0.2	0.1	0.1	= 1547
55-64 Combined	97.8	1.6	0.5	---	---	0.1	= 2775
Males	97.9	1.4	0.5	---	---	0.2	= 1245
Females	97.6	1.8	0.5	0.1	---	0.1	= 1530
65-74 Combined	98.6	1.0	0.3	---	---	---	= 2181
Males	98.5	1.1	0.4	---	---	---	= 946
Females	98.6	1.0	0.2	0.1	---	0.1	= 1235
75-84 Combined	99.3	0.6	---	---	---	0.1	= 984
Males	99.4	0.6	---	---	---	---	= 354
Females	99.2	0.6	---	---	---	0.2	= 630
85 + Combined	100.0	---	---	---	---	---	= 182
Males	100.0	---	---	---	---	---	= 68
Females	100.0	---	---	---	---	---	= 114

(1) See appendix A

B3.3

Q34B. Number of members 6 through 12 years old. (1)

	1972 - 1986						
	None 1	One 2	Two 3	Three 4	4 - 6 5	DK-NA 6	N's
All Ages	76.5	13.8	7.0	1.8	0.5	0.3	=19614
18-24 Combined	87.0	9.1	2.8	0.6	0.2	0.3	= 2468
Males	86.6	9.6	2.6	0.9	0.2	0.2	= 1162
Females	87.4	8.7	2.9	0.4	0.2	0.4	= 1306
25-34 Combined	64.1	19.7	11.9	3.0	0.6	0.6	= 4696
Males	76.2	14.1	7.2	1.8	0.2	0.5	= 2070
Females	54.6	24.1	15.6	4.0	1.0	0.7	= 2626
35-44 Combined	47.5	28.7	16.6	4.9	1.7	0.6	= 3451
Males	49.9	26.1	16.9	4.8	1.7	0.5	= 1552
Females	45.5	30.9	16.3	5.0	1.7	0.6	= 1899
45-54 Combined	79.6	14.4	4.8	0.9	0.2	0.1	= 2877
Males	77.5	15.3	5.6	1.0	0.5	0.1	= 1330
Females	81.4	13.5	4.0	0.8	0.1	0.2	= 1547
55-64 Combined	94.9	4.0	0.6	0.2	0.1	0.1	= 2775
Males	93.4	5.5	0.6	0.3	---	0.2	= 1245
Females	96.1	2.8	0.7	0.1	0.1	0.1	= 1530
65-74 Combined	97.5	1.6	0.8	---	0.1	---	= 2181
Males	97.7	1.7	0.5	---	0.1	---	= 946
Females	97.3	1.5	1.1	---	0.1	0.1	= 1235
75-84 Combined	99.0	0.9	---	---	---	0.1	= 984
Males	98.6	1.4	---	---	---	---	= 354
Females	99.2	0.6	---	---	---	0.2	= 630
85 + Combined	99.5	0.5	---	---	---	---	= 182
Males	100.0	---	---	---	---	---	= 68
Females	99.1	0.9	---	---	---	---	= 114

(1) See appendix A

B3.4

Q34C. Number of members 13 to 17 years old. (1)

	None 1	One 2	Two 3	Three 4	4 - 8 5	NA 6	N's
All Ages	79.5	12.9	5.7	1.4	0.3	0.2	=19614
18-24 Combined	78.8	13.9	5.3	1.5	0.3	0.2	= 2468
Males	73.2	17.8	6.5	1.9	0.3	0.2	= 1162
Females	83.8	10.4	4.3	1.1	0.2	0.2	= 1306
25-34 Combined	92.0	5.9	1.5	0.3	---	0.3	= 4696
Males	95.4	3.4	0.8	0.1	---	0.2	= 2070
Females	89.3	8.0	2.1	0.3	---	0.3	= 2626
35-44 Combined	51.3	26.7	16.3	4.3	0.9	0.5	= 3451
Males	61.7	21.5	12.7	3.2	0.5	0.3	= 1552
Females	42.8	31.0	19.2	5.2	1.3	0.6	= 1899
45-54 Combined	63.9	23.1	9.8	2.4	0.5	0.2	= 2877
Males	60.8	23.7	11.9	2.9	0.6	0.2	= 1330
Females	66.6	22.7	8.1	1.9	0.5	0.3	= 1547
55-64 Combined	89.0	8.6	1.9	0.3	---	0.1	= 2775
Males	86.0	10.6	2.7	0.6	---	0.2	= 1245
Females	91.5	6.9	1.2	0.1	0.1	0.1	= 1530
65-74 Combined	95.9	3.6	0.4	---	---	0.1	= 2181
Males	95.9	3.5	0.4	0.1	---	0.1	= 946
Females	95.9	3.6	0.3	---	---	0.2	= 1235
75-84 Combined	98.5	1.0	0.2	0.2	---	0.1	= 984
Males	99.7	---	---	0.3	---	---	= 354
Females	97.8	1.6	0.3	0.2	---	0.2	= 630
85 + Combined	99.5	---	0.5	---	---	---	= 182
Males	100.0	---	---	---	---	---	= 68
Females	99.1	---	0.9	---	---	---	= 114

The table is headed: 1972 - 1986

(1) See appendix A

B3.5

Q34D. Number of members over 17 years old. (1)

	1972 - 1986					
	One 1	Two 2	Three 3	4 - 8 4	NA 5	N's
All Ages	21.8	59.5	12.9	5.6	0.1	=19614
18-24 Combined	13.3	48.7	23.2	14.7	0.1	= 2468
Males	13.3	40.5	28.7	17.4	0.1	= 1162
Females	13.3	56.0	18.2	12.3	0.2	= 1306
25-34 Combined	19.7	71.6	6.3	2.4	0.1	= 4696
Males	17.2	72.4	7.1	3.3	---	= 2070
Females	21.6	71.0	5.6	1.6	0.1	= 2626
35-44 Combined	17.6	67.1	11.9	3.1	0.2	= 3451
Males	14.9	72.9	9.6	2.4	0.1	= 1552
Females	19.7	62.5	13.8	3.7	0.3	= 1899
45-54 Combined	15.4	52.2	21.5	10.7	0.1	= 2877
Males	14.5	54.4	20.3	10.8	---	= 1330
Females	16.2	50.4	22.6	10.7	0.2	= 1547
55-64 Combined	20.6	59.5	14.5	5.3	0.1	= 2775
Males	14.9	61.1	17.0	6.8	0.1	= 1245
Females	25.3	58.2	12.4	4.0	0.1	= 1530
65-74 Combined	34.4	55.1	7.7	2.6	0.1	= 2181
Males	18.8	67.8	10.3	3.1	0.1	= 946
Females	46.4	45.4	5.7	2.3	0.2	= 1235
75-84 Combined	55.2	38.3	5.4	1.1	---	= 984
Males	32.2	59.3	6.5	2.0	---	= 354
Females	68.1	26.5	4.8	0.6	---	= 630
85 + Combined	62.6	28.0	8.2	1.1	---	= 182
Males	51.5	45.6	2.9	---	---	= 68
Females	69.3	17.5	11.4	1.8	---	= 114

(1) See appendix A

B3.6

Q35A. How many persons in the household are not related to you
       in any way? (1)

	1972 - 1986						
	None 1	One 2	Two 3	Three 4	4 - 8 5	NA 6	N's
All Ages	93.3	4.6	1.0	0.4	0.3	0.6	=16271
18-24 Combined	84.4	10.5	2.9	0.9	0.7	0.6	= 2246
Males	83.6	10.3	3.9	0.7	1.0	0.6	= 1030
Females	85.1	10.7	2.1	1.1	0.4	0.7	= 1216
25-34 Combined	91.4	5.9	1.2	0.4	0.3	0.8	= 4146
Males	89.2	7.5	1.6	0.7	0.5	0.5	= 1732
Females	93.0	4.8	0.9	0.2	0.2	1.0	= 2414
35-44 Combined	95.0	3.3	0.4	0.3	0.3	0.6	= 3138
Males	94.3	3.8	0.6	0.5	0.3	0.6	= 1358
Females	95.6	3.0	0.3	0.2	0.2	0.7	= 1780
45-54 Combined	96.4	2.4	0.6	0.2	0.1	0.4	= 2539
Males	95.8	2.9	0.5	0.3	0.2	0.3	= 1156
Females	96.9	1.9	0.7	0.1	0.1	0.4	= 1383
55-64 Combined	96.7	2.2	0.5	0.2	0.1	0.3	= 2241
Males	97.3	1.9	0.6	---	0.1	0.2	= 1067
Females	96.2	2.5	0.5	0.3	0.2	0.3	= 1174
65-74 Combined	96.5	2.3	0.5	0.2	0.1	0.4	= 1448
Males	97.0	1.9	0.4	0.1	---	0.5	= 771
Females	95.9	2.7	0.6	0.3	0.3	0.3	= 677
75-84 Combined	96.6	2.5	0.4	---	---	0.4	= 445
Males	97.5	1.2	0.4	---	---	0.8	= 241
Females	95.6	3.9	0.5	---	---	---	= 204
85 + Combined	95.6	4.4	---	---	---	---	= 68
Males	97.0	3.0	---	---	---	---	= 33
Females	94.3	5.7	---	---	---	---	= 35

(1) See appendix A

38

B3.7

Q171. As you know, many older people share a home with
        their grown children. Do you think this is generally
        a good idea or a bad idea? (1)

	1973 - 1986				
	A good idea 1	A bad idea 2	Depends 3	DK-NA 4	N's
All Ages	38.3	47.0	14.0	0.3	=11984
18-24 Combined	51.2	35.8	12.2	0.8	= 1538
Males	54.0	34.1	10.9	1.0	= 698
Females	48.8	37.3	13.2	0.7	= 840
25-34 Combined	44.5	41.3	13.7	0.6	= 2914
Males	45.4	41.6	12.4	0.6	= 1263
Females	43.7	41.1	14.7	0.5	= 1651
35-44 Combined	43.1	41.4	14.8	0.7	= 2149
Males	43.7	42.0	13.8	0.5	= 981
Females	42.6	40.9	15.7	0.8	= 1168
45-54 Combined	37.2	49.0	13.2	0.6	= 1678
Males	38.9	48.0	12.1	1.0	= 735
Females	35.8	49.7	14.1	0.3	= 943
55-64 Combined	29.5	55.4	14.3	0.8	= 1646
Males	31.3	55.0	12.7	1.0	= 722
Females	28.0	55.7	15.6	0.6	= 924
65-74 Combined	23.0	62.0	14.2	0.8	= 1336
Males	25.9	60.3	13.1	0.7	= 572
Females	20.8	63.2	15.1	0.9	= 764
75-84 Combined	21.6	59.6	18.0	0.8	= 612
Males	28.5	54.2	16.4	0.9	= 214
Females	17.8	62.6	18.8	0.8	= 398
85 + Combined	26.1	51.4	18.9	3.6	= 111
Males	17.9	66.7	15.4	---	= 39
Females	30.6	43.1	20.8	5.6	= 72

(1) See appendix A

39

B4.1

Q274A. Death of relatives during last five years.

		1978 - 1984						
	None	1-2+ in prior 4	1 last year	1 last, 1-2+ in last 4Y	2+ last year	2+ last, 1-2+ in last 4Y	NA	N's
	1	2	3	4	5	6	7	
All Ages	63.8	23.7	6.4	3.7	1.1	0.8	0.6	= 7506
18-24 Combined	88.0	7.6	3.0	0.3	0.2	---	0.9	= 906
Males	91.4	5.6	1.5	0.5	0.3	---	0.8	= 396
Females	85.3	9.2	4.1	0.2	0.2	---	1.0	= 510
25-34 Combined	78.8	13.9	4.9	1.3	0.4	0.2	0.5	= 1924
Males	81.4	10.8	5.5	1.5	0.2	0.2	0.4	= 821
Females	77.0	16.1	4.5	1.2	0.5	0.2	0.5	= 1103
35-44 Combined	65.4	23.3	8.0	1.9	0.5	0.4	0.5	= 1392
Males	64.0	24.1	8.3	2.5	0.6	0.2	0.3	= 639
Females	66.7	22.6	7.7	1.5	0.4	0.5	0.7	= 753
45-54 Combined	50.7	31.3	7.9	6.0	2.6	0.8	0.6	= 970
Males	53.6	29.5	7.5	6.6	1.9	0.7	0.2	= 427
Females	48.4	32.8	8.3	5.5	3.1	0.9	0.9	= 543
55-64 Combined	45.9	36.2	7.0	6.3	1.8	2.3	0.6	= 990
Males	47.5	36.1	5.7	7.1	1.2	1.9	0.5	= 421
Females	44.6	36.2	7.9	5.6	2.3	2.6	0.7	= 569
65-74 Combined	46.0	34.9	7.5	8.3	1.7	1.1	0.6	= 842
Males	45.8	34.1	8.1	7.5	1.8	2.1	0.6	= 334
Females	46.1	35.4	7.1	8.9	1.6	0.4	0.6	= 508
75-84 Combined	47.9	33.5	9.3	6.1	1.0	1.7	0.5	= 409
Males	42.2	35.9	9.4	8.6	1.6	1.6	0.8	= 128
Females	50.5	32.4	9.3	5.0	0.7	1.8	0.4	= 281
85 + Combined	49.3	32.9	4.1	8.2	2.7	1.4	1.4	= 73
Males	35.0	40.0	5.0	10.0	5.0	5.0	---	= 20
Females	54.7	30.2	3.8	7.5	1.9	---	1.9	= 53

B4.2

Q274B. Number of relatives dying since respondent
        16 years old and prior to the last five years.

	1978 - 1984				
	None 1	One 2	Two 3	3 - 9 4	N's
All Ages	49.9	16.5	10.6	23.0	= 7506
18-24 Combined	97.7	2.1	0.2	----	= 906
Males	99.0	1.0	----	----	= 396
Females	96.7	2.9	0.4	----	= 510
25-34 Combined	83.9	13.3	2.3	0.5	= 1924
Males	86.1	11.7	2.2	---	= 821
Females	82.2	14.4	2.4	0.9	= 1103
35-44 Combined	56.5	30.2	9.3	3.9	= 1392
Males	58.8	29.4	9.2	2.5	= 639
Females	54.6	30.9	9.4	5.0	= 753
45-54 Combined	27.5	29.6	20.7	22.2	= 970
Males	28.3	31.9	20.6	19.2	= 427
Females	26.9	27.8	20.8	24.5	= 543
55-64 Combined	11.6	16.8	24.2	47.4	= 990
Males	13.8	17.3	27.3	41.6	= 421
Females	10.0	16.3	22.0	51.7	= 569
65-74 Combined	6.4	8.6	16.0	69.0	= 842
Males	6.9	9.9	16.8	66.5	= 334
Females	6.1	7.7	15.6	70.7	= 508
75-84 Combined	4.6	3.9	9.0	82.4	= 409
Males	7.8	6.3	10.2	75.8	= 128
Females	3.2	2.8	8.5	85.4	= 281
85 + Combined	4.1	1.4	12.3	82.2	= 73
Males	5.0	---	5.0	90.0	= 20
Females	3.8	1.9	15.1	79.2	= 53

B4.3

Q275C. Death of child or child's spouse.

	1978 - 1986						
	No death reported 1	Died 6+ yrs ago 2	Died 1-5 yrs ago 3	Died last year 4	DK-NA 5		N's
All Ages	89.4	6.5	1.9	0.8	1.3	=	5448
18-24 Combined	92.4	0.4	1.7	1.7	3.8	=	237
Males	92.8	---	---	---	7.2	=	69
Females	92.3	0.6	2.4	2.4	2.4	=	168
25-34 Combined	95.9	1.4	1.0	0.3	1.4	=	1256
Males	97.9	0.6	---	---	1.5	=	468
Females	94.7	1.8	1.6	0.5	1.4	=	788
35-44 Combined	94.2	3.5	1.3	0.4	0.6	=	1187
Males	95.4	2.1	1.3	0.8	0.4	=	523
Females	93.2	4.7	1.2	0.2	0.8	=	664
45-54 Combined	89.8	5.6	2.1	0.9	1.6	=	869
Males	93.6	4.3	0.5	0.5	1.1	=	375
Females	86.8	6.7	3.2	1.2	2.0	=	494
55-64 Combined	86.7	9.0	1.8	0.8	1.8	=	855
Males	91.0	6.2	1.4	---	1.4	=	355
Females	83.6	11.0	2.0	1.4	2.0	=	500
65-74 Combined	82.5	12.8	2.7	1.3	0.7	=	673
Males	84.7	9.8	2.9	1.1	1.5	=	275
Females	80.9	14.8	2.5	1.5	0.3	=	398
75-84 Combined	70.2	21.6	5.0	1.9	1.3	=	319
Males	75.2	17.8	4.0	1.0	2.0	=	101
Females	67.9	23.4	5.5	2.3	0.9	=	218
85 + Combined	57.7	26.9	9.6	3.8	1.9	=	52
Males	69.2	23.1	7.7	---	---	=	13
Females	53.8	28.2	10.3	5.1	2.6	=	39

42

B4.4

Q275D. Death of sibling or sibling-in-law.

	1978 - 1986						
	No death reported 1	Died 6+ yrs ago 2	Died 1-5 yrs ago 3	Died last year 4	DK-NA 5		N's
All Ages	68.3	14.7	11.0	5.2	0.9	=	7117
18-24 Combined	95.0	0.6	2.3	0.8	1.4	=	879
Males	95.8	---	2.3	0.8	1.0	=	384
Females	94.3	1.0	2.2	0.8	1.6	=	495
25-34 Combined	90.6	3.1	3.6	2.0	0.6	=	1850
Males	91.5	2.4	3.0	2.7	0.4	=	789
Females	90.0	3.6	4.1	1.5	0.8	=	1061
35-44 Combined	82.8	8.6	5.5	2.2	0.9	=	1288
Males	83.8	8.2	5.1	2.0	0.9	=	587
Females	82.0	9.0	5.8	2.3	0.9	=	701
45-54 Combined	65.3	14.9	12.5	6.2	1.2	=	907
Males	66.9	15.3	11.3	5.5	1.0	=	399
Females	64.0	14.6	13.4	6.7	1.4	=	508
55-64 Combined	42.6	27.8	20.0	8.4	1.2	=	930
Males	44.1	28.8	18.5	7.3	1.3	=	399
Females	41.4	27.1	21.1	9.2	1.1	=	531
65-74 Combined	27.2	33.1	25.5	13.9	0.4	=	801
Males	28.1	33.1	23.3	15.1	0.3	=	317
Females	26.7	33.1	26.9	13.0	0.4	=	484
75-84 Combined	16.4	45.5	25.6	12.3	0.3	=	391
Males	12.4	42.1	29.8	14.9	0.8	=	121
Females	18.1	47.0	23.7	11.1	---	=	270
85 + Combined	14.1	46.5	26.8	11.3	1.4	=	71
Males	10.5	36.8	31.6	21.1	---	=	19
Females	15.4	50.0	25.0	7.7	1.9	=	52

43

B4.5

Q276A. Number of traumatic events (deaths, divorces, unemployments, and
       hospitalizations/disabilities) happening to respondent last year.

	None 1	One 2	Two 3	Three 4	Four 5	NA 6	N's
1978 - 1986							
All Ages	58.0	31.5	6.5	0.3	---	3.6	= 7506
18-24 Combined	54.2	34.9	7.5	0.4	---	3.0	= 906
Males	52.8	36.6	7.8	0.3	---	2.5	= 396
Females	55.3	33.5	7.3	0.6	---	3.3	= 510
25-34 Combined	61.2	28.6	6.1	0.6	0.1	3.4	= 1924
Males	63.9	27.5	4.9	0.7	---	2.9	= 821
Females	59.1	29.4	7.1	0.5	0.1	3.8	= 1103
35-44 Combined	61.3	28.4	5.8	0.4	0.1	4.1	= 1392
Males	62.8	28.2	5.0	0.3	---	3.8	= 639
Females	60.0	28.6	6.5	0.4	0.1	4.4	= 753
45-54 Combined	55.8	31.6	7.9	0.2	---	4.4	= 970
Males	55.3	31.9	8.9	---	---	4.0	= 427
Females	56.2	31.5	7.2	0.4	---	4.8	= 543
55-64 Combined	56.4	32.7	7.6	0.2	---	3.1	= 990
Males	56.3	32.5	8.1	0.2	---	2.9	= 421
Females	56.4	32.9	7.2	0.2	---	3.3	= 569
65-74 Combined	55.7	35.0	5.1	0.1	---	4.0	= 842
Males	55.7	34.1	6.0	0.3	---	3.9	= 334
Females	55.7	35.6	4.5	---	---	4.1	= 508
75-84 Combined	54.0	38.4	4.9	---	---	2.7	= 409
Males	46.9	46.1	4.7	---	---	2.3	= 128
Females	57.3	34.9	5.0	---	---	2.8	= 281
85 + Combined	56.2	31.5	9.6	---	---	2.7	= 73
Males	55.0	30.0	15.0	---	---	---	= 20
Females	56.6	32.1	7.5	---	---	3.8	= 53

B4.6

Q275E. Death of spouse.

	1978 - 1986					N's
	No death reported 1	Died 6+ yrs ago 2	Died 1-5 yrs ago 3	Died last year 4	DK-NA 5	
All Ages	84.6	9.2	3.6	1.4	1.2	= 6220
18-24 Combined	98.2	0.3	0.3	---	1.2	= 328
Males	100.0	---	---	---	---	= 107
Females	97.3	0.5	0.5	---	1.8	= 221
25-34 Combined	97.6	0.6	0.5	0.4	0.9	= 1496
Males	99.0	---	0.2	0.2	0.7	= 597
Females	96.7	1.0	0.8	0.6	1.0	= 899
35-44 Combined	97.4	1.5	0.6	0.1	0.5	= 1285
Males	98.3	0.3	1.0	---	0.3	= 581
Females	96.6	2.4	0.3	0.1	0.6	= 704
45-54 Combined	90.4	3.8	3.0	1.4	1.4	= 925
Males	95.3	1.7	1.5	0.7	0.7	= 401
Females	86.6	5.3	4.2	1.9	1.9	= 524
55-64 Combined	79.8	10.7	5.4	2.1	1.9	= 941
Males	89.5	5.1	2.6	1.0	1.8	= 391
Females	72.9	14.7	7.5	2.9	2.0	= 550
65-74 Combined	62.8	23.9	9.3	2.9	1.1	= 788
Males	77.7	12.1	5.7	3.2	1.3	= 314
Females	53.0	31.6	11.6	2.7	1.1	= 474
75-84 Combined	35.1	44.4	12.7	5.9	1.8	= 387
Males	55.4	24.0	9.9	7.4	3.3	= 121
Females	25.9	53.8	13.9	5.3	1.1	= 266
85 + Combined	20.0	65.7	7.1	4.3	2.9	= 70
Males	42.1	36.8	5.3	10.5	5.3	= 19
Females	11.8	76.5	7.8	2.0	2.0	= 51

B4.7

Q276B. Number of traumatic events (deaths, divorces, unemployments, and hospitalizations/disabilities) happening to respondent during last five years.

		None 1	One 2	Two 3	Three 4	Four 5	NA 6	N's
\multicolumn{9}{l}{1978 - 1986}
All Ages		25.7	41.8	23.6	4.6	0.6	3.6	= 7506
18-24	Combined	28.3	42.7	21.0	4.7	0.3	3.0	= 906
	Males	26.5	45.5	22.0	3.5	---	2.5	= 396
	Females	29.6	40.6	20.2	5.7	0.6	3.3	= 510
25-34	Combined	30.0	39.2	20.2	6.1	1.1	3.4	= 1924
	Males	31.4	41.5	18.8	4.5	0.9	2.9	= 821
	Females	28.9	37.4	21.2	7.3	1.3	3.8	= 1103
35-44	Combined	27.8	39.2	21.2	6.7	1.1	4.1	= 1392
	Males	27.4	39.1	22.5	6.4	0.8	3.8	= 639
	Females	28.2	39.2	20.1	6.9	1.3	4.4	= 753
45-54	Combined	21.6	40.9	27.3	5.1	0.6	4.4	= 970
	Males	22.2	42.2	26.2	4.7	0.7	4.0	= 427
	Females	21.2	40.0	28.2	5.3	0.6	4.8	= 543
55-64	Combined	21.8	44.2	27.9	2.9	---	3.1	= 990
	Males	20.9	45.4	28.3	2.6	---	2.9	= 421
	Females	22.5	43.4	27.6	3.2	---	3.3	= 569
65-74	Combined	22.1	45.7	26.5	1.5	0.1	4.0	= 842
	Males	22.5	44.3	27.2	2.1	---	3.9	= 334
	Females	21.9	46.7	26.0	1.2	0.2	4.1	= 508
75-84	Combined	19.6	49.6	27.6	0.5	---	2.7	= 409
	Males	14.1	50.8	31.3	1.6	---	2.3	= 128
	Females	22.1	49.1	26.0	---	---	2.8	= 281
85 +	Combined	20.5	43.8	32.9	---	---	2.7	= 73
	Males	10.0	40.0	50.0	---	---	---	= 20
	Females	24.5	45.3	26.4	---	---	3.8	= 53

B4.8

Q277A. Number of traumatic events (divorces, unemployments,
        hospitalizations/disabilities) happening to
        respondent's relatives during last year.

		1978 - 1984			
	None 1	One 2	Two 3	Three 4	N's
All Ages	38.7	40.1	18.1	3.0	= 6043
18-24 Combined	37.8	37.5	20.9	3.8	= 770
Males	41.0	36.9	18.6	3.5	= 339
Females	35.3	38.1	22.7	3.9	= 431
25-34 Combined	31.6	40.0	23.2	5.2	= 1545
Males	33.3	37.5	22.9	6.4	= 643
Females	30.4	41.8	23.4	4.4	= 902
35-44 Combined	35.2	43.1	18.7	3.0	= 1091
Males	38.7	42.4	16.5	2.4	= 509
Females	32.1	43.6	20.6	3.6	= 582
45-54 Combined	33.1	42.2	21.9	2.8	= 782
Males	36.2	43.7	18.7	1.5	= 343
Females	30.8	41.0	24.4	3.9	= 439
55-64 Combined	41.9	41.3	15.0	1.8	= 816
Males	46.5	39.6	12.7	1.2	= 346
Females	38.5	42.6	16.6	2.3	= 470
65-74 Combined	52.5	37.7	9.2	0.6	= 665
Males	49.6	41.0	9.0	0.4	= 268
Females	54.4	35.5	9.3	0.8	= 397
75-84 Combined	58.5	36.4	5.1	---	= 316
Males	54.0	40.0	6.0	---	= 100
Females	60.6	34.7	4.6	---	= 216
85 + Combined	72.4	25.9	1.7	---	= 58
Males	68.4	26.3	5.3	---	= 19
Females	74.4	25.6	---	---	= 39

B4.9

Q277B. Number of traumatic events (divorces, unemployments,
        hospitalizations/disabilities) happening to
        respondent's relatives during last five years.

		1978 - 1984			
	None 1	One 2	Two 3	Three 4	N's
All Ages	18.5	36.2	31.5	13.8	= 6043
18-24 Combined	17.4	33.6	34.4	14.5	= 770
Males	17.1	40.1	29.8	13.0	= 339
Females	17.6	28.5	38.1	15.8	= 431
25-34 Combined	13.2	31.4	34.9	20.5	= 1545
Males	14.3	31.7	35.5	18.5	= 643
Females	12.4	31.2	34.5	22.0	= 902
35-44 Combined	14.2	34.8	37.4	13.6	= 1091
Males	15.7	35.8	37.5	11.0	= 509
Females	12.9	34.0	37.3	15.8	= 582
45-54 Combined	13.0	36.4	33.4	17.1	= 782
Males	15.2	40.8	32.7	11.4	= 343
Females	11.4	33.0	33.9	21.6	= 439
55-64 Combined	20.6	38.5	31.7	9.2	= 816
Males	24.3	36.1	31.5	8.1	= 346
Females	17.9	40.2	31.9	10.0	= 470
65-74 Combined	30.4	44.1	19.8	5.7	= 665
Males	26.5	46.3	20.9	6.3	= 268
Females	33.0	42.6	19.1	5.3	= 397
75-84 Combined	36.7	49.4	11.4	2.5	= 316
Males	38.0	46.0	15.0	1.0	= 100
Females	36.1	50.9	9.7	3.2	= 216
85 + Combined	60.3	31.0	8.6	---	= 58
Males	52.6	31.6	15.8	---	= 19
Females	64.1	30.8	5.1	---	= 39

48

B4.10

Q278A. Total number of traumatic events happening to respondent
        and relatives last year?

			1978 - 1984				
	None 1	One 2	Two 3	Three 4	4 - 6 5	NA 6	N's
All Ages	25.3	32.6	24.1	11.3	3.3	3.5	= 6043
18-24 Combined	23.2	29.2	27.7	12.9	3.5	3.5	= 770
Males	24.5	30.1	26.0	12.7	3.8	2.9	= 339
Females	22.3	28.5	29.0	13.0	3.2	3.9	= 431
25-34 Combined	21.7	32.4	23.1	15.0	4.3	3.4	= 1545
Males	23.2	32.7	21.9	14.3	4.7	3.3	= 643
Females	20.7	32.3	23.9	15.5	4.1	3.4	= 902
35-44 Combined	24.7	33.1	24.2	10.7	3.7	3.7	= 1091
Males	26.5	35.6	23.2	8.8	2.9	2.9	= 509
Females	23.0	30.9	25.1	12.4	4.3	4.3	= 582
45-54 Combined	21.1	32.9	26.3	11.4	4.3	4.0	= 782
Males	20.4	36.4	26.8	10.5	2.9	2.9	= 343
Females	21.6	30.1	26.0	12.1	5.5	4.8	= 439
55-64 Combined	26.2	33.8	23.8	10.4	2.6	3.2	= 816
Males	26.9	36.7	21.7	10.1	1.4	3.2	= 346
Females	25.7	31.7	25.3	10.6	3.4	3.2	= 470
65-74 Combined	33.1	33.7	22.0	6.0	1.7	3.6	= 665
Males	31.7	34.3	22.0	6.0	2.2	3.7	= 268
Females	34.0	33.2	21.9	6.0	1.3	3.5	= 397
75-84 Combined	37.0	32.6	21.8	5.1	0.3	3.2	= 316
Males	33.0	32.0	25.0	8.0	---	2.0	= 100
Females	38.9	32.9	20.4	3.7	0.5	3.7	= 216
85 + Combined	44.8	34.5	12.1	3.4	1.7	3.4	= 58
Males	36.8	42.1	10.5	5.3	5.3	---	= 19
Females	48.7	30.8	12.8	2.6	---	5.1	= 39

B4.11

Q278B. Total number of traumatic events happening to respondent
        and relatives during last five years?

	1978 - 1984							
	None 1	One 2	Two 3	Three 4	4 - 7 5	NA 6		N's
All Ages	6.2	17.4	26.1	24.0	22.8	3.5	=	6043
18-24 Combined	6.8	18.2	24.7	23.8	23.1	3.5	=	770
Males	6.5	19.5	24.2	25.4	21.5	2.9	=	339
Females	7.0	17.2	25.1	22.5	24.4	3.9	=	431
25-34 Combined	5.4	15.9	23.5	23.9	27.9	3.4	=	1545
Males	5.9	16.0	25.0	26.0	23.8	3.3	=	643
Females	5.0	15.9	22.4	22.5	30.8	3.4	=	902
35-44 Combined	5.0	14.8	27.3	23.3	25.8	3.7	=	1091
Males	4.7	16.3	30.5	21.4	24.2	2.9	=	509
Females	5.3	13.6	24.6	24.9	27.3	4.3	=	582
45-54 Combined	4.2	14.5	23.9	26.1	27.4	4.0	=	782
Males	5.2	14.9	26.5	28.9	21.6	2.9	=	343
Females	3.4	14.1	21.9	23.9	31.9	4.8	=	439
55-64 Combined	6.4	16.8	26.7	27.1	19.9	3.2	=	816
Males	6.1	18.5	25.1	29.2	17.9	3.2	=	346
Females	6.6	15.5	27.9	25.5	21.3	3.2	=	470
65-74 Combined	8.6	23.9	29.5	21.4	13.1	3.6	=	665
Males	7.8	21.3	29.9	23.5	13.8	3.7	=	268
Females	9.1	25.7	29.2	19.9	12.6	3.5	=	397
75-84 Combined	10.4	25.0	34.8	20.9	5.7	3.2	=	316
Males	8.0	24.0	32.0	28.0	6.0	2.0	=	100
Females	11.6	25.5	36.1	17.6	5.6	3.7	=	216
85 + Combined	19.0	29.3	24.1	19.0	5.2	3.4	=	58
Males	10.5	26.3	26.3	26.3	10.5	---	=	19
Females	23.1	30.8	23.1	15.4	2.6	5.1	=	39

GENDER, WORK ROLES, AND ATTITUDES ON SEXUALITY

GENDER

The gender, or sex, distributions in the General Social Survey approximate those in the U.S. Census. (U.S. Bureau of the Census, 1987, p. 14) The census shows that more males are born, but that the proportion of females in the population is greater than the male by about age 18. The imbalance between the sexes continues to grow throughout life, with a ratio of almost two women for every man in the later years. While various reasons have been given for the greater survivorship of women, scientists have not yet rendered a definitive explanation of the difference.

WORK ROLES

Although from 30 to 42 percent of the women in the GSS report "keeping house," the increasing rate of women's participation in the work force is suggested when one examines the tables on present and past work status. When asked "did you ever work for as long as one year," the proportion of women responding "yes" is greatest for the younger age groups. Among the 18-24 year olds a higher ratio of women than men answer this question affirmatively, suggesting that women GSS respondents have a more active work force participation rate in early life than men do.

The peak years of full-time labor force participation by both sexes in the GSS are 25-54, after which time the rate drops sharply for both. During these years close to 80 percent or more of the men work full-time and between 38 and 42 percent of the women do also, while another 12 to 15 percent of the women work part-time. Although a large majority of the men past 65 describe themselves as retired, less than half of the women do so even after age 85.

Table C1.4 needs to be interpreted from the point of view of the wife responding about her husband and the husband responding about his wife. The table is understood most easily if one starts by examining the column labelled "keeping house" and then moving on to the other columns. Among the 18-24 year olds, for example, 44 percent of the husbands (Col. 6) say that their wives are keeping house and 35.9 percent say that their wives are working full-time (Col. 1).

When the 18-24 year olds in tables C1.3 and C1.4 are compared, it appears that there may be a discrepancy between the way wives and husbands define work. Whereas 44 percent of the husbands report their wives as "keeping house" (table C1.4 Col. 6) only 30 percent of the wives say they are "keeping house" (table C1.3 Col. 6).

The 35-64 year old age groups might be called the "war generations" because over half report having had some military service. A relatively low proportion of the 18-24 year olds report having had military service. Three percent of the women in the World War II and Korean War generations (age 55-64) report military experience.

ATTITUDES ON SEXUALITY

The age groups exhibit clear differences in attitude regarding early teen sexual relations. The differing proportions who choose "always wrong" appear to form three clusters - the 18-34 year olds, the 35-54 years olds, and 55 and above. Each cluster demonstrates increasingly conservative attitudes, and these differences persist throughout the tables on sexual attitudes.

The generational differences suggest a possible area of investigation. Does the clustering of age groups appear in other areas than that of sexuality? Are there age markers of difference in attitudes that persist across subjects? Do these differences persist over time, or are they merely artifacts of recent changes in attitudes?

More women than men in nearly every age group consider early teen sexual relations "always wrong." Generally, the greater conservatism of women persists thoughout all the questions on sexuality. There is one notable exception, however - male attitudes converge with female in regard to sexual relations between two adults of the same sex (homosexual relations). In the youngest age groups higher percentages of women than men accept homosexual relations.

Age and sex differences persist in attitudes on pornography. Women view pornography more unfavorably than men and are more opposed to it. Over two-thirds of most age groups feel that they have at least some information on the issue, a large majority feels pornography should be illegal for the young (under 18), and substantial proportions of each age groups feels their opinions on the issue are firm. Still, 40 to 66 percent of each age segment considers that issue of pornography "not very important" or "not important at all," and a majority thinks that sexual materials do provide information about sex.

The percentage of persons who say they have seen an X-rated film has dropped almost 8 points over the term of the survey (between 1972-76 and 1982-86). The youngest

group of males has fallen nearly 20 percent (from 53 percent
to 33 percent), and the youngest females 6 percent (from 36
percent down to 30 percent) - the sexes are now more alike
than they were in the earlier period of the survey.
Whatever importance people attach to the issue, there is
less exposure to pornography now than there was in the past.
(Tables which show changes between the three sets of years -
1972-76, 1977-81, and 1982-86 - are identified by Footnote
1. These tables may be obtained from the authors at cost by
writing them at 108 Main St. North, Bethlehem, CT 06751)

The General Social Survey includes a long series of
questions regarding attitudes toward abortion. These are
omitted from the the present volume because the results can
be readily summarized. The proportions of respondents
approving and disapproving varies with the reasons given.
Typically, if a specific problem is involved (risk to the
pregnant woman's health or pregnancy resulting from a rape),
a large majority approve of an abortion. If the
circumstances reflect practical considerations (poverty in
the family, being married and not wanting more children, or
not wanting to marry), opinion is more evenly divided but a
majority is opposed. When abortion is simply the choice of
the individual ("the woman wants it for any reason"),
two-thirds oppose the idea.

C1.1

Q20.   Respondent's sex?

| | 1972 - 1986 | | |
	Male 1	Female 2	N's
All Ages	44.5	55.5	=19614
18-24 yrs. old	47.1	52.9	= 2468
25-34 yrs. old	44.1	55.9	= 4696
35-44 yrs. old	45.0	55.0	= 3451
45-54 yrs. old	46.2	53.8	= 2877
55-64 yrs. old	44.9	55.1	= 2775
65-74 yrs. old	43.4	56.6	= 2181
75-84 yrs. old	36.0	64.0	= 984
85 & OVER	37.4	62.6	= 182

C1.2

Q1C. IF RETIRED, IN SCHOOL, KEEPING HOUSE, OR OTHER:
      Did you ever work for as long as one year? (1)

| | 1972 - 1986 | | | |
	Yes 1	No 2	DK-NA 3	N's
All Ages	79.9	20.0	0.1	= 7674
18-24 Combined	44.6	55.3	0.1	= 808
Males	39.3	60.3	0.4	= 229
Females	46.6	53.4	---	= 579
25-34 Combined	75.8	24.0	0.3	= 1172
Males	84.0	16.0	---	= 94
Females	75.0	24.7	0.3	= 1078
35-44 Combined	80.7	19.1	0.3	= 792
Males	92.5	5.7	1.9	= 53
Females	79.8	20.0	0.1	= 739
45-54 Combined	80.8	19.0	0.3	= 790
Males	94.9	3.1	2.0	= 98
Females	78.8	21.2	---	= 692
55-64 Combined	88.3	11.6	0.1	= 1206
Males	98.5	1.2	0.3	= 324
Females	84.6	15.4	---	= 882
65-74 Combined	89.1	10.9	---	= 1809
Males	99.7	0.3	---	= 745
Females	81.7	18.3	---	= 1064
75-84 Combined	85.9	14.1	---	= 921
Males	99.7	0.3	---	= 314
Females	78.7	21.3	---	= 607
85 + Combined	79.0	21.0	---	= 176
Males	100.0	----	---	= 63
Females	67.3	32.7	---	= 113

(1) See appendix A

57

C1.3

Q1. Last week were you working full time, part time, going to school or
what? (1) (2)

				1972 - 1986				
	Working full time 1	Working part time 2	Temp. not working 3	Retired 4	Student 5	Keeping house 6	Other 7	N's
All Ages	46.0	9.3	5.7	10.9	2.8	24.0	1.8	=19614
18-24 Combined	45.4	13.7	8.2	----	15.2	16.6	1.0	= 2468
Males	54.0	13.9	12.4	----	17.8	1.0	0.9	= 1162
Females	37.7	13.4	4.5	----	12.9	30.4	1.1	= 1306
25-34 Combined	58.4	9.8	6.8	0.1	2.6	21.8	0.5	= 4696
Males	79.1	5.9	10.5	0.2	3.0	0.7	0.6	= 2070
Females	42.2	12.9	3.9	---	2.2	38.4	0.4	= 2626
35-44 Combined	61.4	9.7	6.0	0.3	1.2	20.7	0.7	= 3451
Males	84.5	3.4	8.7	0.6	1.0	0.6	1.2	= 1552
Females	42.4	14.9	3.7	0.1	1.3	37.2	0.4	= 1899
45-54 Combined	57.6	8.7	6.3	2.1	0.5	22.9	2.0	= 2877
Males	79.5	4.3	8.9	3.7	0.3	0.5	2.9	= 1330
Females	38.7	12.5	4.1	0.6	0.6	42.2	1.3	= 1547
55-64 Combined	42.8	8.1	5.5	12.4	0.3	27.5	3.2	= 2775
Males	60.2	5.1	8.7	20.6	0.1	1.0	4.3	= 1245
Females	28.8	10.6	3.0	5.7	0.5	49.1	2.4	= 1530
65-74 Combined	7.8	7.2	2.0	49.9	---	31.9	1.1	= 2181
Males	11.7	7.5	2.0	76.6	---	1.2	1.0	= 946
Females	4.9	7.0	1.9	29.5	0.1	55.4	1.2	= 1235
75-84 Combined	1.5	4.6	0.3	53.3	---	38.8	1.5	= 984
Males	2.8	7.9	0.6	87.9	---	0.8	---	= 354
Females	0.8	2.7	0.2	33.8	---	60.2	2.4	= 630
85 + Combined	1.6	1.6	---	59.3	---	33.5	3.8	= 182
Males	4.4	2.9	---	85.3	---	7.4	---	= 68
Females	---	0.9	---	43.9	---	49.1	6.1	= 114

(1) See appendix A
(2) See appendix B

58

C1.4

Q4. Last week was your (wife/husband) working full time, part time, going
to school, keeping house, or what? (1) (2)

	1972 - 1986							N's
	Working fulltime 1	Working parttime 2	Temp not working 3	Retired 4	Student 5	Keeping House 6	Other 7	
All Ages	52.2	8.1	4.1	8.8	0.9	24.4	1.5	=12405
18-24 Combined	63.8	8.0	6.9	0.1	3.8	16.1	1.3	= 890
Males	35.9	11.9	3.4	---	4.4	44.1	0.3	= 320
Females	79.5	5.8	8.8	0.2	3.5	0.4	1.9	= 570
25-34 Combined	64.4	7.6	4.8	0.1	1.5	21.0	0.5	= 3158
Males	36.1	12.7	2.4	---	1.5	47.2	0.1	= 1374
Females	86.2	3.7	6.7	0.1	1.5	0.8	0.9	= 1784
35-44 Combined	62.9	8.9	3.8	0.5	0.8	21.9	1.3	= 2583
Males	35.4	16.5	1.5	---	0.9	45.4	0.3	= 1224
Females	87.6	2.1	5.8	0.9	0.7	0.7	2.2	= 1359
45-54 Combined	58.7	8.5	5.2	3.6	0.5	21.9	1.7	= 2191
Males	35.4	15.0	3.0	0.2	0.8	45.2	0.4	= 1061
Females	80.5	2.4	7.2	6.8	0.2	----	2.9	= 1130
55-64 Combined	40.3	8.6	3.5	16.9	0.1	27.3	3.3	= 1971
Males	27.7	11.7	1.9	2.9	0.1	53.8	1.9	= 995
Females	53.2	5.4	5.0	31.3	---	0.4	4.7	= 976
65-74 Combined	12.3	6.9	1.1	40.9	0.1	37.4	1.3	= 1234
Males	10.8	7.1	0.6	17.2	0.1	63.2	1.1	= 723
Females	14.5	6.7	2.0	74.6	---	0.8	1.6	= 511
75-84 Combined	4.7	4.9	0.3	42.4	---	44.8	2.9	= 344
Males	4.9	5.3	---	18.7	---	68.0	3.1	= 225
Females	4.2	4.2	0.8	87.4	---	0.8	2.5	= 119
85 + Combined	8.8	---	---	41.2	---	47.1	2.9	= 34
Males	11.1	---	---	33.3	---	55.6	---	= 27
Females	----	---	---	71.4	---	14.3	14.3	= 7

(1) See appendix A
(2) See appendix B

C1.5

Q46. Have you ever been on active duty for military training or service for two consecutive months or more?
IF YES: What was your total time on active duty? (1)

	1974 - 1985					
	None 1	< 2 yrs. 2	2-4 yrs. 3	> 4 yrs. 4	DK-NA 5	N's
All Ages	79.7	4.3	11.6	4.0	0.4	=12091
18-24 Combined	94.6	2.6	2.2	0.4	0.2	= 1521
Males	89.9	4.9	4.5	0.7	---	= 710
Females	98.8	0.5	0.2	0.1	0.4	= 811
25-34 Combined	84.9	3.5	8.5	2.7	0.4	= 2956
Males	67.6	7.2	19.0	6.1	0.2	= 1255
Females	97.7	0.7	0.7	0.3	0.6	= 1701
35-44 Combined	75.9	5.5	14.0	4.2	0.4	= 2164
Males	48.1	12.0	30.4	9.2	0.3	= 976
Females	98.8	0.3	0.4	0.1	0.4	= 920
45-54 Combined	67.5	6.1	20.4	5.5	0.5	= 1701
Males	31.8	12.5	43.1	11.9	0.6	= 781
Females	97.9	0.5	1.1	----	0.4	= 920
55-64 Combined	68.1	4.8	18.4	8.1	0.5	= 1681
Males	30.8	10.2	39.9	18.3	0.7	= 736
Females	97.1	0.5	1.7	0.2	0.4	= 945
65-74 Combined	83.4	2.8	9.5	3.9	0.3	= 1343
Males	63.4	5.8	21.3	9.2	0.3	= 573
Females	98.3	0.6	0.8	---	0.3	= 770
75-84 Combined	87.7	4.1	4.4	3.0	0.8	= 610
Males	69.1	11.2	11.2	7.6	0.9	= 223
Females	98.4	----	0.5	0.3	0.8	= 387
85 + Combined	84.3	9.6	2.6	1.7	1.7	= 115
Males	60.0	25.0	7.5	5.0	2.5	= 40
Females	97.3	1.3	---	---	1.3	= 75

(1) See appendix A

C2.1

Q217A. What if they are in their early teens, say 14 to 16 years old? In
that case, do you think sex relations before marriage are always
wrong, almost always wrong, wrong only sometimes, or not wrong at all?

			1986			
	Always wrong	Almost always wrong	Sometimes wrong	Not wrong at all	DK-NA	N's
	1	2	3	4	5	
All Ages	65.7	18.6	10.9	3.2	1.6	= 1463
18-24 Combined	44.1	23.5	27.2	4.4	0.7	= 136
Males	35.1	22.8	33.3	7.0	1.8	= 57
Females	50.6	24.1	22.8	2.5	---	= 79
25-34 Combined	51.7	25.3	17.7	3.4	1.8	= 379
Males	51.7	20.2	20.8	5.1	2.2	= 178
Females	51.7	29.9	14.9	2.0	1.5	= 201
35-44 Combined	64.8	22.3	8.6	4.3	---	= 301
Males	60.8	22.3	10.8	6.2	---	= 130
Females	67.8	22.2	7.0	2.9	---	= 171
45-54 Combined	70.2	19.1	4.8	3.7	2.1	= 188
Males	60.7	25.0	6.0	6.0	2.4	= 84
Females	77.9	14.4	3.8	1.9	1.9	= 104
55-64 Combined	81.6	8.6	4.0	3.4	2.3	= 174
Males	70.7	13.3	5.3	6.7	4.0	= 75
Females	89.9	5.1	3.0	1.0	1.0	= 99
65-74 Combined	79.7	10.2	6.2	1.1	2.8	= 177
Males	75.8	10.6	7.6	1.5	4.5	= 66
Females	82.0	9.9	5.4	0.9	1.8	= 111
75-84 Combined	88.2	6.5	2.2	---	3.2	= 93
Males	89.3	7.1	3.6	---	---	= 28
Females	87.7	6.2	1.5	---	4.6	= 65
85 + Combined	86.7	13.3	---	---	---	= 15
Males	100.0	----	---	---	---	= 1
Females	85.7	14.3	---	---	---	= 14

C2.2

Q217. There's been a lot of discussion about the way morals and
attitudes about sex are changing in this country. If a man
and woman have sex relations before marriage, do you think
it is always wrong, almost always wrong, wrong only sometimes,
or not wrong at all? (1)

	1972 - 1986					
	Always wrong 1	Almost always wrong 2	Sometimes wrong 3	Not wrong at all 4	DK-NA 5	N's
All Ages	29.3	10.1	21.8	35.4	3.4	=13695
18-24 Combined	12.9	6.3	30.0	49.1	1.8	= 1649
Males	11.2	5.1	28.4	53.8	1.4	= 777
Females	14.3	7.3	31.3	44.8	2.2	= 872
25-34 Combined	16.3	7.5	24.1	50.3	1.8	= 3345
Males	14.2	6.0	22.5	55.7	1.7	= 1492
Females	17.9	8.8	25.5	46.0	1.8	= 1853
35-44 Combined	27.1	10.2	20.9	39.2	2.7	= 2412
Males	22.0	9.4	21.4	44.4	2.7	= 1080
Females	31.2	10.7	20.5	35.0	2.6	= 1332
45-54 Combined	32.0	13.3	21.7	28.7	4.2	= 2029
Males	25.3	12.9	22.0	35.4	4.4	= 962
Females	38.1	13.7	21.4	22.7	4.1	= 1067
55-64 Combined	40.1	13.3	19.6	22.5	4.5	= 1915
Males	33.5	12.4	20.4	29.2	4.6	= 857
Females	45.4	14.1	18.9	17.1	4.5	= 1058
65-74 Combined	47.5	11.5	17.3	18.3	5.3	= 1523
Males	40.1	11.8	18.4	24.8	4.9	= 653
Females	53.1	11.3	16.6	13.4	5.6	= 870
75-84 Combined	55.5	10.6	12.6	14.8	6.5	= 697
Males	40.6	10.2	14.5	25.4	9.4	= 256
Females	64.2	10.9	11.6	8.6	4.8	= 441
85 + Combined	59.2	9.6	16.0	8.0	7.2	= 125
Males	54.5	13.6	15.9	11.4	4.5	= 44
Females	61.7	7.4	16.0	6.2	8.6	= 81

(1) See appendix A

C2.3

Q218. What is your opinion about a married person having sexual relations
with someone other than the marriage partner -- is it always wrong,
almost always wrong, wrong only sometimes, or not wrong at all? (1)

	Always wrong 1	Almost always wrong 2	Sometimes wrong 3	Not wrong at all 4	DK-NA 5	N's
			1973 - 1985			
All Ages	70.8	14.4	10.2	3.2	1.5	=11941
18-24 Combined	61.8	17.9	15.6	3.7	1.0	= 1549
Males	57.5	18.2	18.1	5.0	1.2	= 736
Females	65.7	17.6	13.4	2.5	0.9	= 813
25-34 Combined	63.3	18.9	12.3	4.2	1.3	= 2775
Males	60.8	19.0	14.3	4.7	1.2	= 1203
Females	65.2	18.8	10.8	3.8	1.5	= 1572
35-44 Combined	65.7	16.5	12.1	4.2	1.5	= 2101
Males	61.6	17.2	14.7	5.6	1.0	= 935
Females	69.0	15.9	10.1	3.2	1.9	= 1166
45-54 Combined	72.0	13.9	9.6	2.6	2.0	= 1731
Males	65.9	15.2	12.1	3.9	2.9	= 794
Females	77.2	12.7	7.5	1.5	1.2	= 937
55-64 Combined	79.0	10.7	7.0	2.2	1.1	= 1737
Males	74.5	11.8	9.3	2.9	1.4	= 785
Females	82.8	9.8	5.0	1.6	0.8	= 952
65-74 Combined	84.5	7.3	4.7	1.9	1.6	= 1345
Males	79.8	9.3	6.2	2.9	1.9	= 593
Females	88.3	5.7	3.5	1.2	1.3	= 752
75-84 Combined	85.1	7.5	4.3	1.0	2.1	= 584
Males	80.5	8.6	6.2	1.4	3.3	= 210
Females	87.7	7.0	3.2	0.8	1.3	= 374
85 + Combined	87.4	2.5	4.2	0.8	5.0	= 119
Males	89.6	2.1	6.3	---	2.1	= 48
Females	85.9	2.8	2.8	1.4	7.0	= 71

(1) See appendix A

C2.4

Q219. What about sexual relations between two adults of the same sex--do you
think it is always wrong, almost always wrong, wrong only sometimes, or
not wrong at all? (1)

	1973 - 1985						
	Always wrong	Almost always wrong	Sometimes wrong	Not wrong at all	Other	NA	N's
	1	2	3	4	5	6	
All Ages	69.4	5.2	6.9	13.4	0.7	4.4	=11941
18-24 Combined	59.5	7.0	10.3	19.1	0.7	3.5	= 1549
Males	62.5	7.1	8.3	17.8	1.0	3.4	= 736
Females	56.7	6.9	12.1	20.3	0.5	3.6	= 813
25-34 Combined	59.8	6.0	10.0	20.0	0.7	3.5	= 2775
Males	60.5	7.3	9.6	19.6	0.4	2.5	= 1203
Females	59.2	5.0	10.3	20.3	0.9	4.3	= 1572
35-44 Combined	66.1	6.0	7.7	15.0	0.9	4.3	= 2101
Males	67.1	5.9	7.3	16.0	1.0	2.8	= 935
Females	65.3	6.2	8.1	14.2	0.8	5.5	= 1166
45-54 Combined	72.1	5.5	6.4	10.6	1.0	4.3	= 1731
Males	71.8	5.0	6.4	11.5	0.6	4.7	= 794
Females	72.4	6.0	6.4	9.9	1.3	4.1	= 937
55-64 Combined	78.8	3.7	4.1	8.4	0.4	4.6	= 1737
Males	78.0	3.6	3.6	10.1	0.6	4.2	= 785
Females	79.4	3.9	4.5	7.0	0.2	4.9	= 952
65-74 Combined	82.5	2.9	2.4	5.7	0.4	6.2	= 1345
Males	82.1	3.9	2.9	4.6	0.5	6.1	= 593
Females	82.7	2.1	2.0	6.5	0.4	6.3	= 752
75-84 Combined	83.7	3.4	2.1	3.8	0.5	6.5	= 584
Males	81.4	4.3	1.9	5.2	0.5	6.7	= 210
Females	85.0	2.9	2.1	2.9	0.5	6.4	= 374
85 + Combined	84.0	1.7	3.4	3.4	---	7.6	= 119
Males	85.4	---	6.3	2.1	---	6.3	= 48
Females	83.1	2.8	1.4	4.2	---	8.5	= 71

(1) See appendix A

C2.5

Q224. How much information do you have about the pornography issue - do you
        have all of the information you need, most of the information, some
        of the information, or very little information?

	1984					
	All info R needs 1	Most info 2	Some info 3	V. little info 4	DK-NA 5	N's
All Ages	14.2	20.5	36.9	25.9	2.4	= 1467
18-24 Combined	12.0	24.0	31.3	30.3	2.4	= 208
Males	15.5	29.1	25.2	28.2	1.9	= 103
Females	8.6	19.0	37.1	32.4	2.9	= 105
25-34 Combined	12.9	21.0	37.9	26.4	1.7	= 348
Males	10.6	29.3	34.1	24.4	1.6	= 123
Females	14.2	16.4	40.0	27.6	1.8	= 225
35-44 Combined	14.7	27.3	39.9	17.4	0.7	= 293
Males	15.7	32.8	35.1	16.4	---	= 134
Females	13.8	22.6	44.0	18.2	1.3	= 159
45-54 Combined	12.5	18.2	43.2	23.9	2.3	= 176
Males	19.4	19.4	36.1	23.6	1.4	= 72
Females	7.7	17.3	48.1	24.0	2.9	= 104
55-64 Combined	15.1	19.3	38.0	25.0	2.6	= 192
Males	15.0	22.5	40.0	22.5	---	= 80
Females	15.2	17.0	36.6	26.8	4.5	= 112
65-74 Combined	17.4	14.2	33.5	30.3	4.5	= 155
Males	20.0	18.3	28.3	28.3	5.0	= 60
Females	15.8	11.6	36.8	31.6	4.2	= 95
75-84 Combined	19.8	7.4	30.9	37.0	4.9	= 81
Males	8.7	8.7	43.5	39.1	---	= 23
Females	24.1	6.9	25.9	36.2	6.9	= 58
85 + Combined	14.3	7.1	14.3	50.0	14.3	= 14
Males	----	---	50.0	50.0	----	= 2
Females	16.7	8.3	8.3	50.0	16.7	= 12

C2.6

Q220B. I'm going to read some opinions about the
effects of looking at or reading sexual
materials. As I read each one, please tell
me if you think sexual materials do or do
not have that effect.
Sexual materials lead to breakdown of
morals. (1)

	1973 - 1986			
	Yes 1	No 2	DK-NA 3	N's
All Ages	57.2	36.3	6.6	=11984
18-24 Combined	42.7	52.5	4.8	= 1538
Males	37.2	59.2	3.6	= 698
Females	47.3	46.9	5.8	= 840
25-34 Combined	45.9	49.2	4.9	= 2914
Males	40.3	55.4	4.3	= 1263
Females	50.2	44.5	5.3	= 1651
35-44 Combined	53.3	40.7	6.0	= 2149
Males	46.2	49.0	4.8	= 981
Females	59.3	33.7	6.9	= 1168
45-54 Combined	62.0	31.8	6.1	= 1678
Males	56.2	38.5	5.3	= 735
Females	66.6	26.6	6.8	= 943
55-64 Combined	69.1	23.6	7.3	= 1646
Males	64.4	30.3	5.3	= 722
Females	72.7	18.4	8.9	= 924
65-74 Combined	73.4	16.8	9.8	= 1336
Males	69.2	22.4	8.4	= 572
Females	76.4	12.7	10.9	= 764
75-84 Combined	76.5	12.3	11.3	= 612
Males	71.5	18.7	9.8	= 214
Females	79.1	8.8	12.1	= 398
85 + Combined	73.9	8.1	18.0	= 111
Males	82.1	5.1	12.8	= 39
Females	69.4	9.7	20.8	= 72

(1) See appendix A

C2.7

Q220C. I'm going to read some opinions about the
        effects of looking at or reading sexual
        materials. As I read each one, please tell
        me if you think sexual materials do or do
        not have that effect.
                Sexual materials lead people to commit
                rape. (1)

		1973 - 1986		
	Yes 1	No 2	DK-NA 3	N's
All Ages	53.8	37.7	8.5	=11984
18-24 Combined	44.7	48.8	6.6	= 1538
Males	39.4	55.6	5.0	= 698
Females	49.0	43.1	7.9	= 840
25-34 Combined	43.3	50.0	6.7	= 2914
Males	35.9	58.4	5.8	= 1263
Females	49.1	43.6	7.3	= 1651
35-44 Combined	48.1	44.2	7.7	= 2149
Males	41.1	52.9	6.0	= 981
Females	53.9	36.9	9.2	= 1168
45-54 Combined	57.8	33.7	8.5	= 1678
Males	50.6	41.8	7.6	= 735
Females	63.4	27.5	9.1	= 943
55-64 Combined	64.9	26.8	8.3	= 1646
Males	58.4	35.7	5.8	= 722
Females	69.9	19.8	10.3	= 924
65-74 Combined	68.7	19.5	11.8	= 1336
Males	64.2	25.2	10.7	= 572
Females	72.1	15.2	12.7	= 764
75-84 Combined	71.6	12.9	15.5	= 612
Males	64.0	22.4	13.6	= 214
Females	75.6	7.8	16.6	= 398
85 + Combined	67.6	11.7	20.7	= 111
Males	71.8	7.7	20.5	= 39
Females	65.3	13.9	20.8	= 72

(1) See appendix A

C2.8

Q220D. I'm going to read some opinions about the
effects of looking at or reading sexual
materials. As I read each one, please tell
me if you think sexual materials do or do
not have that effect.
Sexual materials provide an outlet for
bottled-up impulses. (1)

	1973 - 1986			
	Yes 1	No 2	DK-NA 3	N's
All Ages	57.6	29.5	12.9	=11984
18-24 Combined	60.9	31.3	7.9	= 1538
Males	59.9	33.7	6.4	= 698
Females	61.7	29.3	9.0	= 840
25-34 Combined	60.0	30.6	9.4	= 2914
Males	60.8	31.5	7.7	= 1263
Females	59.3	30.0	10.7	= 1651
35-44 Combined	58.5	32.2	9.3	= 2149
Males	60.4	31.4	8.2	= 981
Females	56.9	32.9	10.2	= 1168
45-54 Combined	55.9	30.8	13.3	= 1678
Males	57.8	33.3	8.8	= 735
Females	54.4	28.7	16.9	= 943
55-64 Combined	55.4	29.0	15.6	= 1646
Males	58.0	30.6	11.4	= 722
Females	53.4	27.7	18.9	= 924
65-74 Combined	57.3	23.3	19.5	= 1336
Males	58.0	25.5	16.4	= 572
Females	56.7	21.6	21.7	= 764
75-84 Combined	47.1	24.3	28.6	= 612
Males	46.7	31.3	22.0	= 214
Females	47.2	20.6	32.2	= 398
85 + Combined	50.5	17.1	32.4	= 111
Males	64.1	10.3	25.6	= 39
Females	43.1	20.8	36.1	= 72

(1) See appendix A

C2.9

Q222. Have you seen an X-rated movie in the
       last year? (1)

		1973 - 1986		
	Yes 1	No 2	DK-NA 3	N's
All Ages	20.1	79.4	0.6	=11984
18-24 Combined	36.5	63.3	0.2	= 1538
Males	45.1	54.4	0.4	= 698
Females	29.3	70.7	---	= 840
25-34 Combined	28.1	71.3	0.6	= 2914
Males	35.2	64.1	0.6	= 1263
Females	22.7	76.7	0.6	= 1651
35-44 Combined	23.1	76.5	0.4	= 2149
Males	28.2	71.7	0.1	= 981
Females	18.8	80.6	0.6	= 1168
45-54 Combined	16.6	82.8	0.6	= 1678
Males	21.8	77.6	0.7	= 735
Females	12.5	87.0	0.5	= 943
55-64 Combined	9.2	89.9	0.9	= 1646
Males	12.9	86.0	1.1	= 722
Females	6.4	93.0	0.6	= 924
65-74 Combined	5.7	93.6	0.7	= 1336
Males	7.7	91.8	0.5	= 572
Females	4.2	95.0	0.8	= 764
75-84 Combined	3.1	96.6	0.3	= 612
Males	5.1	93.9	0.9	= 214
Females	2.0	98.0	---	= 398
85 + Combined	2.7	94.6	2.7	= 111
Males	7.7	92.3	---	= 39
Females	---	95.8	4.2	= 72

(1) See appendix A

C2.10

Q223. How important is the pornography issue to you - would you say
it is one of the most important, important, not very important,
not important at all?

	1984						
	One of most Imp 1	Important 2	Not very imp 3	Not imp at all 4	DK-NA 5		N's
All Ages	11.0	32.7	39.3	15.1	2.0	=	1467
18-24 Combined	4.8	26.9	49.5	17.3	1.4	=	208
Males	3.9	18.4	54.4	22.3	1.0	=	103
Females	5.7	35.2	44.8	12.4	1.9	=	105
25-34 Combined	6.6	30.5	46.3	15.8	0.9	=	348
Males	2.4	20.3	56.9	20.3	---	=	123
Females	8.9	36.0	40.4	13.3	1.3	=	225
35-44 Combined	11.3	32.1	44.4	11.3	1.0	=	293
Males	9.7	29.1	50.0	11.2	---	=	134
Females	12.6	34.6	39.6	11.3	1.9	=	159
45-54 Combined	14.2	41.5	31.3	10.2	2.8	=	176
Males	11.1	30.6	41.7	13.9	2.8	=	72
Females	16.3	49.0	24.0	7.7	2.9	=	104
55-64 Combined	16.7	35.9	27.6	16.7	3.1	=	192
Males	11.3	32.5	35.0	21.3	---	=	80
Females	20.5	38.4	22.3	13.4	5.4	=	112
65-74 Combined	16.1	33.5	29.0	17.4	3.9	=	155
Males	13.3	28.3	38.3	16.7	3.3	=	60
Females	17.9	36.8	23.2	17.9	4.2	=	95
75-84 Combined	14.8	28.4	32.1	22.2	2.5	=	81
Males	13.0	26.1	39.1	21.7	---	=	23
Females	15.5	29.3	29.3	22.4	3.4	=	58
85 + Combined	7.1	42.9	21.4	14.3	14.3	=	14
Males	---	----	50.0	50.0	----	=	2
Females	8.3	50.0	16.7	8.3	16.7	=	12

C2.11

Q225. How firm are you about (your opinion on/the way you feel about)
pornography - would you feel you are very likely to change (your
opinion), somewhat likely to change, somewhat unlikely to change
or very unlikely to change your opinion?

	1984					
	Change very likely 1	Somewhat likely 2	Somewhat unlikely 3	Change very unlikely 4	DK-NA 5	N's
All Ages	2.5	14.0	28.4	51.9	3.1	= 1467
18-24 Combined	6.3	23.1	31.7	35.6	3.4	= 208
Males	6.8	21.4	33.0	35.9	2.9	= 103
Females	5.7	24.8	30.5	35.2	3.8	= 105
25-34 Combined	3.4	15.8	36.8	42.2	1.7	= 348
Males	4.1	14.6	42.3	37.4	1.6	= 123
Females	3.1	16.4	33.8	44.9	1.8	= 225
35-44 Combined	2.4	18.4	30.7	46.4	2.0	= 293
Males	0.7	21.6	33.6	43.3	0.7	= 134
Females	3.8	15.7	28.3	49.1	3.1	= 159
45-54 Combined	0.6	10.2	25.6	61.4	2.3	= 176
Males	---	13.9	29.2	55.6	1.4	= 72
Females	1.0	7.7	23.1	65.4	2.9	= 104
55-64 Combined	2.1	6.3	22.9	64.6	4.2	= 192
Males	2.5	8.8	33.8	53.8	1.3	= 80
Females	1.8	4.5	15.2	72.3	6.3	= 112
65-74 Combined	---	9.0	17.4	69.7	3.9	= 155
Males	---	11.7	13.3	71.7	3.3	= 60
Females	---	7.4	20.0	68.4	4.2	= 95
75-84 Combined	---	4.9	19.8	66.7	8.6	= 81
Males	---	8.7	21.7	69.6	---	= 23
Females	---	3.4	19.0	65.5	12.1	= 58
85 + Combined	---	---	7.1	78.6	14.3	= 14
Males	---	---	50.0	50.0	---	= 2
Females	---	---	----	83.3	16.7	= 12

71

C2.12

Q221. Which of these statements comes closest to your
       feelings about pornography laws? Distribution
       of pornography should be .... (1)

		1973 - 1986			
		Illegal to all 1	Illegal > 18 2	Legal 3	DK-NA 4	N's
All Ages		41.2	50.5	6.7	1.6	=11984
18-24	Combined	20.4	69.6	9.4	0.6	= 1538
	Males	11.9	75.4	12.2	0.6	= 698
	Females	27.5	64.9	7.0	0.6	= 840
25-34	Combined	26.3	66.1	6.6	1.1	= 2914
	Males	16.8	74.3	7.8	1.1	= 1263
	Females	33.5	59.8	5.6	1.0	= 1651
35-44	Combined	35.8	57.4	6.0	0.8	= 2149
	Males	26.6	64.9	7.5	0.9	= 981
	Females	43.6	51.0	4.6	0.8	= 1168
45-54	Combined	48.2	44.3	5.5	2.0	= 1678
	Males	38.2	53.5	6.1	2.2	= 735
	Females	55.9	37.2	5.0	1.9	= 943
55-64	Combined	56.1	34.4	7.2	2.2	= 1646
	Males	49.6	38.9	9.6	1.9	= 722
	Females	61.3	31.0	5.4	2.4	= 924
65-74	Combined	63.7	27.1	6.8	2.4	= 1336
	Males	54.9	34.3	8.9	1.9	= 572
	Females	70.3	21.7	5.2	2.7	= 764
75-84	Combined	69.0	22.2	5.1	3.8	= 612
	Males	65.0	26.6	5.6	2.8	= 214
	Females	71.1	19.8	4.8	4.3	= 398
85 +	Combined	70.3	14.4	2.7	12.6	= 111
	Males	69.2	15.4	5.1	10.3	= 39
	Females	70.8	13.9	1.4	13.9	= 72

(1) See appendix A

SOCIOECONOMIC STATUS

OCCUPATIONAL LEVEL

Socioeconomic variables in the GSS include occupation, education, income, social class self-definition, and housing. The occupational classifications follow the U.S. occupational title system. (Davis and Smith, 1986, p. 25) For the present volume the GSS occupational categories were combined into two major groups - white collar and blue collar - with the white collar further defined as "professional," "administrative," and "other." For further information on the groupings see Appendix B.

While little change in the proportion of persons reporting blue collar occupations appears over the term of the survey, the growth in white collar occupations becomes apparent in the higher ratios of the 25-55 year old age groups employed in white collar areas. Men across all ages are more likely to be employed in blue collar fields than women. Blue collar employment is most common among the 18-25 year old men, but for women it is most common among the old age groups.

With reference to occupational prestige, occupations with prestige ranges from 30-39 and 40-49 claim the highest proportions of persons. The former is typified by skilled crafts, mechanics, and trades, and the latter most often represents office and sales personnel. Younger persons and women appear more frequently in the lower prestige occupations, with only one exception applying to women. A higher proportion of women fall in the 60-69 point category. This level that includes school teachers, registered nurses and other health practitioners along with engineers, authors, and the like.

The highest proportion of women in the three most prestigious occupational categories are in the 25-34 and 35-44 year age groups. Women in the 85+ generation do overmatch these two groups, but this could reflect sampling, or perhaps the fact that long life tends to be associated with higher educational and income levels. For men, like women, the higher prestige jobs (score of 50 and up) appear most often in the younger age groups. These data show the results of the trend toward more highly skilled jobs in the occupational marketplace.

Industry patterns for the age groups show the shift away from primary industry (agriculture, mining, fisheries, and forestry), transportation, and manufacturing The change is toward trade (retail/wholesale), government, and service fields. Women show greater employment in service and trade areas whereas men show higher involvement in manufacturing, transportation, and agriculture. The patterns in all three occupational tables - white collar/blue collar, prestige, and industry - are similar for respondents and spouses.

EDUCATION

The most significant educational data relate to the growth in the number of years of school completed by the younger population. Relatively large proportions of the older age groups completed 8th. grade or less and small proportions completed high school. By contrast, close to 80 percent of the younger age groups have completed high school. Similarly, the proportions of the younger population attending college, completing college, and continuing beyond college (post college) are considerably above those in the older population.

In all age groups more women than men have completed high school, but after high school the balance shifts toward higher proportions of men continuing to college and beyond.

The younger age groups (54 and below) are more in favor of increased expenditures for education than the old, with the highest proportions of those in favor appearing among the 25-34 year olds. Grouping of age categories suggests that there may be two population opinion clusters - 18-54 and 55-85 - or possibly three, 18-44, 55-74, and 75-85+ - with reference to expenditures for education.

INCOME

The majority of most age groups considers its income in early life to have been "average." The exceptions are the 45-54 and 55-64 years olds, who show higher proportions saying "below average," perhaps reflecting the effects of the depression in their thinking about their early income status. Some change in the perception of relative income status also appears over the course of the survey - higher proportions of persons have responded recently that their income is "above average."

Women and men in most age groups differ little in how they think about their relative income status. Still, one third or more of most age groups have been obliged to rely on government benefits for income at some time, with considerable shifts over the term of the survey. The proportion saying they have drawn benefits has increased from 33.7 percent in 1972-76 to 38.4 percent in 1982-86. The most marked changes are among the 25-34 year olds, where

44.5 percent report receiving such benefits in 1985-86 compared to 34.2 percent in 1973-76. This group is followed by the 35-44 year olds, where 42.4 percent report receiving benefits in 1982-86 compared to only 34.9 percent in 1972-76. The changes undoubtedly reflect the cumulative effect of adding individuals who have received benefits in previous years, but it also suggests an expansion of government programs for the American population. During the 1982-1986 period, 50 percent or more of the men in the two age groups specified report having received benefits at some time in their lives.

Prior to retirement the number of earners in a family is a major factor in determining family income. The age groups most frequently reporting only one or two earners are the 25-34 and 35-44 year olds (over half of the persons age 55 and up report "none" because of retirement). The 45 to 54 year olds show the highest percentage of three or more earners. Men and women in this age group generally report like numbers of earners, as they do among 25-34 year olds. The greatest dissimilarity between the sexes occurs in the groups age 55 and up, where from 5 to 9 percent more women than men report no earners. Surprisingly, though, more than 25 percent of the 85+ age group reports at least one earner.

One of the sharpest changes over the period of the survey appears in the figures on income. The proportion reporting incomes of $15,000 or less drops from 65 percent in 1973-76 to 35 percent in 1982-86, while the proportion reporting incomes of $25,000 or more rises from 8 percent in 1973-86 to nearly 35 percent in 1982-86.

The peak income years, with the highest proportions of persons earning $25,000 or more, are 35-44 and 45-54. The highest ratios of persons with lower incomes ($10,000 or less) are in the older ages. Members of the older age groups refuse to disclose their incomes more often than others.

Consistently higher percentages of women report lower incomes than men, the only exception being in the 85+ age group. Higher proportions of men than women also report incomes of $20,000 and above. This gap has persisted over the course of the survey.

Subjective feelings about income offer an interesting area of investigation. Do they reflect objective circumstances of income? About 75 percent of the respondents feel that their financial situation has improved or stayed the same, but there has been a slight drop over the period (39 percent in 1972-76 said "better" but only 36.6 percent said "better" in 1982-86). Much of this change is accounted for by the older age groups, 55 and above. The age group showing the sharpest downtrend is the 85+, which dropped from 30.5 percent "better" in 1972-76 down to 8.6 percent "better" in 1982-86. The 55-64 year olds deomonstrate the second greatest decline, falling from 33 percent "better" in 1972-76 down to 26.5 percent in 1982-86.

Except for the youngest age group, smaller proportions of women than men say that their financial situation is "better." Conversely, in all but one age group higher percentages of women than men say their income is "worse." This difference has increased for nearly all age groups over the period.

In spite of some decline in assessment of their financial situation, there has been little change in the proportion of respondents who consider their incomes average. Over the period of the survey over half of the respondents have said that their income is average. Men, however, are somewhat more likely than women to say that their income is above average, and, correspondingly, higher proportions of women say that their income is below average. Still, relatively high percentages of women do describe their income as average. They may do this because they are comparing themselves to other women rather than to men.

As in the case of reports of actual income, the age groups that show the highest proportions claiming "above average" income are the 35-44 and 45-54 year olds. Their assessment of their relative income status, therefore, appears realistic.

As to satisfaction with income, close to 75 percent of the respondents say that they are more or less satisfied or pretty well satisfied. This percentage is similar to the percentage of respondents who say that their income is better or has stayed the same.

There has been no marked change in satisfaction with income over the period. Approximately the same proportions of persons in each age and gender group express the same levels of satisfaction with their incomes in the most recent survey years as in the earliest years. The one exception is among 55-64 year olds, where there's a 9 percent increase in the proportion who say they're not at all satisfied.

As age advances, increasingly large percentages of persons express satisfaction with their incomes. The younger age groups express the greatest dissatisfaction with their incomes. Even though women have lower incomes than, men they differ little from men with respect to the percentages within age groups expressing satisfaction or dissatisfaction.

Social Security spending is strongly endorsed by the respondents and has continued to be so over the period. Women at most ages are more likely than men to say that too little is spent on Social Security. Attitudes on welfare have swung quite widely during the term of the survey, ranging from simple majority support (51% "about right" or "too little" spending on welfare) in 1972-76, to majority opposition from 1977-81 (58% "too much"), and back to stronger endorsement in 1982-86 (almost 67% "too little" or "about right").

SOCIAL CLASS IDENTIFICATION; SUCCESS IN LIFE

The General Social Survey differs somewhat from other national polls regarding proportions of persons who term themselves "working class." A Fortune magazine poll in the 1940s found that 80 percent of the public chose the self-designation of "middle class, while the New York Times-CBS Survey in the late 70s showed self-designations of 35 percent "middle class," 34 percent "working class," while 25 percent refused to select any class. (Robertson, 1981) The General Social Survey shows a nearly even split between "middle class" and "working class, with 46.5 percent "working lass", 45 percent "middle class," 3 percent "upper" and 5 percent "lower class." The younger GSS respondents more often describe themselves as members of the "working class," whereas older age groups lean toward the "middle class" identification. Older women choose "middle class" more frequently than men, but a slightly higher percentage of older women than men describe themselves as "lower class."

When it comes to opinion on how one gets ahead in life, the GSS shows that the American public endorses "hard work" as the reason for success - approximately two-thirds choose it. There is little support for "lucky breaks" and "help" as reasons for getting ahead, but more men than women choose these alternatives, perhaps as a way of attributing lack of personal advancement to factors beyond the individual's control.

SOCIAL CHARACTERISTICS OF RESIDENCE

A single family home is the norm for all age groups except for the very youngest. This latter group more commonly reports residing in an apartment or two unit dwelling and paying rent. The elderly report more frequent residence in apartments than most other age groups do, but are frequently owners rather than renters.

The GSS interviewers assess quality of housing by comparing the residence of the respondent with other residences in the neighborhood. (Davis and Smith, 1986, p. 76) Most residences are given a rating of "average." "Above average" is most frequently applied to the residences of the older age groups with the exception of the 85+, where the residences of a rather high proportion of men are classified as "below average, possibly because there were few respondents."

Ownership of residence is the most common pattern after age 35. In five of the age groups, however, women are more often renters than men. A large majority (80 to 85 percent) of the respondents report having phones in their homes, but the youngest age group is most likely to report having none. More men than women, too, report having no phone.

D1.1.1

Q2A. What kind of work do you (did you normally) do? That is, what
      (is/was) job called? (1) (2)

	W. collar, Prof. 1	W. collar, Admin. 2	W. collar, Other 3	Blue Collar 4	N's
1972 - 1986					
All Ages	15.6	15.9	19.8	48.6	=18017
18-24 Combined	9.5	11.1	23.8	55.7	= 2007
Males	9.2	11.1	8.0	71.7	= 1014
Females	9.8	11.1	39.9	39.3	= 993
25-34 Combined	19.8	14.2	22.3	43.8	= 4402
Males	19.5	16.8	7.4	56.3	= 2049
Females	20.0	11.8	35.2	32.9	= 2353
35-44 Combined	19.9	17.9	20.4	41.8	= 3289
Males	20.6	23.8	4.7	50.9	= 1543
Females	19.2	12.8	34.2	33.7	= 1746
45-54 Combined	14.3	18.9	19.5	47.3	= 2712
Males	15.4	22.5	5.0	57.1	= 1317
Females	13.2	15.5	33.2	38.1	= 1395
55-64 Combined	12.4	16.9	18.4	52.3	= 2630
Males	12.6	20.8	6.5	60.1	= 1239
Females	12.2	13.4	29.0	45.4	= 1391
65-74 Combined	11.8	15.9	14.7	57.6	= 1980
Males	10.0	18.8	4.7	66.6	= 943
Females	13.5	13.2	23.8	49.5	= 1037
75-84 Combined	14.6	16.9	13.6	54.9	= 852
Males	12.0	20.2	5.1	62.7	= 351
Females	16.4	14.6	19.6	49.5	= 501
85 + Combined	16.6	13.1	17.2	53.1	= 145
Males	11.8	19.1	2.9	66.2	= 68
Females	20.8	7.8	29.9	41.6	= 77

(1) See appendix A
(2) See appendix B

D1.1.2

Q2B. Prestige of respondent's occupation. (2)

| | 1972 - 1986 | | | | | | | |
	Low 10-19 1	20-29 2	30-39 3	40-49 4	50-59 5	60-69 6	High 70 + 7	N's
All Ages	9.7	15.7	26.1	25.5	12.3	8.6	2.1	=18017
18-24 Combined	13.7	21.8	30.7	22.9	7.3	3.2	0.5	= 2007
Males	19.4	23.4	26.9	19.7	7.8	2.1	0.7	= 1014
Females	7.8	20.1	34.6	26.1	6.7	4.3	0.3	= 993
25-34 Combined	7.0	13.7	26.9	27.4	13.0	9.7	2.3	= 4402
Males	7.8	12.7	27.7	25.7	15.6	7.0	3.5	= 2049
Females	6.4	14.5	26.3	28.9	10.7	12.0	1.2	= 2353
35-44 Combined	6.7	12.9	24.1	26.3	15.1	11.4	3.4	= 3289
Males	6.4	10.1	24.9	23.6	20.1	9.5	5.4	= 1543
Females	7.0	15.4	23.5	28.8	10.7	13.1	1.5	= 1746
45-54 Combined	10.0	14.5	27.0	24.2	13.6	8.7	2.1	= 2712
Males	9.6	10.9	27.9	22.6	18.0	8.0	3.0	= 1317
Females	10.4	17.8	26.1	25.7	9.5	9.3	1.2	= 1395
55-64 Combined	11.2	16.3	26.3	25.1	11.9	7.3	1.9	= 2630
Males	9.0	12.7	25.1	28.6	15.7	6.1	2.8	= 1239
Females	13.2	19.5	27.4	22.1	8.5	8.3	1.1	= 1391
65-74 Combined	12.8	19.0	23.5	24.7	10.7	7.8	1.5	= 1980
Males	11.3	13.8	25.6	28.0	14.1	4.7	2.5	= 943
Females	14.2	23.7	21.6	21.8	7.6	10.6	0.5	= 1037
75-84 Combined	12.4	17.5	22.8	24.5	10.7	10.2	1.9	= 852
Males	8.8	11.7	22.5	31.9	14.8	6.0	4.3	= 351
Females	15.0	21.6	23.0	19.4	7.8	13.2	0.2	= 501
85 + Combined	11.0	13.8	17.2	32.4	9.0	11.7	4.8	= 145
Males	10.3	10.3	14.7	39.7	13.2	4.4	7.4	= 68
Females	11.7	16.9	19.5	26.0	5.2	18.2	2.6	= 77

(2) See appendix B

D1.1.3

Q2C. Respondent's industry. (1) (2)

			1972 - 1986				
	Primary Industry 1	Manufa- cturing 2	Transp/ Communic. 3	Trade 4	Service 5	Govt. 6	N's
All Ages	10.0	24.1	6.0	17.5	35.6	7.0	=17972
18-24 Combined	8.9	23.1	4.1	27.7	30.1	6.0	= 2001
Males	15.9	27.6	5.6	24.9	18.0	8.0	= 1014
Females	1.7	18.4	2.6	30.6	42.6	4.1	= 987
25-34 Combined	9.2	21.7	6.4	17.1	38.6	7.1	= 4393
Males	17.2	26.0	8.1	13.3	25.6	9.9	= 2046
Females	2.3	18.0	4.8	20.5	49.9	4.6	= 2347
35-44 Combined	8.9	23.9	6.5	15.2	38.4	7.2	= 3276
Males	16.3	28.7	8.6	11.8	25.0	9.6	= 1538
Females	2.3	19.6	4.6	18.2	50.2	5.1	= 1738
45-54 Combined	10.7	27.0	6.1	15.8	32.8	7.6	= 2706
Males	18.9	31.0	8.5	10.3	21.5	9.8	= 1313
Females	2.9	23.2	3.7	21.0	43.5	5.6	= 1393
55-64 Combined	10.1	25.8	6.1	16.6	33.6	7.7	= 2624
Males	19.9	28.1	9.4	12.5	19.7	10.4	= 1233
Females	1.5	23.7	3.2	20.3	45.9	5.4	= 1391
65-74 Combined	12.5	24.6	5.6	16.1	34.7	6.4	= 1977
Males	24.3	26.8	8.9	11.8	20.1	8.1	= 941
Females	1.8	22.7	2.5	20.0	48.1	4.9	= 1036
75-84 Combined	12.6	23.6	6.7	16.9	34.2	5.9	= 850
Males	26.9	24.3	10.9	10.3	19.4	8.3	= 350
Females	2.6	23.2	3.8	21.6	44.6	4.2	= 500
85 + Combined	16.6	22.1	7.6	13.1	36.6	4.1	= 145
Males	27.9	16.2	10.3	10.3	26.5	8.8	= 68
Females	6.5	27.3	5.2	15.6	45.5	---	= 77

(1) See appendix A
(2) See appendix B

D1.2.1

Q5A. What kind of work (does/did) you [SPOUSE] normally do? That is,
what (is/was) (his/her) job called? (1) (2)

	1972 - 1986				
	W. collar, Prof. 1	W. collar, Admin. 2	W. collar, Other 3	Blue Collar 4	N's
All Ages	15.6	17.9	17.9	48.6	=11343
18-24 Combined	7.1	12.5	19.0	61.4	= 785
Males	5.4	10.3	52.9	31.4	= 223
Females	7.8	13.3	5.5	73.3	= 562
25-34 Combined	19.3	15.2	18.5	47.0	= 2928
Males	21.6	10.0	37.3	31.1	= 1156
Females	17.8	18.5	6.3	57.4	= 1772
35-44 Combined	19.0	18.6	19.0	43.4	= 2408
Males	21.0	11.9	36.7	30.4	= 1057
Females	17.5	23.8	5.1	53.6	= 1351
45-54 Combined	15.8	21.4	16.4	46.4	= 2037
Males	16.1	16.1	30.9	36.9	= 913
Females	15.6	25.7	4.6	54.1	= 1124
55-64 Combined	11.1	20.6	16.9	51.4	= 1815
Males	14.2	16.3	29.5	40.0	= 843
Females	8.3	24.4	6.0	61.3	= 972
65-74 Combined	11.0	17.8	16.9	54.3	= 1064
Males	12.5	13.8	27.6	46.1	= 558
Females	9.3	22.1	5.1	63.4	= 506
75-84 Combined	14.0	15.1	18.3	52.7	= 279
Males	16.8	13.7	28.0	41.6	= 161
Females	10.2	16.9	5.1	67.8	= 118
85 + Combined	25.9	18.5	18.5	37.0	= 27
Males	30.0	20.0	15.0	35.0	= 20
Females	14.3	14.3	28.6	42.9	= 7

(1) See appendix A
(2) See appendix B

D1.2.2

Q5B. Prestige of respondent's spouse's occupation. (2)

	1972 - 1986							
	Low 10-19 1	20-29 2	30-39 3	40-49 4	50-59 5	60-69 6	High 70 + 7	N's
All Ages	7.8	13.5	27.3	26.7	14.0	8.4	2.2	=11343
18-24 Combined	10.2	19.4	32.2	25.7	8.3	3.3	0.9	= 785
Males	4.9	20.2	37.2	27.8	5.4	4.0	0.4	= 223
Females	12.3	19.0	30.2	24.9	9.4	3.0	1.1	= 562
25-34 Combined	6.0	11.9	28.9	27.8	13.1	9.7	2.6	= 2928
Males	5.9	13.7	26.7	29.8	8.3	14.3	1.4	= 1156
Females	6.1	10.7	30.2	26.6	16.3	6.7	3.4	= 1772
35-44 Combined	6.0	11.0	25.6	27.8	16.2	10.9	2.5	= 2408
Males	6.9	14.2	23.0	30.7	9.6	14.8	0.9	= 1057
Females	5.3	8.6	27.6	25.5	21.5	7.8	3.7	= 1351
45-54 Combined	8.5	14.1	23.8	25.4	17.3	8.2	2.7	= 2037
Males	9.0	18.8	22.5	27.5	10.7	10.2	1.3	= 913
Females	8.1	10.2	24.9	23.7	22.6	6.6	3.9	= 1124
55-64 Combined	9.9	14.8	27.2	26.3	14.2	6.1	1.5	= 1815
Males	8.2	18.9	29.9	23.8	9.5	9.0	0.7	= 843
Females	11.3	11.2	24.9	28.5	18.2	3.6	2.3	= 972
65-74 Combined	10.7	15.5	29.4	25.0	10.9	6.8	1.7	= 1064
Males	12.0	18.8	29.4	24.2	7.0	7.9	0.7	= 558
Females	9.3	11.9	29.4	25.9	15.2	5.5	2.8	= 506
75-84 Combined	6.5	16.8	29.0	26.9	8.2	10.4	2.2	= 279
Males	8.7	18.6	30.4	23.0	3.1	14.9	1.2	= 161
Females	3.4	14.4	27.1	32.2	15.3	4.2	3.4	= 118
85 + Combined	18.5	----	18.5	33.3	11.1	14.8	3.7	= 27
Males	20.0	----	15.0	25.0	15.0	20.0	5.0	= 20
Females	14.3	----	28.6	57.1	----	----	---	= 7

(2) See appendix B

D1.2.3

Q5C. Spouse's industry. (1) (2)

	1972 - 1986						
	Primary Industry 1	Manufa- cturing 2	Transp/ Communic. 3	Trade 4	Service 5	Govt. 6	N's
All Ages	11.6	25.3	7.0	16.9	32.2	7.0	=11292
18-24 Combined	14.9	25.0	6.0	22.3	22.2	9.5	= 779
Males	1.8	15.4	2.3	29.4	44.8	6.3	= 221
Females	20.1	28.9	7.5	19.5	13.3	10.8	= 558
25-34 Combined	11.4	23.3	7.6	15.2	34.9	7.6	= 2918
Males	2.2	18.3	3.7	19.2	52.5	4.1	= 1149
Females	17.4	26.5	10.1	12.6	23.5	9.9	= 1769
35-44 Combined	10.8	24.6	7.9	15.2	34.6	6.9	= 2394
Males	3.2	19.0	3.3	18.0	52.4	4.0	= 1050
Females	16.7	28.9	11.5	12.9	20.8	9.1	= 1344
45-54 Combined	11.0	27.3	6.5	17.5	31.8	6.0	= 2032
Males	2.9	21.5	3.4	22.0	46.0	4.3	= 911
Females	17.6	32.0	9.0	13.8	20.2	7.3	= 1121
55-64 Combined	12.4	27.0	6.5	18.5	28.7	7.0	= 1803
Males	2.4	23.8	3.3	24.8	40.4	5.3	= 836
Females	21.0	29.7	9.2	13.0	18.5	8.6	= 967
65-74 Combined	12.4	26.0	5.7	17.5	31.8	6.6	= 1060
Males	3.1	23.7	3.6	21.4	42.6	5.6	= 556
Females	22.6	28.6	7.9	13.3	19.8	7.7	= 504
75-84 Combined	9.7	25.1	6.8	18.3	37.3	2.9	= 279
Males	0.6	19.3	4.3	21.7	50.3	3.7	= 161
Females	22.0	33.1	10.2	13.6	19.5	1.7	= 118
85 + Combined	11.1	14.8	11.1	18.5	44.4	---	= 27
Males	5.0	10.0	5.0	25.0	55.0	---	= 20
Females	28.6	28.6	28.6	----	14.3	---	= 7

(1) See appendix A
(2) See appendix B

D2.1.1

Q12. What is the highest grade in elementary school or high school that you
      finished and got credit for? (1) (2)

	1972 - 1986							
	8th grade or less 1	Some HS 2	HS grad 3	Some college 4	College grad. 5	Post college 6	DK-NA 7	N's
All Ages	15.1	17.6	33.5	18.1	9.1	6.4	0.2	=19614
18-24 Combined	2.1	22.0	41.8	25.9	6.8	1.2	0.2	= 2468
Males	1.9	23.5	40.4	26.5	6.2	1.5	---	= 1162
Females	2.3	20.8	43.1	25.3	7.4	0.8	0.3	= 1306
25-34 Combined	3.6	13.1	37.5	22.9	13.9	8.9	0.1	= 4696
Males	3.4	11.6	33.5	24.2	15.7	11.5	---	= 2070
Females	3.8	14.3	40.7	21.9	12.5	6.7	0.1	= 2626
35-44 Combined	7.9	14.6	35.8	20.0	11.0	10.4	0.3	= 3451
Males	9.2	13.4	28.5	21.3	12.4	14.8	0.3	= 1552
Females	6.7	15.6	41.8	18.9	9.8	6.9	0.3	= 1899
45-54 Combined	14.5	20.4	35.1	15.1	7.9	6.9	0.2	= 2877
Males	17.0	18.8	28.6	15.6	9.8	10.1	0.1	= 1330
Females	12.3	21.7	40.6	14.6	6.2	4.2	0.3	= 1547
55-64 Combined	23.5	19.9	31.8	13.3	5.8	5.6	0.1	= 2775
Males	25.8	17.9	27.1	13.7	6.7	8.4	0.2	= 1245
Females	21.7	21.6	35.6	12.9	5.0	3.3	0.1	= 1530
65-74 Combined	37.5	21.0	22.9	9.6	5.3	3.3	0.3	= 2181
Males	40.1	19.3	20.7	10.0	5.0	4.4	0.4	= 946
Females	35.5	22.3	24.6	9.2	5.6	2.5	0.2	= 1235
75-84 Combined	49.0	16.9	13.2	11.2	6.5	2.4	0.8	= 984
Males	53.4	16.4	9.9	6.8	8.2	4.5	0.8	= 354
Females	46.5	17.1	15.1	13.7	5.6	1.3	0.8	= 630
85 + Combined	52.2	13.2	13.2	9.9	5.5	2.7	3.3	= 182
Males	64.7	7.4	8.8	8.8	4.4	2.9	2.9	= 68
Females	44.7	16.7	15.8	10.5	6.1	2.6	3.5	= 114

(1) See appendix A
(2) See appendix B

89

D2.1.2

Q16. Respondent's degree. (1)

	< high school 1	High school 2	Junior college 3	Bachelor 4	Graduate 5	DK-NA 6	N's
1972 - 1986							
All Ages	32.0	50.1	2.7	10.3	4.6	0.3	=19614
18-24 Combined	23.2	66.0	3.3	6.6	0.3	0.6	= 2468
Males	24.4	65.0	2.9	6.8	0.2	0.7	= 1162
Females	22.1	67.0	3.6	6.4	0.5	0.5	= 1306
25-34 Combined	16.1	57.4	4.7	16.4	5.2	0.1	= 4696
Males	14.6	54.9	4.7	18.6	7.1	---	= 2070
Females	17.3	59.4	4.7	14.7	3.7	0.2	= 2626
35-44 Combined	21.6	54.1	2.8	13.2	7.9	0.4	= 3451
Males	20.6	49.9	2.8	15.4	10.8	0.4	= 1552
Females	22.5	57.5	2.7	11.4	5.5	0.4	= 1899
45-54 Combined	33.8	49.6	1.8	8.5	6.0	0.3	= 2877
Males	34.2	43.8	2.1	10.7	8.9	0.3	= 1330
Females	33.5	54.5	1.6	6.7	3.5	0.3	= 1547
55-64 Combined	42.3	45.4	1.2	6.7	4.1	0.3	= 2775
Males	43.1	41.0	0.9	8.4	6.3	0.3	= 1245
Females	41.6	48.9	1.5	5.4	2.4	0.3	= 1530
65-74 Combined	58.1	31.9	1.2	5.8	2.6	0.4	= 2181
Males	59.2	30.5	1.0	4.7	4.0	0.6	= 946
Females	57.2	33.0	1.5	6.6	1.5	0.2	= 1235
75-84 Combined	66.7	22.8	1.1	5.9	2.8	0.7	= 984
Males	70.3	16.1	0.8	6.8	5.4	0.6	= 354
Females	64.6	26.5	1.3	5.4	1.4	0.8	= 630
85 + Combined	70.3	19.8	1.6	3.8	3.8	0.5	= 182
Males	75.0	14.7	---	2.9	5.9	1.5	= 68
Females	67.5	22.8	2.6	4.4	2.6	---	= 114

(1) See appendix A

90

D2.2

Q69G. We are faced with many problems in this country, none of
which can be solved easily or inexpensively. I'm going
to name some of these problems, and for each one I'd
like you to tell me whether you think we're spending too
much money on it, too little money, or about the right
amount.

Improving the nation's education system.

		1973 - 1986			
	Too little 1	About right 2	Too much 3	DK-NA 4	N's
All Ages	54.5	33.5	8.2	3.8	=18006
18-24 Combined	60.3	34.3	3.2	2.2	= 2268
Males	60.5	34.4	3.3	1.7	= 1049
Females	60.0	34.2	3.0	2.7	= 1219
25-34 Combined	64.3	29.3	4.1	2.3	= 4338
Males	63.1	29.9	5.5	1.5	= 1888
Females	65.3	28.8	3.1	2.8	= 2450
35-44 Combined	60.2	31.2	6.5	2.1	= 3211
Males	56.4	33.8	7.8	2.0	= 1444
Females	63.3	29.0	5.5	2.2	= 1767
45-54 Combined	52.9	33.5	9.4	4.2	= 2561
Males	52.0	32.7	11.9	3.4	= 1161
Females	53.7	34.1	7.3	4.9	= 1400
55-64 Combined	46.0	37.5	12.0	4.5	= 2523
Males	45.8	36.4	15.0	2.9	= 1119
Females	46.2	38.3	9.7	5.8	= 1404
65-74 Combined	40.8	37.3	15.2	6.7	= 2023
Males	38.5	37.0	18.6	5.8	= 872
Females	42.6	37.4	12.7	7.3	= 1151
75-84 Combined	35.8	39.3	15.1	9.9	= 909
Males	31.9	39.6	21.2	7.4	= 326
Females	37.9	39.1	11.7	11.3	= 583
85 + Combined	32.9	38.2	16.2	12.7	= 173
Males	30.2	44.4	12.7	12.7	= 63
Females	34.5	34.5	18.2	12.7	= 110

D3.1

Q26. Thinking about the time when you were 16 years old, compared with
American families in general then, would you say your family income
was -- below average, average or above average? (1)
(PROBE: Just your best guess.)

	Far below average 1	Below average 2	Average 3	Above average 4	Far above average 5	DK-NA 6	N's
1972 - 1986							
All Ages	7.5	23.4	52.7	13.8	1.5	1.1	=19605
18-24 Combined	3.4	16.4	59.3	18.6	1.5	0.9	= 2468
Males	2.3	17.0	58.3	20.0	1.9	0.6	= 1162
Females	4.3	15.9	60.3	17.4	1.1	1.1	= 1306
25-34 Combined	4.9	21.4	54.9	16.6	1.6	0.6	= 4693
Males	4.4	21.8	54.0	18.0	1.4	0.4	= 2067
Females	5.3	21.1	55.6	15.5	1.7	0.8	= 2626
35-44 Combined	6.8	24.6	52.5	13.3	1.7	1.0	= 3447
Males	6.9	26.6	50.0	14.1	1.5	0.8	= 1551
Females	6.7	23.0	54.6	12.7	1.8	1.2	= 1896
45-54 Combined	9.3	26.3	49.9	12.0	1.4	1.1	= 2877
Males	9.2	27.2	48.8	12.6	1.5	0.7	= 1330
Females	9.4	25.5	50.9	11.4	1.4	1.4	= 1547
55-64 Combined	11.0	28.3	47.1	10.5	1.7	1.3	= 2773
Males	11.4	29.7	45.0	10.8	1.8	1.3	= 1244
Females	10.7	27.1	48.8	10.3	1.6	1.4	= 1529
65-74 Combined	11.0	24.1	51.8	9.9	1.5	1.7	= 2181
Males	10.1	25.7	51.2	9.9	1.6	1.5	= 946
Females	11.6	22.9	52.3	10.0	1.4	1.9	= 1235
75-84 Combined	9.0	23.6	51.9	12.3	1.4	1.7	= 984
Males	8.8	25.1	48.6	14.4	1.1	2.0	= 354
Females	9.2	22.7	53.8	11.1	1.6	1.6	= 630
85 + Combined	9.9	19.2	54.4	13.7	0.5	2.2	= 182
Males	10.3	23.5	50.0	13.2	1.5	1.5	= 68
Females	9.6	16.7	57.0	14.0	---	2.6	= 114

(1) See appendix A

D3.2

Q194. Did you ever--because of sicknessss, unemployment,
       or any other reason -- receive anything like
       welfare, unemployment insurance, or other aid from
       government agencies? (1)

	1973 - 1984			
	Yes 1	No 2	DK-NA 3	N's
All Ages	35.7	64.1	0.2	=12055
18-24 Combined	32.1	67.8	0.1	= 1588
Males	31.8	68.2	---	= 736
Females	32.4	67.4	0.2	= 852
25-34 Combined	39.0	60.9	0.2	= 2849
Males	43.0	56.7	0.2	= 1239
Females	35.8	64.0	0.1	= 1610
35-44 Combined	37.0	62.9	0.1	= 2092
Males	41.1	58.8	0.1	= 951
Females	33.7	66.3	0.1	= 1141
45-54 Combined	38.6	61.1	0.3	= 1804
Males	41.2	58.6	0.2	= 816
Females	36.4	63.3	0.3	= 988
55-64 Combined	35.0	64.8	0.2	= 1714
Males	39.2	60.6	0.3	= 771
Females	31.6	68.3	0.1	= 943
65-74 Combined	33.6	66.2	0.2	= 1347
Males	37.0	62.8	0.2	= 610
Females	30.7	69.1	0.3	= 737
75-84 Combined	24.6	75.4	---	= 557
Males	24.3	75.7	---	= 218
Females	24.8	75.2	---	= 339
85 + Combined	27.9	71.2	1.0	= 104
Males	29.5	68.2	2.3	= 44
Females	26.7	73.3	---	= 60

(1) See appendix A

D3.3

Q187B. During the last few years, has your financial
        situation been getting better, worse, or has
        it stayed the same? (1)

	1972 - 1986				
	Better	Worse	Stayed the same	DK-NA	N's
	1	2	3	4	
All Ages	37.8	22.5	38.8	0.9	=19614
18-24 Combined	44.9	20.2	33.5	1.4	= 2468
Males	44.8	18.4	35.4	1.4	= 1162
Females	44.9	21.7	31.9	1.5	= 1306
25-34 Combined	48.6	20.3	30.6	0.5	= 4696
Males	53.1	18.2	28.3	0.4	= 2070
Females	45.0	21.9	32.5	0.6	= 2626
35-44 Combined	40.8	24.5	33.9	0.7	= 3451
Males	45.0	22.2	32.3	0.4	= 1552
Females	37.4	26.4	35.2	0.9	= 1899
45-54 Combined	37.1	25.2	37.0	0.7	= 2877
Males	38.5	24.4	36.5	0.6	= 1330
Females	35.9	25.9	37.4	0.8	= 1547
55-64 Combined	30.9	24.4	43.6	1.1	= 2775
Males	35.7	22.7	40.8	0.9	= 1245
Females	27.1	25.9	45.8	1.2	= 1530
65-74 Combined	19.9	23.0	55.9	1.1	= 2181
Males	21.5	23.3	53.9	1.4	= 946
Females	18.7	22.8	57.5	1.0	= 1235
75-84 Combined	22.9	17.7	58.3	1.1	= 984
Males	25.4	15.0	57.6	2.0	= 354
Females	21.4	19.2	58.7	0.6	= 630
85 + Combined	17.0	17.6	63.2	2.2	= 182
Males	17.6	16.2	64.7	1.5	= 68
Females	16.7	18.4	62.3	2.6	= 114

(1) See appendix A

D3.4

Q36. Just thinking about your family now -- those people in the
household who are related to you . . . How many persons in
the family, including yourself, earned any money last year
from any job or employment? (1)

				1972 - 1986			
	None 1	One 2	Two 3	Three 4	4 - 8 5	NA 6	N's
All Ages	14.8	39.7	32.1	7.7	4.6	1.1	=19614
18-24 Combined	3.8	35.3	35.5	14.1	10.2	1.2	= 2468
Males	2.0	33.7	32.7	17.3	13.2	1.1	= 1162
Females	5.4	36.8	38.0	11.2	7.5	1.2	= 1306
25-34 Combined	3.5	46.9	44.3	3.1	1.4	0.8	= 4696
Males	1.6	46.9	45.8	3.7	1.3	0.7	= 2070
Females	5.0	46.9	43.1	2.6	1.5	1.0	= 2626
35-44 Combined	3.0	40.2	37.9	10.8	7.4	0.8	= 3451
Males	1.4	43.4	40.1	8.9	5.8	0.5	= 1552
Females	4.3	37.6	36.1	12.4	8.6	1.0	= 1899
45-54 Combined	5.7	36.0	33.1	15.7	8.4	1.1	= 2877
Males	4.2	35.6	34.6	15.5	8.7	1.4	= 1330
Females	7.0	36.3	31.7	15.8	8.1	0.9	= 1547
55-64 Combined	15.5	46.4	28.5	5.8	2.6	1.2	= 2775
Males	10.7	45.0	32.1	7.6	3.3	1.4	= 1245
Females	19.3	47.6	25.5	4.4	2.1	1.1	= 1530
65-74 Combined	51.5	34.1	10.9	1.9	0.5	1.1	= 2181
Males	48.3	34.2	13.5	2.1	0.7	1.1	= 946
Females	53.9	34.0	8.9	1.7	0.2	1.2	= 1235
75-84 Combined	71.7	21.3	5.1	---	0.2	1.6	= 984
Males	67.2	24.0	6.8	---	0.3	1.7	= 354
Females	74.3	19.8	4.1	---	0.2	1.6	= 630
85 + Combined	68.1	23.6	4.4	0.5	0.5	2.7	= 182
Males	63.2	27.9	4.4	1.5	---	2.9	= 68
Females	71.1	21.1	4.4	---	0.9	2.6	= 114

(1) See appendix A

95

D3.5

Q37. In which of these groups did your total family income, from all sources, fall last year before taxes, that is? (1)

	< $5K	$5K to $9999	$10k to $14999	$15k to $19999	$20k to $24999	$25k or more	Refused	DK-NA	N's
	1	2	3	4	5	6	7	8	
All Ages	13.6	17.4	17.3	12.2	10.4	21.4	3.3	4.3	=18006
18-24 Combined	18.7	21.7	18.2	11.2	8.0	13.2	1.5	7.6	= 2268
Males	16.0	20.7	16.7	12.3	8.6	16.8	1.3	7.6	= 1049
Females	20.9	22.6	19.4	10.3	7.5	10.1	1.6	7.5	= 1219
25-34 Combined	8.4	15.9	21.7	15.9	13.1	21.0	2.0	1.9	= 4338
Males	6.8	13.9	23.3	16.6	14.5	21.9	2.2	0.8	= 1888
Females	9.6	17.5	20.5	15.4	12.0	20.4	1.8	2.8	= 2450
35-44 Combined	5.9	11.2	17.3	14.3	13.1	33.4	2.6	2.2	= 3211
Males	3.5	9.4	16.6	15.4	14.3	37.4	2.5	0.9	= 1444
Females	7.8	12.6	17.8	13.4	12.2	30.2	2.7	3.3	= 1767
45-54 Combined	8.0	13.2	15.3	13.1	11.7	31.4	3.5	3.8	= 2561
Males	5.9	11.3	14.8	14.2	13.3	35.1	3.7	1.8	= 1161
Females	9.8	14.9	15.6	12.1	10.4	28.3	3.4	5.5	= 1400
55-64 Combined	13.0	18.6	16.6	11.1	10.6	21.1	4.7	4.4	= 2523
Males	9.2	16.0	16.6	11.8	12.2	28.1	3.9	2.1	= 1119
Females	16.0	20.7	16.5	10.5	9.3	15.6	5.3	6.1	= 1404
65-74 Combined	26.9	25.9	14.1	6.9	4.7	9.4	5.8	6.3	= 2023
Males	21.1	27.4	17.3	7.7	4.8	12.3	5.6	3.8	= 872
Females	31.3	24.7	11.7	6.3	4.6	7.2	5.9	8.3	= 1151
75-84 Combined	35.3	26.1	10.6	4.1	3.7	4.4	6.3	9.6	= 909
Males	26.1	30.4	15.3	5.5	4.3	8.6	5.5	4.3	= 326
Females	40.5	23.7	7.9	3.3	3.4	2.1	6.7	12.5	= 583
85 + Combined	39.3	17.3	7.5	2.3	1.7	5.2	8.1	18.5	= 173
Males	41.3	20.6	9.5	3.2	3.2	3.2	6.3	12.7	= 63
Females	38.2	15.5	6.4	1.8	0.9	6.4	9.1	21.8	= 110

(1) See appendix A

D3.6

Q188. Compared with American families in general, would you say your family
income is far below average, below average, average, above average,
or far above average?
(PROBE: Just your best guess.)

	Far below average 1	Below average 2	Average 3	Above average 4	Far above average 5	DK-NA 6	N's
			1972 - 1986				
All Ages	4.8	22.9	52.6	17.2	1.6	0.9	=19614
18-24 Combined	4.7	23.7	55.0	14.9	1.2	0.5	= 2468
Males	4.0	23.0	54.0	17.1	1.5	0.4	= 1162
Females	5.4	24.3	56.0	12.9	0.9	0.5	= 1306
25-34 Combined	4.5	22.8	53.3	17.6	1.2	0.5	= 4696
Males	4.0	22.1	50.8	21.2	1.6	0.3	= 2070
Females	4.9	23.5	55.3	14.7	0.9	0.7	= 2626
35-44 Combined	4.6	18.9	50.4	23.2	2.2	0.7	= 3451
Males	4.1	16.0	47.7	28.6	2.9	0.6	= 1552
Females	5.1	21.2	52.6	18.9	1.6	0.7	= 1899
45-54 Combined	4.6	20.8	50.3	21.2	2.5	0.6	= 2877
Males	4.1	19.8	46.5	25.9	3.4	0.4	= 1330
Females	4.9	21.7	53.6	17.3	1.7	0.8	= 1547
55-64 Combined	4.8	23.5	53.0	16.1	1.7	0.9	= 2775
Males	4.5	19.8	51.1	21.4	2.6	0.7	= 1245
Females	5.1	26.5	54.5	11.9	1.0	1.0	= 1530
65-74 Combined	5.8	29.1	53.0	9.4	1.1	1.7	= 2181
Males	5.8	28.6	51.2	11.7	1.4	1.3	= 946
Females	5.7	29.5	54.4	7.6	0.8	1.9	= 1235
75-84 Combined	4.3	26.9	55.6	9.9	0.8	2.5	= 984
Males	2.8	29.1	52.0	13.3	0.8	2.0	= 354
Females	5.1	25.7	57.6	7.9	0.8	2.9	= 630
85 + Combined	6.0	20.9	58.2	10.4	---	4.4	= 182
Males	8.8	19.1	58.8	11.8	---	1.5	= 68
Females	4.4	21.9	57.9	9.6	---	6.1	= 114

D3.7

Q187A. We are interested in how people are getting along
        financially these days. So far as you and your family
        are concerned, would you say that you are pretty well
        satisfied with you financial situation, more or less
        satisfied, or not satisfied at all? (1)

		1972 - 1986			
	Pretty well satisfied 1	More or less satisfied 2	Not at all satisfied 3	DK-NA 4	N's
All Ages	30.3	44.0	25.3	0.4	=19614
18-24 Combined	26.0	44.4	29.3	0.3	= 2468
Males	26.6	45.1	28.1	0.3	= 1162
Females	25.4	43.7	30.5	0.4	= 1306
25-34 Combined	21.4	46.5	31.8	0.3	= 4696
Males	22.1	45.9	31.6	0.4	= 2070
Females	20.9	46.9	31.9	0.3	= 2626
35-44 Combined	25.6	44.4	29.8	0.2	= 3451
Males	25.6	45.5	28.8	0.1	= 1552
Females	25.7	43.5	30.5	0.3	= 1899
45-54 Combined	32.6	44.5	22.4	0.5	= 2877
Males	32.3	44.6	22.6	0.5	= 1330
Females	32.9	44.3	22.2	0.6	= 1547
55-64 Combined	37.6	41.8	19.9	0.7	= 2775
Males	38.5	41.9	19.0	0.6	= 1245
Females	36.9	41.6	20.7	0.8	= 1530
65-74 Combined	40.1	42.3	17.3	0.3	= 2181
Males	42.4	39.5	17.9	0.2	= 946
Females	38.4	44.4	16.8	0.4	= 1235
75-84 Combined	47.1	39.6	12.6	0.7	= 984
Males	46.9	40.4	12.1	0.6	= 354
Females	47.1	39.2	12.9	0.8	= 630
85 + Combined	51.6	36.8	9.3	2.2	= 182
Males	57.4	30.9	11.8	---	= 68
Females	48.2	40.4	7.9	3.5	= 114

(1) See appendix A

98

D3.8

Q69M. We are faced with many problems in this country, none of
which can be solved easily or inexpensively. I'm going
to name some of these problems, and for each one I'd
like you to tell me whether you think we're spending too
much money on it, too little money, or about the right
amount.

Social Security.

	Too little 1	About right 2	Too much 3	DK-NA 4	N's
1984 - 1986					
All Ages	54.0	35.1	6.7	4.2	= 4457
18-24 Combined	57.7	30.3	7.6	4.4	= 501
Males	52.4	34.2	9.1	4.3	= 231
Females	62.2	27.0	6.3	4.4	= 270
25-34 Combined	61.3	27.1	7.3	4.4	= 1100
Males	53.9	31.9	10.4	3.8	= 473
Females	66.8	23.4	4.9	4.8	= 627
35-44 Combined	54.5	31.9	9.7	3.9	= 875
Males	48.7	34.7	13.7	2.8	= 386
Females	59.1	29.7	6.5	4.7	= 489
45-54 Combined	54.5	35.9	5.6	4.0	= 574
Males	54.9	36.8	6.0	2.3	= 266
Females	54.2	35.1	5.2	5.5	= 308
55-64 Combined	51.1	38.2	5.6	5.1	= 587
Males	44.7	42.0	7.6	5.7	= 264
Females	56.3	35.0	4.0	4.6	= 323
65-74 Combined	45.6	48.2	3.2	3.0	= 504
Males	44.0	51.3	2.6	2.1	= 191
Females	46.6	46.3	3.5	3.5	= 313
75-84 Combined	38.2	52.8	4.1	4.9	= 267
Males	35.4	51.9	7.6	5.1	= 79
Females	39.4	53.2	2.7	4.8	= 188
85 + Combined	42.9	46.9	4.1	6.1	= 49
Males	50.0	50.0	---	---	= 12
Females	40.5	45.9	5.4	8.1	= 37

D4.1

Q184. If you were asked to use one of four names for your social
        class, which would you say you belong in: the lower class,
        the working class, the middle class, or the upper class? (1)

	1972 - 1986					
	Lower class 1	Working class 2	Middle class 3	Upper class 4	DK-NA 5	N's
All Ages	5.0	46.5	45.0	3.0	0.6	=18072
18-24 Combined	5.9	51.1	40.4	2.3	0.4	= 2270
Males	5.0	52.6	39.4	2.7	0.3	= 1068
Females	6.7	49.8	41.2	2.0	0.4	= 1202
25-34 Combined	4.2	51.9	41.8	1.9	0.3	= 4324
Males	3.0	53.3	41.4	2.0	0.3	= 1956
Females	5.2	50.7	42.1	1.7	0.2	= 2368
35-44 Combined	4.0	47.8	44.6	3.1	0.5	= 3180
Males	3.6	46.6	45.8	3.4	0.5	= 1460
Females	4.4	48.8	43.7	2.8	0.4	= 1720
45-54 Combined	4.4	47.0	44.5	3.3	0.8	= 2642
Males	3.9	47.6	44.7	3.3	0.6	= 1245
Females	4.9	46.5	44.5	3.2	0.9	= 1397
55-64 Combined	4.8	45.3	46.1	3.1	0.6	= 2547
Males	4.6	45.2	46.5	3.1	0.6	= 1166
Females	4.9	45.4	45.8	3.2	0.7	= 1381
65-74 Combined	7.2	38.2	49.9	3.9	0.8	= 2010
Males	7.6	42.2	45.7	3.5	1.0	= 880
Females	6.9	35.0	53.1	4.2	0.7	= 1130
75-84 Combined	6.0	28.8	58.8	5.0	1.4	= 921
Males	6.6	32.7	55.6	4.2	0.9	= 333
Females	5.6	26.5	60.7	5.4	1.7	= 588
85 + Combined	7.9	29.8	52.2	7.9	2.2	= 178
Males	6.1	43.9	40.9	6.1	3.0	= 66
Females	8.9	21.4	58.9	8.9	1.8	= 112

(1) See appendix A

D4.2

Q197. Some people say that people get ahead by their own hard work; others say that lucky breaks or help from other people are more important. Which do you think is most important? (1)

			1973 - 1985			
	Hard work	Both equally	Luck or help	Other	DK-NA	N's
	1	2	3	4	5	
All Ages	63.0	24.2	11.5	0.3	1.0	=11941
18-24 Combined	63.8	22.7	12.7	0.3	0.5	= 1549
Males	60.5	24.0	14.4	0.5	0.5	= 736
Females	66.8	21.5	11.2	0.1	0.4	= 813
25-34 Combined	64.0	23.6	11.4	0.3	0.6	= 2775
Males	61.7	24.4	12.6	0.6	0.7	= 1203
Females	65.8	23.0	10.5	0.1	0.6	= 1572
35-44 Combined	63.0	25.7	10.2	0.1	1.0	= 2101
Males	58.4	28.3	12.5	0.2	0.5	= 935
Females	66.7	23.5	8.3	0.1	1.4	= 1166
45-54 Combined	61.0	25.9	11.5	0.5	1.1	= 1731
Males	61.0	24.6	12.8	0.5	1.1	= 794
Females	61.0	27.1	10.4	0.4	1.1	= 937
55-64 Combined	61.8	24.8	12.0	0.5	0.9	= 1737
Males	61.1	23.3	14.0	0.8	0.8	= 785
Females	62.4	26.1	10.3	0.3	0.9	= 952
65-74 Combined	63.5	22.5	12.3	0.1	1.6	= 1345
Males	59.2	23.6	15.0	0.3	1.9	= 593
Females	66.9	21.5	10.2	---	1.3	= 752
75-84 Combined	64.4	22.3	11.0	---	2.4	= 584
Males	61.9	22.4	12.4	---	3.3	= 210
Females	65.8	22.2	10.2	---	1.9	= 374
85 + Combined	57.1	26.9	8.4	---	7.6	= 119
Males	58.3	29.2	6.3	---	6.3	= 48
Females	56.3	25.4	9.9	---	8.5	= 71

(1) See appendix A

D5.1

Q55. Dwelling type. (2)

	1982 - 1986								N's
	Trailer	Detached 1-fam. H	2 Units	3-4 Fam house	Row house	Apart-ment	Other	NA	
	1	2	3	4	5	6	7	8	
All Ages	6.5	63.9	6.9	2.0	4.5	14.4	0.9	1.0	= 7543
18-24 Combined	7.7	48.5	7.8	3.3	4.3	25.8	1.5	1.1	= 844
Males	9.1	52.7	5.6	3.8	3.5	22.8	1.8	0.8	= 395
Females	6.5	44.8	9.8	2.9	4.9	28.5	1.3	1.3	= 449
25-34 Combined	6.2	55.3	8.9	3.4	5.3	19.0	1.1	0.7	= 1938
Males	6.6	55.3	7.7	4.1	4.5	19.9	0.8	1.2	= 836
Females	6.0	55.4	9.9	2.8	5.8	18.4	1.4	0.4	= 1102
35-44 Combined	5.5	70.5	6.4	1.6	4.3	9.8	0.6	1.1	= 1407
Males	6.7	69.6	6.7	2.2	3.0	9.6	0.5	1.6	= 625
Females	4.6	71.2	6.1	1.2	5.4	10.0	0.8	0.8	= 782
45-54 Combined	5.2	72.7	4.7	1.1	3.9	10.4	0.5	1.5	= 965
Males	4.6	72.7	3.7	0.7	3.9	12.2	0.2	1.8	= 433
Females	5.6	72.7	5.5	1.5	3.9	8.8	0.8	1.1	= 532
55-64 Combined	7.6	72.8	5.5	1.0	4.3	7.8	0.2	0.9	= 1025
Males	6.8	74.9	5.0	1.1	3.8	7.0	0.5	0.9	= 442
Females	8.2	71.2	5.8	0.9	4.6	8.4	---	0.9	= 583
65-74 Combined	7.3	66.9	6.5	1.4	4.7	11.6	0.9	0.6	= 850
Males	6.6	70.1	5.7	0.9	4.8	9.6	1.5	0.9	= 334
Females	7.8	64.9	7.0	1.7	4.7	13.0	0.6	0.4	= 516
75-84 Combined	7.2	64.4	6.0	0.7	3.7	15.5	1.2	1.4	= 433
Males	5.2	71.9	3.0	0.7	5.2	11.9	1.5	0.7	= 135
Females	8.1	61.1	7.4	0.7	3.0	17.1	1.0	1.7	= 298
85 + Combined	4.9	59.3	8.6	1.2	2.5	21.0	1.2	1.2	= 81
Males	4.2	54.2	16.7	---	4.2	20.8	---	---	= 24
Females	5.3	61.4	5.3	1.8	1.8	21.1	1.8	1.8	= 57

(2) See appendix B

D5.2.1

Q56A. Compared to houses/apartments in the neighborhood,
would you say the house/apartment is . . . .

| | 1982 - 1984 | | | | |
	Above average 1	Average 2	Below average 3	DK-NA 4	N's
All Ages	16.5	69.4	11.9	2.2	= 4553
18-24 Combined	10.2	71.0	16.7	2.2	= 551
Males	10.1	68.9	19.5	1.5	= 267
Females	10.2	72.9	14.1	2.8	= 284
25-34 Combined	14.1	70.7	13.4	1.9	= 1186
Males	11.3	73.3	12.1	3.3	= 486
Females	16.0	68.9	14.3	0.9	= 700
35-44 Combined	14.7	73.1	9.9	2.3	= 825
Males	14.7	71.3	10.5	3.5	= 373
Females	14.6	74.6	9.5	1.3	= 452
45-54 Combined	24.0	63.5	10.2	2.3	= 567
Males	27.2	59.0	11.3	2.5	= 239
Females	21.6	66.8	9.5	2.1	= 328
55-64 Combined	18.3	70.5	9.4	1.9	= 630
Males	19.0	71.3	8.5	1.2	= 258
Females	17.7	69.9	9.9	2.4	= 372
65-74 Combined	20.0	65.5	12.0	2.6	= 501
Males	17.2	69.0	11.3	2.5	= 203
Females	21.8	63.1	12.4	2.7	= 298
75-84 Combined	21.1	66.0	9.3	3.6	= 247
Males	20.3	65.8	12.7	1.3	= 79
Females	21.4	66.1	7.7	4.8	= 168
85 + Combined	13.0	67.4	17.4	2.2	= 46
Males	7.1	64.3	28.6	---	= 14
Females	15.6	68.8	12.5	3.1	= 32

D5.2.2

Q244. May I have your name and (one of your) telephone number(s) just in case
I have left something out in this interview?
IF TELEPHONE NUMBER IS GIVEN, ASK:
Is this phone located in your own home?

	No phone 1	Refused 2	Phone in home 3	Phone elsewhere 4	Phone, DK where 5	DK-NA 6	N's
All Ages	6.8	2.5	87.2	2.5	0.5	0.2	=18006
18-24 Combined	13.3	1.7	79.4	4.6	0.7	0.3	= 2268
Males	12.3	1.5	79.9	5.2	0.7	0.4	= 1049
Females	14.2	1.9	79.0	4.0	0.7	0.2	= 1219
25-34 Combined	8.3	2.8	84.7	3.3	0.7	0.3	= 4338
Males	9.0	2.1	84.7	3.4	0.6	0.1	= 1888
Females	7.7	3.3	84.6	3.3	0.7	0.4	= 2450
35-44 Combined	5.5	2.8	88.0	2.3	1.0	0.3	= 3211
Males	6.2	2.7	86.8	3.1	1.0	0.1	= 1444
Females	5.0	2.9	89.0	1.7	1.0	0.5	= 1767
45-54 Combined	4.6	2.4	89.6	2.4	0.8	0.2	= 2561
Males	5.7	2.0	88.5	2.9	0.8	0.1	= 1161
Females	3.8	2.8	90.4	1.9	0.9	0.2	= 1400
55-64 Combined	4.4	2.6	90.2	1.6	0.9	0.2	= 2523
Males	6.2	2.9	87.3	2.3	1.1	0.3	= 1119
Females	3.1	2.4	92.5	1.0	0.8	0.2	= 1404
65-74 Combined	5.4	1.9	91.1	0.8	0.6	0.1	= 2023
Males	6.9	1.8	89.6	0.8	0.8	0.1	= 872
Females	4.3	1.9	92.3	0.9	0.4	0.2	= 1151
75-84 Combined	3.0	3.4	91.5	1.2	0.9	---	= 909
Males	5.8	2.8	89.3	1.5	0.6	---	= 326
Females	1.4	3.8	92.8	1.0	1.0	---	= 583
85 + Combined	5.8	3.5	89.0	0.6	0.6	0.6	= 173
Males	11.1	1.6	85.7	---	1.6	---	= 63
Females	2.7	4.5	90.9	0.9	---	0.9	= 110

1973 - 1986

D5.3

Q57. (Do you/Does your family) own your (home/apartment),
       pay rent, or what?

		1985 - 1986			
	Own or is buying 1	Pays rent 2	Other 3	DK-NA 4	N's
All Ages	62.2	34.9	1.7	1.2	= 2990
18-24 Combined	36.2	60.8	2.7	0.3	= 293
Males	38.3	58.6	2.3	0.8	= 128
Females	34.5	62.4	3.0	---	= 165
25-34 Combined	45.2	51.9	1.9	1.1	= 752
Males	44.9	52.3	2.6	0.3	= 350
Females	45.5	51.5	1.2	1.7	= 402
35-44 Combined	67.9	30.2	1.0	0.9	= 582
Males	69.4	29.8	0.8	---	= 252
Females	66.7	30.6	1.2	1.5	= 330
45-54 Combined	74.9	22.1	1.3	1.8	= 398
Males	75.3	23.7	0.5	0.5	= 194
Females	74.5	20.6	2.0	2.9	= 204
55-64 Combined	78.5	19.0	1.3	1.3	= 395
Males	81.0	15.8	1.6	1.6	= 184
Females	76.3	21.8	0.9	0.9	= 211
65-74 Combined	73.4	22.9	2.0	1.7	= 349
Males	79.4	18.3	0.8	1.5	= 131
Females	69.7	25.7	2.8	1.8	= 218
75-84 Combined	69.4	26.3	2.7	1.6	= 186
Males	69.6	23.2	3.6	3.6	= 56
Females	69.2	27.7	2.3	0.8	= 130
85 + Combined	77.1	20.0	2.9	---	= 35
Males	70.0	30.0	---	---	= 10
Females	80.0	16.0	4.0	---	= 25

PRIMORDIAL GROUP

NATIVITY

As might be expected, the percentage of foreign born respondents is greatest among the older age groups. The same is true of foreign born parents. Among the older groups, slightly more women than men were born abroad, whereas slightly more older men than women report foreign born parents. Seventy-five percent of the younger generation specifies European ancestry, but this is a decline compared to the older age groups. At the same time, the percentages reporting South American, North American, African, and Asian ancestry generally increase in the youngest age group.

RELIGION

The proportions of both young and old who report having been raised with a specific religious affiliation is very high, and there's little difference among age groups. About 95 percent of persons who are 65+ report having been raised with a specific religious affiliation, and 93 percent of the 18-24 years olds do also. The rate for the intervening ages is between 90 and 95 percent. The percentage mentioning Protestant or Jewish religious ancestry is lower in the younger population than it is in the older, whereas the percentage with a Catholic background or no religious upbringing increases among the young. The figures on spouse religious upbringing are similar to those for the respondents themselves.

As to present religious preference, over 90 percent of the overall group expresses a preference, but only 85 percent of the 18-24 year olds do so. More men than women at all ages say they have no religious preference. Over the term of the survey there has been a slight decline in the percentage of 18-24 year olds reporting no preference. More women than men attribute no preference to their spouses. When young and old groups are compared, figures on spouse religious preference suggest an increased rate of religious intermarriage.

Strength of religious conviction as indicated by attendance at services shows the lowest level to be among the 18-24 year olds, where 57 percent report attending at least monthly. By comparison, 70 percent of the older age groups report attending at least monthly.

Nearly twice the proportion of the older age groups than the younger exhibit significant religous conviction in terms of strong membership in the preferred religious group. Conversely, nearly twice the number of younger persons say they are not very strong in their commitment. The rate for "somewhat strong" is almost the same for every age cluster - about 10 percent. More women than men report a strong membership in their religious denomination.

In spite of the lack of strong conviction on the part of young, the belief in life after death is quite widespread. Seventy percent or more of all age groups except the youngest express the belief, and even for the youngest segments the rate is over 67 percent. Again, women show greater conviction than men, exceeding them by 3 to 5 percentage points in most age components.

RACE

The proportion of persons reporting "white" as their race ranges from about 90 percent of the older age groups down to about 84 percent of the younger. The proportion who say "black" increases from about 10 percent within the 55+ generation to 13 percent among the young. The ratios of women stating that they are black is slightly higher among the youth than it is among the elders. The proportion of persons reporting "other," though small, is greatest among the younger age segments.

With regard to improving the condition of black persons, the largest percentage of each age group considers that about the right amount of money is being spent on this effort. The younger respondents, however, are more likely than others to feel that too little is being spent. Comparison of the figures in this table with those in the table where individuals describe their political leanings as "conservative, moderate, or liberal," shows that the proportion of the youngest age cluster saying "too little" is being spent corresponds to the percentage which describes itself as "liberal." At the same time, the percentage of older persons who are most favorable to blacks (those who say "too little") is above the percentage who describe themselves as liberal. This suggests that more older persons who consider themselves politically moderate or conservative favor improvement of the condition of blacks. Slightly smaller ratios of women than men say that "too much" is being spent to improve the conditions of black persons.

E1.1

Q27. Were you born in this country?

	1977 - 1986			
	Yes 1	No 2	DK-NA 3	N's
All Ages	93.3	6.5	0.2	=12050
18-24 Combined	94.8	5.1	0.1	= 1434
Males	95.0	4.8	0.2	= 642
Females	94.6	5.3	0.1	= 792
25-34 Combined	93.6	6.3	0.1	= 3021
Males	93.9	6.0	0.1	= 1391
Females	93.3	6.6	0.1	= 1702
35-44 Combined	92.7	6.9	0.4	= 2192
Males	93.3	6.7	---	= 991
Females	92.2	7.2	0.7	= 1201
45-54 Combined	93.6	6.1	0.2	= 1614
Males	94.1	5.5	0.4	= 740
Females	93.2	6.6	0.1	= 874
55-64 Combined	94.6	5.1	0.4	= 1671
Males	95.8	4.0	0.1	= 717
Females	93.6	5.9	0.5	= 954
65-74 Combined	93.2	6.7	0.1	= 1350
Males	91.6	8.2	0.2	= 538
Females	94.2	5.7	0.1	= 812
75-84 Combined	88.2	11.8	---	= 645
Males	83.7	16.3	---	= 209
Females	90.4	9.6	---	= 436
85 + Combined	83.7	16.3	---	= 123
Males	82.1	17.9	---	= 39
Females	84.5	15.5	---	= 84

E1.2.1

Q28. Were both your parents born in this country? (2)

	1977 - 1986					
	Both in U.S 1	One in U.S 2	DK, one or both 3	Neither 4	NA 5	N's
All Ages	81.0	6.0	0.3	12.4	0.2	=12050
18-24 Combined	89.1	4.7	0.4	5.6	0.1	= 1434
Males	88.3	5.1	0.3	6.1	0.2	= 642
Females	89.8	4.3	0.5	5.3	0.1	= 792
25-34 Combined	88.2	4.3	0.3	7.1	0.1	= 3021
Males	88.4	4.3	0.4	6.8	0.1	= 1319
Females	88.0	4.3	0.2	7.2	0.2	= 1702
35-44 Combined	85.9	5.3	0.4	8.0	0.4	= 2192
Males	85.3	6.4	0.3	8.0	0.1	= 991
Females	86.5	4.5	0.4	8.0	0.6	= 1201
45-54 Combined	80.1	6.9	0.1	12.6	0.2	= 1614
Males	80.5	6.6	---	12.6	0.3	= 740
Females	79.7	7.2	0.2	12.7	0.1	= 874
55-64 Combined	72.2	8.3	0.4	18.7	0.4	= 1671
Males	70.4	8.9	0.4	20.1	0.1	= 717
Females	73.6	7.8	0.4	17.7	0.5	= 954
65-74 Combined	69.1	7.3	0.4	22.9	0.2	= 1350
Males	65.4	8.6	0.2	25.7	0.2	= 538
Females	71.6	6.5	0.6	21.1	0.2	= 812
75-84 Combined	65.6	8.1	0.5	25.7	0.2	= 645
Males	58.4	8.1	0.5	33.0	---	= 209
Females	69.0	8.0	0.5	22.2	0.2	= 436
85 + Combined	62.6	7.3	---	30.1	---	= 123
Males	61.5	7.7	---	30.8	---	= 39
Females	63.1	7.1	---	29.8	---	= 84

(2) See appendix B

E1.2.2

Q30. From what countries or part of the world did your ancestors
       come? (2)

	North America 1	South America 2	Europe 3	Africa 4	Asia 5	Other 6	N's
1972 - 1986							
All Ages	8.3	3.9	79.1	6.8	0.9	1.0	=15307
18-24 Combined	9.2	6.4	73.6	8.6	1.0	1.1	= 1932
Males	8.4	5.5	75.6	8.1	1.1	1.3	= 905
Females	9.9	7.2	71.8	9.2	1.0	1.0	= 1027
25-34 Combined	9.2	5.3	75.2	7.6	1.5	1.2	= 3697
Males	8.6	4.6	76.6	7.5	1.3	1.4	= 1619
Females	9.6	5.8	74.1	7.7	1.6	1.2	= 2078
35-44 Combined	8.5	4.7	78.4	6.4	1.3	0.8	= 2666
Males	7.5	4.4	79.4	6.2	1.4	1.2	= 1208
Females	9.3	4.9	77.6	6.5	1.2	0.5	= 1458
45-54 Combined	8.4	3.5	79.9	6.8	0.6	0.8	= 2278
Males	6.9	3.2	80.1	7.9	0.8	1.1	= 1064
Females	9.7	3.7	79.7	5.8	0.4	0.6	= 1214
55-64 Combined	8.0	2.0	83.5	5.1	0.6	0.7	= 2158
Males	6.6	2.5	84.9	4.7	0.6	0.7	= 992
Females	9.3	1.6	82.3	5.5	0.5	0.8	= 1166
65-74 Combined	6.8	1.1	84.6	6.4	0.4	0.8	= 1686
Males	6.2	1.3	84.4	6.4	0.5	1.2	= 764
Females	7.3	0.9	84.7	6.4	0.3	0.4	= 922
75-84 Combined	5.8	1.2	87.7	4.6	0.1	0.7	= 747
Males	5.3	1.4	88.4	4.2	0.4	0.4	= 285
Females	6.1	1.1	87.2	4.8	---	0.9	= 462
85 + Combined	7.7	1.4	80.4	7.0	---	3.5	= 143
Males	5.4	1.8	80.4	7.1	---	5.4	= 56
Females	9.2	1.1	80.5	6.9	---	2.3	= 87

(2) See appendix B

E2.1

Q115. In what religion were you raised?

	1973 - 1986						
	Protestant 1	Catholic 2	Jewish 3	None 4	Other 5	DK-NA 6	N's
All Ages	65.7	27.5	2.4	3.0	1.1	0.3	=18006
18-24 Combined	60.9	31.7	1.3	4.8	0.9	0.4	= 2268
Males	62.3	30.3	1.9	4.1	0.8	0.6	= 1049
Females	59.6	32.8	0.8	5.3	1.1	0.3	= 1219
25-34 Combined	61.4	31.5	2.3	3.3	1.2	0.3	= 4338
Males	61.1	31.5	2.3	3.3	1.5	0.3	= 1888
Females	61.6	31.5	2.3	3.3	0.9	0.4	= 2450
35-44 Combined	64.3	28.8	2.2	3.1	1.2	0.3	= 3211
Males	63.7	28.0	2.6	3.9	1.5	0.2	= 1444
Females	64.8	29.4	1.9	2.4	1.1	0.5	= 1767
45-54 Combined	66.7	26.1	2.5	3.1	1.2	0.4	= 2561
Males	64.7	27.1	2.3	3.7	1.6	0.5	= 1161
Females	68.4	25.2	2.6	2.6	0.9	0.3	= 1400
55-64 Combined	68.8	24.7	2.9	2.2	1.1	0.3	= 2523
Males	66.3	26.5	3.0	2.3	1.6	0.2	= 1119
Females	70.9	23.2	2.7	2.1	0.7	0.4	= 1404
65-74 Combined	72.4	22.3	2.6	1.6	0.9	0.2	= 2023
Males	70.5	23.3	3.0	1.8	1.3	0.1	= 872
Females	73.8	21.6	2.3	1.5	0.6	0.3	= 1151
75-84 Combined	75.4	18.4	3.7	1.4	0.7	0.4	= 909
Males	71.8	20.6	4.0	2.1	1.2	0.3	= 326
Females	77.4	17.2	3.6	1.0	0.3	0.5	= 583
85 + Combined	72.3	17.3	4.6	5.2	---	0.6	= 173
Males	68.3	19.0	3.2	9.5	---	---	= 63
Females	74.5	16.4	5.5	2.7	---	0.9	= 110

112

E2.2

Q117. In what religion was your (husband/wife) raised? (1)

	Prot. 1	Cath. 2	Jewish 3	None 4	Other 5	DK-NA 6	N's
All Ages	65.3	26.8	2.4	3.1	1.1	1.3	=11256
18-24 Combined	61.2	28.2	1.0	5.7	1.5	2.5	= 812
Males	64.9	27.3	0.7	5.0	0.4	1.8	= 282
Females	59.2	28.7	1.1	6.0	2.1	2.8	= 530
25-34 Combined	61.0	30.5	2.0	3.7	1.2	1.5	= 2881
Males	63.3	30.4	1.4	2.3	1.1	1.4	= 1235
Females	59.2	30.6	2.6	4.7	1.3	1.6	= 1646
35-44 Combined	63.3	28.8	2.3	2.7	1.5	1.4	= 2379
Males	63.6	29.7	2.3	2.0	1.5	1.0	= 1126
Females	63.0	28.1	2.2	3.4	1.5	1.8	= 1253
45-54 Combined	67.1	25.3	2.4	2.6	1.3	1.2	= 1925
Males	68.2	26.4	1.8	0.9	1.9	0.9	= 907
Females	66.0	24.4	3.0	4.2	0.8	1.6	= 1018
55-64 Combined	69.0	23.3	2.9	3.3	0.6	0.8	= 1776
Males	69.4	24.2	3.1	1.8	0.9	0.6	= 883
Females	68.6	22.4	2.8	4.8	0.2	1.1	= 893
65-74 Combined	71.3	22.6	2.9	1.8	0.6	0.7	= 1136
Males	72.0	22.8	2.8	1.0	0.7	0.6	= 667
Females	70.4	22.4	3.0	3.0	0.4	0.9	= 469
75-84 Combined	75.2	17.8	4.1	1.3	0.6	1.0	= 314
Males	73.8	18.9	4.9	1.0	0.5	1.0	= 206
Females	77.8	15.7	2.8	1.9	0.9	0.9	= 108
85 + Combined	72.7	21.2	---	3.0	3.0	---	= 33
Males	76.9	19.2	---	3.8	---	---	= 26
Females	57.1	28.6	---	---	14.3	---	= 7

(1) See appendix A

E3.1

Q104. What is your religious preference? (1)

	1972 - 1986						
	Prot. 1	Cath. 2	Jewish 3	None 4	Other 5	DK-NA 6	N's
All Ages	63.5	25.5	2.3	6.9	1.4	0.3	=19614
18-24 Combined	56.1	28.0	1.3	12.4	2.0	0.3	= 2468
Males	54.8	26.4	1.5	14.7	2.1	0.4	= 1162
Females	57.3	29.3	1.0	10.3	1.9	0.2	= 1306
25-34 Combined	58.3	27.3	2.2	10.2	1.8	0.3	= 4696
Males	54.7	26.6	2.0	13.6	2.7	0.4	= 2070
Females	61.1	27.7	2.4	7.5	1.2	0.2	= 2626
35-44 Combined	61.6	26.5	2.3	7.4	1.7	0.4	= 3451
Males	59.2	25.5	2.6	10.4	1.9	0.4	= 1552
Females	63.5	27.4	2.1	5.0	1.6	0.4	= 1899
45-54 Combined	65.8	26.0	2.3	4.3	1.4	0.2	= 2877
Males	62.2	27.1	1.9	6.8	1.7	0.5	= 1330
Females	69.0	25.0	2.6	2.2	1.2	0.1	= 1547
55-64 Combined	69.0	23.9	2.9	3.2	0.7	0.3	= 2775
Males	66.4	24.7	3.0	4.7	1.0	0.2	= 1245
Females	71.0	23.2	2.8	2.1	0.5	0.3	= 1530
65-74 Combined	70.6	22.7	2.3	3.4	0.9	0.2	= 2181
Males	68.7	22.5	2.3	5.3	1.1	0.1	= 946
Females	72.0	22.8	2.3	1.9	0.7	0.2	= 1235
75-84 Combined	74.7	18.2	3.6	2.7	0.6	0.2	= 984
Males	70.9	18.6	4.2	4.8	1.1	0.3	= 354
Females	76.8	17.9	3.2	1.6	0.3	0.2	= 630
85 + Combined	73.6	18.7	4.9	2.2	0.5	---	= 182
Males	72.1	19.1	4.4	4.4	---	---	= 68
Females	74.6	18.4	5.3	0.9	0.9	---	= 114

(1) See appendix A

114

E3.2

Q116. What is your (SPOUSE'S) religious preference? (1)

	Prot. 1	Cath. 2	Jewish 3	None 4	Other 5	DK-NA 6	N's
			1973 - 1986				
All Ages	64.7	25.8	2.3	5.3	1.3	0.6	=11256
18-24 Combined	62.3	24.4	1.1	9.2	2.0	1.0	= 812
Males	67.7	24.5	0.7	4.6	1.4	1.1	= 282
Females	59.4	24.3	1.3	11.7	2.3	0.9	= 530
25-34 Combined	61.0	27.3	2.0	7.7	1.6	0.4	= 2881
Males	63.9	28.3	1.4	4.9	1.3	0.3	= 1235
Females	58.8	26.5	2.4	9.9	1.8	0.5	= 1646
35-44 Combined	62.6	27.8	2.2	5.3	1.6	0.6	= 2379
Males	62.4	29.2	2.4	3.7	1.8	0.4	= 1126
Females	62.7	26.6	2.0	6.6	1.4	0.7	= 1253
45-54 Combined	65.4	25.7	2.4	4.4	1.4	0.8	= 1925
Males	64.9	27.6	2.1	2.6	1.8	1.0	= 907
Females	65.8	24.1	2.7	5.9	1.0	0.6	= 1018
55-64 Combined	68.3	24.3	2.9	3.3	0.6	0.6	= 1776
Males	68.9	25.5	3.1	1.1	1.0	0.5	= 883
Females	67.7	23.2	2.8	5.4	0.1	0.8	= 893
65-74 Combined	70.2	23.8	2.8	2.1	0.6	0.4	= 1136
Males	70.5	24.7	2.7	1.2	0.6	0.3	= 667
Females	69.9	22.4	3.0	3.4	0.6	0.6	= 469
75-84 Combined	74.8	16.9	4.1	2.9	0.3	1.0	= 314
Males	73.8	18.4	4.9	1.9	0.5	0.5	= 206
Females	76.9	13.9	2.8	4.6	---	1.9	= 108
85 + Combined	75.8	18.2	---	6.1	---	---	= 33
Males	80.8	15.4	---	3.8	---	---	= 26
Females	57.1	28.6	---	14.3	---	---	= 7

(1) See appendix A

E4.1

Q105. How often do you attend religious services? (1) (2)

			1972 - 1986				
	Never	Yearly	Monthly	Weekly	More than weekly	DK-NA	N's
	1	2	3	4	5	6	
All Ages	13.3	21.2	20.4	36.7	8.0	0.4	=19614
18-24 Combined	15.0	27.8	23.6	28.0	5.3	0.4	= 2468
Males	16.4	30.5	24.9	23.3	4.5	0.5	= 1162
Females	13.8	25.3	22.5	32.2	6.0	0.2	= 1306
25-34 Combined	15.2	25.3	22.0	31.0	6.2	0.3	= 4696
Males	17.6	29.3	22.3	25.1	5.4	0.4	= 2070
Females	13.4	22.2	21.7	35.6	6.8	0.3	= 2626
35-44 Combined	13.0	21.0	20.1	37.0	8.5	0.5	= 3451
Males	15.3	25.8	21.4	30.7	6.6	0.3	= 1552
Females	11.1	17.1	19.1	42.1	10.1	0.6	= 1899
45-54 Combined	11.9	19.6	20.3	38.8	9.0	0.5	= 2877
Males	14.3	23.7	22.0	32.6	6.7	0.7	= 1330
Females	9.8	16.0	18.8	44.1	10.9	0.3	= 1547
55-64 Combined	10.6	17.9	19.5	42.2	9.4	0.5	= 2775
Males	11.9	23.5	21.4	35.8	7.0	0.5	= 1245
Females	9.5	13.3	17.9	47.3	11.4	0.5	= 1530
65-74 Combined	12.6	15.4	17.8	44.1	9.8	0.3	= 2181
Males	15.2	20.3	18.5	38.9	6.9	0.2	= 946
Females	10.5	11.7	17.2	48.1	12.1	0.4	= 1235
75-84 Combined	12.4	14.9	15.3	46.6	10.2	0.5	= 984
Males	14.1	19.5	16.4	41.8	7.6	0.6	= 354
Females	11.4	12.4	14.8	49.4	11.6	0.5	= 630
85 + Combined	23.1	12.6	15.9	37.9	8.8	1.6	= 182
Males	27.9	4.4	16.2	44.1	5.9	1.5	= 68
Females	20.2	17.5	15.8	34.2	10.5	1.8	= 114

(1) See appendix A
(2) See appendix B

E4.2

Q107. Would you call yourself a strong or not very strong
(PREFRENCE NAMED IN E3.1)?

	1974 - 1986				
	Strong	Not very strong	Somewhat strong	DK-NA	
	1	2	3	4	N's
All Ages	41.7	46.5	9.3	2.5	=15325
18-24 Combined	31.7	56.4	9.3	2.6	= 1799
Males	28.2	61.1	8.0	2.7	= 804
Females	34.6	52.7	10.4	2.4	= 995
25-34 Combined	34.4	54.5	8.7	2.4	= 3612
Males	30.9	57.4	9.4	2.4	= 1507
Females	37.0	52.4	8.3	2.4	= 2105
35-44 Combined	40.9	47.7	9.0	2.4	= 2699
Males	34.1	54.3	9.0	2.6	= 1173
Females	46.2	42.7	9.0	2.2	= 1526
45-54 Combined	41.9	46.5	9.1	2.4	= 2200
Males	34.1	53.7	9.7	2.5	= 975
Females	48.2	40.8	8.7	2.4	= 1225
55-64 Combined	46.7	40.6	9.8	2.8	= 2217
Males	38.2	49.7	10.0	2.1	= 958
Females	53.1	33.8	9.7	3.4	= 1259
65-74 Combined	52.0	35.5	9.9	2.6	= 1789
Males	42.0	43.8	10.8	3.4	= 740
Females	59.0	29.6	9.2	2.1	= 1049
75-84 Combined	55.8	30.6	10.7	3.0	= 843
Males	44.1	41.4	11.0	3.4	= 290
Females	61.8	25.0	10.5	2.7	= 553
85 + Combined	66.3	21.7	9.6	2.4	= 166
Males	58.6	24.1	15.5	1.7	= 58
Females	70.4	20.4	6.5	2.8	= 108

E4.3

Q108. Do you believe there is a life after death? (1)

| | 1973 - 1986 | | | |
	Yes 1	No 2	DK-NA 3	N's
All Ages	71.0	20.3	8.7	=11984
18-24 Combined	67.4	24.0	8.6	= 1538
Males	66.8	24.6	8.6	= 698
Females	68.0	23.5	8.6	= 840
25-34 Combined	72.4	19.2	8.4	= 2914
Males	70.0	20.9	9.1	= 1263
Females	74.3	17.9	7.9	= 1651
35-44 Combined	72.7	19.4	7.9	= 2149
Males	69.3	22.1	8.6	= 981
Females	75.5	17.1	7.4	= 1168
45-54 Combined	70.1	21.0	8.9	= 1678
Males	67.2	24.2	8.6	= 735
Females	72.4	18.5	9.1	= 943
55-64 Combined	71.1	20.8	8.1	= 1646
Males	67.3	25.2	7.5	= 722
Females	74.0	17.4	8.5	= 924
65-74 Combined	70.4	20.1	9.6	= 1336
Males	63.8	26.2	10.0	= 572
Females	75.3	15.4	9.3	= 764
75-84 Combined	70.8	18.5	10.8	= 612
Males	65.4	22.9	11.7	= 214
Females	73.6	16.1	10.3	= 398
85 + Combined	70.3	10.8	18.9	= 111
Males	76.9	10.3	12.8	= 39
Females	66.7	11.1	22.2	= 72

(1) See appendix A

E5.1

Q21. What race do you consider yourself?

	1972 - 1986			
	White 1	Black 2	Other 3	N's
All Ages	87.5	11.2	1.3	=19614
18-24 Combined	85.7	13.0	1.3	= 2468
Males	87.5	10.9	1.5	= 1162
Females	84.0	14.9	1.1	= 1306
25-34 Combined	86.2	12.0	1.8	= 4696
Males	87.6	10.5	1.8	= 2070
Females	85.0	13.2	1.8	= 2626
35-44 Combined	87.9	10.4	1.7	= 3451
Males	89.7	8.7	1.6	= 1552
Females	86.4	11.8	1.8	= 1899
45-54 Combined	87.5	11.5	1.0	= 2877
Males	86.5	12.0	1.4	= 1330
Females	88.3	11.0	0.7	= 1547
55-64 Combined	88.6	10.3	1.0	= 2775
Males	89.6	9.5	1.0	= 1245
Females	87.9	11.0	1.1	= 1530
65-74 Combined	88.6	10.7	0.7	= 2181
Males	89.0	10.4	0.6	= 946
Females	88.3	11.0	0.7	= 1235
75-84 Combined	91.6	8.1	0.3	= 984
Males	91.0	8.5	0.6	= 354
Females	91.9	7.9	0.2	= 630
85 + Combined	89.6	10.4	---	= 182
Males	88.2	11.8	---	= 68
Females	90.4	9.6	---	= 114

E5.2

Q69H. We are faced with many problems in this country, none of
       which can be solved easily or inexpensively. I'm going
       to name some of these problems, and for each one I'd
       like you to tell me whether you think we're spending too
       much money on it, too little money, or about the right
       amount.
                 Improving the conditions of blacks.

	1973 - 1986				
	Too little 1	About right 2	Too much 3	DK-NA 4	N's
All Ages	27.8	42.2	22.0	8.0	=18006
18-24 Combined	35.1	43.1	14.9	6.9	= 2268
Males	33.3	42.8	17.9	6.0	= 1049
Females	36.6	43.4	12.4	7.6	= 1219
25-34 Combined	31.6	41.9	19.8	6.7	= 4338
Males	30.0	41.9	23.1	4.9	= 1888
Females	32.7	41.9	17.2	8.1	= 2450
35-44 Combined	27.2	42.3	23.8	6.8	= 3211
Males	27.2	39.8	28.9	4.1	= 1444
Females	27.1	44.3	19.6	9.0	= 1767
45-54 Combined	26.6	41.0	25.3	7.1	= 2561
Males	27.8	37.6	29.1	5.5	= 1161
Females	25.6	43.9	22.1	8.4	= 1400
55-64 Combined	22.4	42.8	26.0	8.7	= 2523
Males	23.3	40.1	29.0	7.5	= 1119
Females	21.7	45.0	23.6	9.7	= 1404
65-74 Combined	24.9	41.5	24.0	9.6	= 2023
Males	23.9	40.4	28.1	7.7	= 872
Females	25.7	42.3	20.9	11.1	= 1151
75-84 Combined	19.9	43.8	21.0	15.3	= 909
Males	19.3	45.4	24.5	10.7	= 326
Females	20.2	42.9	19.0	17.8	= 583
85 + Combined	19.7	43.9	14.5	22.0	= 173
Males	12.7	55.6	14.3	17.5	= 63
Females	23.6	37.3	14.5	24.5	= 110

VOTING, PARTY AFFILIATION, AND POLITICAL OUTLOOK
PRESIDENTIAL VOTING

Probably because the GSS is a household survey the percentage of persons who say they have voted in presidential elections is slightly higher than percentages in census reports. (U.S. Bureau of the Census, 1987, p. 229) However, since the survey began in 1972 both the GSS and the U.S. Census show that there has been a decline followed by an increase in the proportion of persons who vote. Ratios of persons who say they voted for the respective candidates are similar to those reported by federal government agencies, with the exception of 1980. In that year the GSS respondents give Carter a slight margin over Reagan even though Reagan won the election - the reason may be related to the Anderson candidacy and the large proportion of women in the sample who said they voted for Carter. (For a technical paper on this problem write Professor Tom Smith at the National Opinion Research Center, University of Chicago, 1155 East 60th Street, Chicago, IL 60637).

More men than women report voting at the beginning of the survey, but the younger women catch up by the end. Generally women have equaled or outperformed men in voting for the winning candidate, but not so the younger women in the Reagan-Carter and Reagan-Mondale election. When George Wallace ran for president in 1968, more men than women in most age groups report that they voted for Wallace. The situation was partially reversed when Anderson ran as a third candidate in 1980 - more women than men in the youngest age group voted for him.

Party identification shows a substantial Democratic majority (54 percent Democrat to 32 percent Republican and 12 percent Independent). This differs from other polls, which show an average of about 40 percent Democrat, 20 percent Republican, and 30 percent Independent since 1972. (Janda et al, 1987, p. 242)

In the GSS higher proportions of the younger age groups identify themselves as Independents. The greater ratios of older persons identifying themselves as Republicans may be a cohort phenomenon rather than indicating increasingly Republican leanings with age.

The largest proportion of the GSS respondents describe their political views as moderate or conservative. This ratio changes with age in the respect that the younger age groups are more likely to identify themselves as liberal. More men than women label their views as conservative, an identification that appears consistent with the data that follows on political attitudes.

ATTITUDES ON POLITICAL ISSUES

Income taxes are considered too high by 60 percent or more of the respondents age 18-64, but less than half of the 65-85+ consider them too high. The difference between the younger and older age groups may be explained in part by the higher proportions of the 65+ respondents who pay no income taxes. Generally less than 1 percent of any age group consider such taxes too low.

The largest proportion of respondents in each age group consider military expenditures "about right;" however, young respondents are more likely than old to select the "too high" choice. More women than men appear in the "don't know/no answer" category.

In spite of some differences the majority of all ages think that too much money is spent on foreign aid. The majority of most of them, however, feel that the U.S. should take an active part in world affairs. Proportionately more women than men think that the U.S. should stay out of world affairs.

Opinion is almost equally divided on the matter of spending money for space exploration, with the "too little" and "about right" choices just about offsetting "too much." When specific age segments are considered, sizable ratios of some think that too much money is spent on exploration. Even the 18-44 year olds, who are most in favor of space exploration, show upwards of 40 percent in opposition. Over half of the women in all age groups, excepting the 65+, are opposed.

124

F1.1

Q62. In 1968, you remember that Humphrey ran for President on
the Democratic ticket against Nixon for the Republicans,
and Wallace as an Independent. Do you remember for sure
whether or not you voted in that election?

	1972 - 1973				
	Voted 1	Did not vote 2	Not eligible 3	DK-NA 4	N's
All Ages	64.0	26.1	8.2	1.6	= 3103
18-24 Combined	2.2	48.8	48.3	0.7	= 414
Males	3.2	43.2	53.2	0.5	= 222
Females	1.0	52.2	42.7	1.0	= 192
25-34 Combined	58.8	35.4	4.7	1.1	= 663
Males	60.1	35.2	4.7	---	= 318
Females	57.7	35.7	4.6	2.0	= 345
35-44 Combined	74.7	21.0	2.3	1.9	= 514
Males	75.1	19.2	3.1	2.6	= 229
Females	74.4	22.5	1.8	1.4	= 285
45-54 Combined	79.2	17.8	1.0	1.9	= 572
Males	82.1	15.4	1.1	1.4	= 280
Females	76.4	20.2	1.0	2.4	= 292
55-64 Combined	82.1	15.0	1.2	1.7	= 481
Males	84.9	12.6	1.3	1.3	= 238
Females	79.4	17.3	1.2	2.1	= 243
65-74 Combined	77.0	20.9	---	2.1	= 326
Males	80.6	18.1	---	1.3	= 160
Females	73.5	23.5	---	3.0	= 166
75-84 Combined	79.3	17.4	---	3.3	= 121
Males	82.0	16.0	---	2.0	= 50
Females	77.5	18.3	---	4.2	= 71
85 + Combined	75.0	25.0	---	---	= 12
Males	100.0	----	---	---	= 7
Females	40.0	60.0	---	---	= 5

F1.2

Q62A. IF VOTED: Did you vote for Humphrey, Nixon, or Wallace?

	1972 - 1973							N's
	Humphrey	Nixon	Wallace	Other	Refused to tell	DK-NA		
	1	2	3	4	5	6		
All Ages	39.6	44.3	11.1	0.8	1.6	2.6	=	1987
18-24 Combined	66.7	33.3	----	---	---	---	=	9
Males	57.1	42.9	----	---	---	---	=	7
Females	100.0	----	----	---	---	---	=	2
25-34 Combined	37.4	43.6	14.6	1.0	1.0	2.3	=	390
Males	34.6	40.8	19.9	2.1	1.6	1.0	=	191
Females	40.2	46.2	9.5	---	0.5	3.5	=	199
35-44 Combined	40.4	41.7	14.1	0.3	1.3	2.3	=	384
Males	39.5	36.6	20.3	0.6	1.7	1.2	=	172
Females	41.0	45.8	9.0	---	0.9	3.3	=	212
45-54 Combined	42.4	41.9	10.4	1.3	1.3	2.6	=	453
Males	40.0	42.6	12.6	0.9	1.7	2.2	=	230
Females	44.8	41.3	8.1	1.8	0.9	3.1	=	223
55-64 Combined	39.0	46.8	7.8	0.8	2.8	2.8	=	395
Males	41.1	43.6	10.9	---	3.0	1.5	=	202
Females	36.8	50.3	4.7	1.6	2.6	4.1	=	193
65-74 Combined	39.0	47.4	8.4	0.4	2.0	2.8	=	251
Males	35.7	46.5	12.4	---	3.1	2.3	=	129
Females	42.6	48.4	4.1	0.8	0.8	3.3	=	122
75-84 Combined	35.4	47.9	10.4	1.0	1.0	4.2	=	96
Males	43.9	43.9	9.8	2.4	---	---	=	41
Females	29.1	50.9	10.9	---	1.8	7.3	=	55
85 + Combined	11.1	88.9	----	---	---	---	=	9
Males	14.3	85.7	----	---	---	---	=	7
Females	----	100.0	----	---	---	---	=	2

F1.3

Q63. In 1972, you remember that McGovern ran for President
on the Democratic ticket against Nixon for the
Republicans. Do you remember for sure whether or not
you voted in that election?

| | 1973 - 1977 | | | | |
	Voted 1	Did not vote 2	Not eligible 3	DK-NA 4	N's
All Ages	65.2	27.3	6.1	1.4	= 7459
18-24 Combined	31.5	32.9	35.4	0.2	= 1025
Males	30.9	33.5	35.7	---	= 499
Females	32.1	32.3	35.2	0.4	= 526
25-34 Combined	59.4	37.3	2.4	0.9	= 1649
Males	60.1	36.9	1.9	1.1	= 719
Females	58.8	37.6	2.8	0.8	= 930
35-44 Combined	68.9	27.2	2.1	1.8	= 1289
Males	70.2	27.6	1.0	1.2	= 573
Females	67.9	27.0	2.9	2.2	= 716
45-54 Combined	74.4	23.5	0.9	1.2	= 1195
Males	77.6	20.8	0.7	0.9	= 544
Females	71.7	25.8	1.1	1.4	= 651
55-64 Combined	79.5	18.1	0.9	1.5	= 1086
Males	81.8	16.8	1.0	0.4	= 505
Females	77.5	19.3	0.9	2.4	= 581
65-74 Combined	77.8	19.9	0.4	1.9	= 835
Males	84.1	13.4	0.5	2.0	= 402
Females	72.1	25.9	0.2	1.8	= 433
75-84 Combined	72.2	23.4	0.3	4.1	= 320
Males	80.0	17.9	---	2.1	= 140
Females	66.1	27.8	0.6	5.6	= 180
85 + Combined	65.0	28.3	1.7	5.0	= 60
Males	85.2	11.1	---	3.7	= 27
Females	48.5	42.4	3.0	6.1	= 33

F1.4

Q63A. IF VOTED: Did you vote for McGovern or Nixon?

			1973 - 1977				
	McGovern	Nixon	Other	Refused	Didn't vote	DK-NA	N's
	1	2	3	4	5	6	
All Ages	36.5	57.3	2.7	0.7	0.5	2.4	= 4872
18-24 Combined	51.4	43.0	3.1	---	0.3	2.2	= 323
Males	51.3	41.6	5.2	---	---	1.9	= 154
Females	51.5	44.4	1.2	---	0.6	2.4	= 169
25-34 Combined	46.7	48.7	2.7	0.6	0.2	1.1	= 980
Males	45.0	48.5	4.2	0.9	0.5	0.9	= 433
Females	48.1	48.8	1.5	0.4	---	1.3	= 547
35-44 Combined	32.0	62.2	2.5	0.4	0.4	2.5	= 891
Males	29.3	64.8	2.7	1.0	0.2	2.0	= 403
Females	34.2	60.0	2.3	---	0.6	2.9	= 488
45-54 Combined	33.2	60.3	3.0	0.8	0.8	1.9	= 889
Males	33.9	58.5	4.0	1.4	0.9	1.2	= 422
Females	32.5	61.9	2.1	0.2	0.6	2.6	= 467
55-64 Combined	30.6	62.6	2.3	1.2	0.3	3.0	= 864
Males	32.2	59.8	2.4	1.7	0.5	3.4	= 413
Females	29.0	65.2	2.2	0.7	0.2	2.7	= 451
65-74 Combined	33.6	58.1	2.8	1.2	0.8	3.5	= 652
Males	33.8	57.9	2.9	1.5	0.9	2.9	= 340
Females	33.3	58.3	2.6	1.0	0.6	4.2	= 312
75-84 Combined	35.0	58.1	2.1	0.4	---	4.3	= 234
Males	36.0	59.6	1.8	0.9	---	1.8	= 114
Females	34.2	56.7	2.5	---	---	6.7	= 120
85 + Combined	20.5	74.4	5.1	---	---	---	= 39
Males	26.1	73.9	---	---	---	---	= 23
Females	12.5	75.0	12.5	---	---	---	= 16

F1.5

Q64. In 1976, you remember that Carter ran for President on the Democratic ticket against Ford for the Republicans. Do you remember for sure whether or not you voted in that election?

	1977 - 1982				
	Voted 1	Did not vote 2	Not eligible 3	DK-NA 4	N's
All Ages	62.2	29.2	7.0	1.7	= 5993
18-24 Combined	19.9	33.4	46.3	0.4	= 769
Males	20.7	35.6	43.5	0.3	= 329
Females	19.3	31.8	48.4	0.5	= 440
25-34 Combined	53.9	42.8	1.8	1.6	= 1470
Males	54.3	42.6	1.5	1.7	= 658
Females	53.6	43.0	2.0	1.5	= 812
35-44 Combined	67.1	29.5	1.5	1.9	= 1027
Males	66.7	29.4	1.5	2.3	= 472
Females	67.4	29.5	1.4	1.6	= 555
45-54 Combined	75.8	21.0	1.3	1.8	= 832
Males	75.6	21.2	1.8	1.3	= 386
Females	76.0	20.9	0.9	2.2	= 446
55-64 Combined	79.6	18.2	1.0	1.2	= 866
Males	84.4	13.1	0.8	1.7	= 358
Females	76.2	21.9	1.2	0.8	= 508
65-74 Combined	75.7	21.9	0.3	2.1	= 672
Males	84.0	14.9	---	1.1	= 275
Females	70.0	26.7	0.5	2.8	= 397
75-84 Combined	75.3	21.0	0.3	3.4	= 295
Males	81.4	13.7	---	4.9	= 102
Females	72.0	24.9	0.5	2.6	= 193
85 + Combined	67.7	25.8	---	6.5	= 62
Males	63.6	22.7	---	13.6	= 22
Females	70.0	27.5	---	2.5	= 40

F1.6

Q64A. IF VOTED: Did you vote for Carter or Ford?

	Carter 1	Ford 2	Other 3	Refused 4	Didn't vote 5	DK-NA 6	N's
1977 - 1982							
All Ages	54.1	41.5	1.0	0.6	0.2	2.6	= 3737
18-24 Combined	45.8	47.7	3.3	---	0.7	2.6	= 153
Males	36.8	57.4	2.9	---	---	2.9	= 68
Females	52.9	40.0	3.5	---	1.2	2.4	= 85
25-34 Combined	57.8	36.6	1.8	0.5	0.3	3.0	= 794
Males	58.5	36.2	1.9	---	0.3	3.1	= 359
Females	57.2	37.0	1.6	0.9	0.2	3.0	= 435
35-44 Combined	55.5	41.2	0.4	0.7	0.1	2.0	= 690
Males	53.7	43.8	0.6	0.6	---	1.3	= 315
Females	57.1	38.9	0.3	0.8	0.3	2.7	= 375
45-54 Combined	52.8	42.9	0.8	0.5	0.2	2.8	= 632
Males	55.1	41.4	0.7	0.3	0.3	2.1	= 292
Females	50.9	44.1	0.9	0.6	---	3.5	= 340
55-64 Combined	54.0	41.7	0.9	0.9	0.1	2.5	= 691
Males	54.8	39.3	0.7	1.3	0.3	3.6	= 303
Females	53.4	43.6	1.0	0.5	---	1.5	= 388
65-74 Combined	52.2	44.5	0.8	1.0	0.2	1.4	= 510
Males	54.7	43.1	1.3	0.4	---	0.4	= 232
Females	50.0	45.7	0.4	1.4	0.4	2.2	= 278
75-84 Combined	54.0	40.6	---	---	---	5.4	= 224
Males	49.4	45.9	---	---	---	4.7	= 85
Females	56.8	37.4	---	---	---	5.8	= 139
85 + Combined	39.5	55.8	---	---	2.3	2.3	= 43
Males	46.7	46.7	---	---	---	6.7	= 15
Females	35.7	60.7	---	---	3.6	---	= 28

130

F1.7

Q65. In 1980, you remember that Carter ran for President on the
Democratic ticket against Reagan for the Republicans, and
Anderson as an independent. Do you remember for sure whether
or not you voted in that election? (2)

	Voted 1	Did not vote 2	Not eligible 3	Refused 4	DK-NA 5	N's
			1982 - 1985			
All Ages	65.6	26.9	6.0	0.2	1.4	= 6080
18-24 Combined	26.0	30.5	42.2	0.1	1.1	= 708
Males	25.1	28.7	44.4	---	1.8	= 338
Females	26.8	32.2	40.3	0.3	0.5	= 370
25-34 Combined	57.8	39.0	1.7	0.1	1.3	= 1559
Males	59.6	38.1	1.2	---	1.1	= 658
Females	56.5	39.6	2.1	0.2	1.6	= 901
35-44 Combined	71.3	25.6	1.3	0.3	1.5	= 1106
Males	69.1	27.5	1.4	0.2	1.8	= 495
Females	73.2	24.1	1.1	0.3	1.3	= 611
45-54 Combined	75.4	22.3	0.9	0.1	1.3	= 777
Males	76.5	21.5	0.6	0.3	1.1	= 349
Females	74.5	22.9	1.2	---	1.4	= 428
55-64 Combined	78.7	19.0	0.8	0.1	1.3	= 851
Males	83.4	15.3	0.3	0.3	0.8	= 367
Females	75.2	21.9	1.2	---	1.7	= 484
65-74 Combined	80.8	16.6	0.9	0.1	1.5	= 673
Males	85.4	12.7	0.7	---	1.1	= 268
Females	77.8	19.3	1.0	0.2	1.7	= 405
75-84 Combined	78.5	18.5	0.3	0.3	2.4	= 340
Males	84.1	14.0	---	0.9	0.9	= 107
Females	76.0	20.6	0.4	---	3.0	= 233
85 + Combined	68.2	24.2	1.5	1.5	4.5	= 66
Males	82.6	13.0	---	---	4.3	= 23
Females	60.5	30.2	2.3	2.3	4.7	= 43

(2) See appendix B

131

F1.8

Q65A. IF VOTED: Did you vote for Carter, Reagan, or Anderson?

	Carter	Reagan	Anderson	Other	Refused	Didn't vote	DK-NA	N's
	1	2	3	4	5	6	7	
1982 - 1985								
All Ages	45.7	44.7	6.3	0.5	1.1	0.3	2.0	= 4000
18-24 Combined	38.4	44.3	14.1	0.5	---	0.5	2.2	= 185
Males	38.4	48.8	10.5	---	---	---	2.3	= 86
Females	38.4	40.4	17.2	1.0	---	1.0	2.0	= 99
25-34 Combined	42.7	44.2	9.3	1.2	1.0	---	1.5	= 904
Males	40.7	44.8	9.9	2.0	0.8	---	1.8	= 393
Females	44.2	43.8	8.8	0.6	1.2	---	1.4	= 511
35-44 Combined	44.1	44.2	7.2	0.8	1.4	0.3	2.2	= 790
Males	37.4	51.2	7.0	0.6	1.8	---	2.0	= 342
Females	49.1	38.8	7.4	0.9	1.1	0.4	2.2	= 448
45-54 Combined	46.6	45.4	4.4	0.3	1.0	0.3	1.9	= 588
Males	42.0	48.0	4.8	0.7	1.9	0.4	2.2	= 269
Females	50.5	43.3	4.1	---	0.3	0.3	1.6	= 319
55-64 Combined	46.2	44.4	4.6	0.1	1.5	0.4	2.7	= 675
Males	44.0	49.5	2.6	0.3	1.6	0.3	1.6	= 307
Females	48.1	40.2	6.3	---	1.4	0.5	3.5	= 368
65-74 Combined	50.8	42.4	4.0	---	1.3	0.2	1.3	= 545
Males	50.7	42.8	4.8	---	1.7	---	---	= 229
Females	50.9	42.1	3.5	---	0.9	0.3	2.2	= 316
75-84 Combined	42.3	52.1	1.1	---	0.7	1.1	2.6	= 267
Males	37.8	58.9	1.1	---	1.1	1.1	---	= 90
Females	44.6	48.6	1.1	---	0.6	1.1	4.0	= 177
85 + Combined	50.0	45.7	2.2	---	---	---	2.2	= 46
Males	52.6	47.4	---	---	---	---	---	= 19
Females	48.1	44.4	3.7	---	---	---	3.7	= 27

F1.9

Q66. In 1984, you remember that Mondale ran for President on the Democratic ticket against Reagan for the Republicans. Do you remember for sure whether or not you voted in that election?

			1985 - 1986			
	Voted	Did not vote	Not eligible	Refused	DK-NA	
	1	2	3	4	5	N's
All Ages	67.9	28.0	2.8	0.2	1.1	= 2990
18-24 Combined	42.3	42.3	14.0	0.3	1.0	= 293
Males	39.1	43.0	17.2	---	0.8	= 128
Females	44.8	41.8	11.5	0.6	1.2	= 165
25-34 Combined	59.0	37.4	2.3	0.3	1.1	= 752
Males	56.3	39.1	2.9	0.6	1.1	= 350
Females	61.4	35.8	1.7	---	1.0	= 402
35-44 Combined	72.3	24.6	2.4	---	0.7	= 582
Males	71.0	25.8	2.8	---	0.4	= 252
Females	73.3	23.6	2.1	---	0.9	= 330
45-54 Combined	73.6	24.1	1.0	---	1.3	= 398
Males	74.2	24.7	1.0	---	---	= 194
Females	73.0	23.5	1.0	---	2.5	= 204
55-64 Combined	77.5	19.7	1.3	---	1.5	= 395
Males	77.2	21.2	1.1	---	0.5	= 184
Females	77.7	18.5	1.4	---	2.4	= 211
65-74 Combined	80.2	18.1	0.9	---	0.9	= 349
Males	89.3	10.7	---	---	---	= 131
Females	74.8	22.5	1.4	---	1.4	= 218
75-84 Combined	74.7	22.0	0.5	1.1	1.6	= 186
Males	80.4	16.1	---	1.8	1.8	= 56
Females	72.3	24.6	0.8	0.8	1.5	= 130
85 + Combined	68.6	31.4	---	---	---	= 35
Males	90.0	10.0	---	---	---	= 10
Females	60.0	40.0	---	---	---	= 25

F1.10

Q66A. IF VOTED: Did you vote for Mondale or Reagan?

		Mondale	Reagan	Other	Refused	Didn't vote	DK-NA		N's
		1	2	3	4	5	6		
All Ages		37.8	58.9	0.6	1.2	0.6	0.8	=	2033
18-24	Combined	32.3	63.7	1.6	0.8	---	1.6	=	124
	Males	18.0	78.0	2.0	---	---	2.0	=	50
	Females	41.9	54.1	1.4	1.4	---	1.4	=	74
25-34	Combined	39.0	57.4	0.9	1.8	0.7	0.2	=	444
	Males	32.5	62.9	1.0	2.5	0.5	0.5	=	197
	Females	44.1	53.0	0.8	1.2	0.8	---	=	247
35-44	Combined	34.2	62.7	0.2	1.7	0.5	0.7	=	421
	Males	28.5	68.7	---	1.7	0.6	0.6	=	179
	Females	38.4	58.3	0.4	1.7	0.4	0.8	=	242
45-54	Combined	38.9	57.3	0.3	1.4	1.0	1.0	=	293
	Males	37.5	55.6	0.7	2.8	2.1	1.4	=	144
	Females	40.3	59.1	---	---	---	0.7	=	149
55-64	Combined	35.7	61.0	1.0	0.3	0.6	1.3	=	308
	Males	35.9	61.3	1.4	0.7	---	0.7	=	142
	Females	35.5	60.8	0.6	---	1.2	1.8	=	166
65-74	Combined	42.9	54.6	0.4	1.1	---	1.1	=	280
	Males	40.2	56.4	0.9	0.9	---	1.7	=	117
	Females	44.8	53.4	---	1.2	---	0.6	=	163
75-84	Combined	39.6	56.8	---	0.7	2.2	0.7	=	139
	Males	40.0	60.0	---	---	---	---	=	45
	Females	39.4	55.3	---	1.1	3.2	1.1	=	94
85 +	Combined	50.0	50.0	---	---	---	---	=	24
	Males	66.7	33.3	---	---	---	---	=	9
	Females	40.0	60.0	---	---	---	---	=	15

1985 - 1986

F2.1

Q61. Generally speaking, do you usually think of yourself as a Republican, Democrat, Independent, or what? (1) (2)

	1972 - 1986					
	Democrat 1	Independent 2	Republican 3	Other 4	DK-NA 5	N's
All Ages	53.6	12.3	32.2	1.5	0.5	=19614
18-24 Combined	49.4	17.7	30.3	2.1	0.4	= 2468
Males	47.8	17.3	32.0	2.5	0.4	= 1162
Females	50.9	18.1	28.9	1.7	0.5	= 1306
25-34 Combined	53.4	15.2	29.1	1.9	0.4	= 4696
Males	50.7	16.9	30.2	2.0	0.2	= 2070
Females	55.4	14.0	28.2	1.8	0.6	= 2626
35-44 Combined	54.7	12.7	30.7	1.7	0.4	= 3451
Males	51.0	14.3	32.2	1.9	0.5	= 1552
Females	57.6	11.3	29.4	1.4	0.3	= 1899
45-54 Combined	55.7	10.8	31.6	1.4	0.5	= 2877
Males	55.9	10.8	31.4	1.7	0.3	= 1330
Females	55.6	10.9	31.7	1.2	0.7	= 1547
55-64 Combined	55.4	7.9	35.2	1.1	0.4	= 2775
Males	55.7	7.8	35.5	0.8	0.2	= 1245
Females	55.1	8.0	35.0	1.3	0.6	= 1530
65-74 Combined	55.0	8.3	35.0	1.1	0.5	= 2181
Males	57.1	7.9	33.1	1.3	0.6	= 946
Females	53.4	8.7	36.5	1.1	0.3	= 1235
75-84 Combined	49.1	8.6	40.8	0.5	1.0	= 984
Males	49.7	6.8	41.2	0.6	1.7	= 354
Females	48.7	9.7	40.5	0.5	0.6	= 630
85 + Combined	40.7	11.5	46.7	1.1	---	= 182
Males	38.2	10.3	51.5	---	---	= 68
Females	42.1	12.3	43.9	1.8	---	= 114

(1) See appendix A
(2) See appendix B

F2.2

Q67. Would you say that your political views are liberal, moderate
      or conservative? (2)

	1974 - 1986				
	Liberal 1	Moderate 2	Conservative 3	DK-NA 4	N's
All Ages	25.7	38.0	31.4	5.0	=15713
18-24 Combined	36.6	37.1	22.4	3.8	= 1960
Males	36.0	36.8	23.7	3.5	= 897
Females	37.2	37.4	21.4	4.0	= 1063
25-34 Combined	32.9	37.2	26.5	3.4	= 3812
Males	35.4	33.2	29.0	2.4	= 1712
Females	31.0	40.5	24.4	4.1	= 2100
35-44 Combined	25.8	35.8	34.7	3.6	= 2801
Males	26.8	30.7	39.6	2.9	= 1285
Females	25.0	40.1	30.6	4.3	= 1516
45-54 Combined	19.3	39.6	36.7	4.4	= 2204
Males	21.3	34.4	41.6	2.7	= 1027
Females	17.5	44.2	32.5	5.9	= 1177
55-64 Combined	18.0	41.2	35.3	5.5	= 2176
Males	19.8	38.0	38.1	4.1	= 979
Females	16.5	43.8	33.1	6.7	= 1197
65-74 Combined	20.2	38.5	33.6	7.8	= 1766
Males	23.7	34.7	35.7	5.9	= 764
Females	17.5	41.4	31.9	9.2	= 1002
75-84 Combined	17.8	37.1	33.6	11.5	= 827
Males	17.9	41.6	34.1	6.4	= 296
Females	17.7	34.7	33.3	14.3	= 531
85 + Combined	10.8	38.3	34.7	16.2	= 167
Males	10.0	36.7	40.0	13.3	= 60
Females	11.2	39.3	31.8	17.8	= 107

(2) See appendix B

F3.1

Q78. Do you consider the amount of federal income tax which you have
to pay as too high, about right, or too low? (1)

	Too high 1	About right 2	Too low 3	R pays none (vol.) 4	DK-NA 5	N's
1976 - 1985						
All Ages	63.6	29.5	0.5	2.4	4.1	= 8963
18-24 Combined	60.4	33.4	0.8	1.9	3.5	= 1133
Males	60.2	34.1	0.8	1.9	3.1	= 522
Females	60.6	32.7	0.8	2.0	3.9	= 611
25-34 Combined	68.4	28.2	0.5	0.5	2.5	= 2143
Males	66.7	31.1	0.7	---	1.5	= 940
Females	69.7	26.0	0.2	0.8	3.2	= 1203
35-44 Combined	69.4	27.6	0.4	0.6	1.9	= 1564
Males	69.5	28.9	0.4	0.3	0.9	= 702
Females	69.3	26.6	0.5	0.9	2.8	= 862
45-54 Combined	72.0	23.9	0.5	1.1	2.5	= 1234
Males	70.5	26.5	0.9	0.9	1.2	= 569
Females	73.2	21.7	0.2	1.4	3.6	= 665
55-64 Combined	65.3	28.9	0.5	1.7	3.6	= 1310
Males	62.9	33.0	1.0	1.4	1.6	= 572
Females	67.2	25.7	---	1.9	5.1	= 738
65-74 Combined	49.1	35.6	0.4	6.3	8.6	= 998
Males	51.1	37.0	0.5	5.8	5.6	= 411
Females	47.7	34.6	0.3	6.6	10.7	= 587
75-84 Combined	39.8	34.2	0.4	12.6	13.0	= 477
Males	41.4	40.8	1.3	9.6	7.0	= 157
Females	39.1	30.9	---	14.1	15.9	= 320
85 + Combined	41.3	32.7	---	11.5	14.4	= 104
Males	34.1	43.9	---	17.1	4.9	= 41
Females	46.0	25.4	---	7.9	20.6	= 63

(1) See appendix A

F4.1

Q69I. We are faced with many problems in this country, none of
which can be solved easily or inexpensively. I'm going
to name some of these problems, and for each one I'd
like you to tell me whether you think we're spending too
much money on it, too little money, or about the right
amount.

The military, armaments and defense. (1)

	Too little 1	About right 2	Too much 3	DK-NA 4	N's
1973 - 1986					
All Ages	23.1	40.6	30.0	6.2	=18006
18-24 Combined	18.4	40.3	36.9	4.4	= 2268
Males	22.4	37.9	37.6	2.1	= 1049
Females	14.9	42.4	36.3	6.3	= 1219
25-34 Combined	20.4	39.9	35.0	4.6	= 4338
Males	24.2	37.1	36.5	2.2	= 1888
Females	17.5	42.1	33.9	6.5	= 2450
35-44 Combined	21.6	41.5	31.7	5.1	= 3211
Males	25.8	38.6	33.1	2.6	= 1444
Females	18.3	43.9	30.6	7.2	= 1767
45-54 Combined	27.2	42.6	25.1	5.2	= 2561
Males	28.9	38.9	29.5	2.7	= 1161
Females	25.8	45.6	21.4	7.3	= 1400
55-64 Combined	28.1	40.2	24.7	7.1	= 2523
Males	31.5	37.7	27.5	3.3	= 1119
Females	25.4	42.2	22.4	10.0	= 1404
65-74 Combined	25.4	40.7	24.8	9.1	= 2023
Males	28.6	38.2	28.0	5.3	= 872
Females	22.9	42.7	22.4	12.0	= 1151
75-84 Combined	24.1	37.8	23.9	14.2	= 909
Males	29.1	41.4	23.0	6.4	= 326
Females	21.3	35.8	24.4	18.5	= 583
85 + Combined	20.2	37.0	23.1	19.7	= 173
Males	22.2	46.0	22.2	9.5	= 63
Females	19.1	31.8	23.6	25.5	= 110

(1) See appendix A

F4.2

Q69J. We are faced with many problems in this country, none of
which can be solved easily or inexpensively. I'm going
to name some of these problems, and for each one I'd
like you to tell me whether you think we're spending too
much money on it, too little money, or about the right
amount.

Foreign aid.

	1973 - 1986				
	Too little 1	About right 2	Too much 3	DK-NA 4	N's
All Ages	4.4	19.5	71.0	5.1	=18006
18-24 Combined	8.9	26.0	59.3	5.9	= 2268
Males	8.1	23.6	64.4	3.8	= 1049
Females	9.5	28.0	54.9	7.6	= 1219
25-34 Combined	5.6	20.3	70.0	4.1	= 4338
Males	5.6	18.9	73.0	2.6	= 1888
Females	5.6	21.5	67.7	5.3	= 2450
35-44 Combined	3.9	19.0	73.3	3.8	= 3211
Males	3.5	19.9	73.8	2.8	= 1444
Females	4.2	18.2	72.9	4.6	= 1767
45-54 Combined	2.9	18.4	74.6	4.1	= 2561
Males	3.4	16.9	76.9	2.8	= 1161
Females	2.5	19.6	72.6	5.3	= 1400
55-64 Combined	2.4	17.4	75.5	4.7	= 2523
Males	2.4	17.8	76.3	3.5	= 1119
Females	2.4	17.0	74.9	5.7	= 1404
65-74 Combined	3.0	17.2	73.1	6.8	= 2023
Males	3.3	16.6	75.9	4.1	= 872
Females	2.7	17.5	70.9	8.9	= 1151
75-84 Combined	2.9	15.7	70.5	10.9	= 909
Males	2.5	13.8	75.2	8.6	= 326
Females	3.1	16.8	67.9	12.2	= 583
85 + Combined	4.6	16.2	65.3	13.9	= 173
Males	1.6	14.3	69.8	14.3	= 63
Females	6.4	17.3	62.7	13.6	= 110

F4.3

Q69A. We are faced with many problems in this country, none
of which can be solved easily or inexpensively. I'm
going to name some of these problems, and for each one
I'd like you to tell me whether you think we're spending
too much money on it, too little money, or about the
right amount.

Space exploration program

		1973 - 1986			
	Too little 1	About right 2	Too much 3	DK-NA 4	N's
All Ages	10.8	36.0	47.9	5.2	=18006
18-24 Combined	12.6	40.9	43.0	3.5	= 2268
Males	18.2	45.2	34.0	2.6	= 1049
Females	7.7	37.2	50.8	4.3	= 1219
25-34 Combined	13.5	38.4	44.4	3.7	= 4338
Males	21.8	41.3	33.9	3.0	= 1888
Females	7.1	36.2	52.5	4.2	= 2450
35-44 Combined	13.9	38.6	44.1	3.4	= 3211
Males	21.1	41.9	34.7	2.4	= 1444
Females	8.0	35.9	51.8	4.2	= 1767
45-54 Combined	11.1	35.6	48.1	5.2	= 2561
Males	17.2	39.2	40.1	3.5	= 1161
Females	6.0	32.6	54.9	6.6	= 1400
55-64 Combined	7.8	33.7	53.3	5.3	= 2523
Males	11.9	39.4	44.7	4.0	= 1119
Females	4.5	29.1	60.1	6.3	= 1404
65-74 Combined	5.6	29.5	56.4	8.6	= 2023
Males	7.9	33.5	53.2	5.4	= 872
Females	3.8	26.5	58.7	10.9	= 1151
75-84 Combined	3.5	27.6	55.8	13.1	= 909
Males	6.7	31.6	53.4	8.3	= 326
Females	1.7	25.4	57.1	15.8	= 583
85 + Combined	2.9	26.0	50.3	20.8	= 173
Males	1.6	27.0	54.0	17.5	= 63
Females	3.6	25.5	48.2	22.7	= 110

F5.1

Q99. Do you think it will be best for the future
      of this country if we take an active part
      in world affairs, or if we stay out of world
      affairs?

	Active part 1	Stay out 2	DK-NA 3	N's
All Ages	63.7	31.5	4.8	=12767
18-24 Combined	60.5	35.3	4.2	= 1572
Males	66.6	30.3	3.2	= 727
Females	55.3	39.6	5.1	= 845
25-34 Combined	66.2	29.5	4.2	= 3127
Males	71.2	25.7	3.1	= 1388
Females	62.3	32.6	5.1	= 1739
35-44 Combined	71.2	25.1	3.7	= 2298
Males	75.5	21.1	3.3	= 1055
Females	67.5	28.4	4.1	= 1243
45-54 Combined	69.2	26.6	4.3	= 1780
Males	74.3	21.7	4.0	= 798
Females	65.0	30.5	4.5	= 982
55-64 Combined	63.4	31.8	4.8	= 1774
Males	69.8	26.3	3.9	= 779
Females	58.3	36.2	5.5	= 995
65-74 Combined	54.4	39.0	6.5	= 1427
Males	61.0	35.5	3.5	= 623
Females	49.4	41.8	8.8	= 804
75-84 Combined	44.1	47.0	8.9	= 666
Males	51.9	43.5	4.6	= 237
Females	39.9	49.0	11.2	= 429
85 + Combined	41.5	48.0	10.6	= 123
Males	45.2	45.2	9.5	= 42
Females	39.5	49.4	11.1	= 81

Column span header: 1973 - 1986

SOCIAL PSYCHOLOGY

SOCIAL PARTICIPATION

The GSS provides information on several forms of social participation, among them organizational memberships and evening social activity. Seventy percent of each age group, excepting the youngest and oldest, hold at least one membership. The highest rates of organizational participation are between age 35 and 54, when over 50 percent of the respondents report at least two memberships. In most age clusters higher percentages of men than women report holding at least one membership. The proportions of individuals who hold memberships have increased over the term of the survey.

The most frequent forms of social visiting are with relatives and neighbors. Compared to these, visiting with friends outside the neighborhood and siblings is less commonly reported. The young are most active in all forms of social visiting, notably with neighbors and friends outside the neighborhood. Women are generally more active than men, and report higher rates of satisfaction with friendships. Though large proportions of all age groups do report a "great deal of satisfaction" with friendships, the ratios specifying this level have declined over the term of the survey.

MORALE

A number of variables in the General Social Survey can be classified under the heading of "morale". Morale has been conceptualized as an affective state; as a cognitive assessment of life quality; and, sometimes as a stable personality trait or the opposite, a transitory mood state.

(Schulz, 1985, p. 539) The GSS provides data quite directly related to the first two, but it can probably be related to the third only following considerable analysis.

Alienation. The term "alienation" generally refers to a situation where people have lost control over a social institution (e.g. the economy during a period of depression), and feel like aliens in the social environment they have created. (Abercrombie et al, 1984, p. 820)

A series of questions plumbing the sense of alienation was asked in 1978 when "stagflation" in the economy was reaching a peak. The sense that the rich get richer and the poor get poorer averaged close to 75 percent in that year. While more than 50 percent believed that what you think doesn't count much any more, only 28 percent felt that they were left out of things going on around them.

Although not a part of the alientation series, a trio of questions about the helpfulness, fairness, and trustworthiness of others has been asked quite often in the survey. A majority feels that others try to be helpful rather than "to look out for themselves." The older age groups generally express more positive feelings on this subject than the younger. At the same time, all groups, excepting the eldest, have responded increasingly favorably over the period. Women are more likely than men to say that others are helpful.

Nearly two-thirds of the total group also feel that people try to be fair. The older age groups respond more positively than others regarding people's fairness, and their more positive feelings have persisted over time. As

143

in the previous question, somewhat higher proportions of women than men believe that people are fair.

Some ambiguity appears to arise when feelings regarding trustworthiness of others are compared with feelings about their helpfulness and fairness. A majority thinks that others can not be trusted, with the youngest expressing the highest rate of doubt. The sense of distrust has increased slightly over the 13 surveys. Larger ratios of women than men have expressed distrust.

Anomia. A series of questions has addressed the problem of anomia, a feeling that has been described as arising in individuals and society at large when social norms are weak, absent, or conflicting. (Merton, 1968, p. 217) One set of questions was asked in three years, 1973, 1974, and 1976, and the other in eight of the years over the full term of the survey.

With respect to the first set of questions, the older age groups have placed considerably more emphasis on money than the younger. As to ethical means of making money, close to 70 percent of each age group has taken an ethical stand. A majority of the older age groups think that one should live for today, but a majority of the younger (under 65+) disagreed. In most age clusters higher proportions of women than men took an ethical stand in regard to making money, but higher proportions of women acknowledged the importance of money (said that, next to health, money is most important).

Close to 70 percent or more of each age group thought that "a person these days doesn't know whom he can count on," with more women than men exhibiting this uncertainty.

A majority of all groups agreed that people don't really care what happens to the next fellow. Still, only a minority wondered whether things are worthwhile any more, though women again expressed more doubt than men.

In terms of the questions asked in eight surveys, a majority of each age group feels that the lot of the average man is getting worse. Women are more negative on this subject than men, and the young, oddly - because of their comparatively limited experience - more negative than the old. This doesn't discourage feelings about the desirability of bringing children into the world, though - even larger majorities of each age group thinks it's fair to bring a child into the world. In most of the age groups, however, a larger percentage of women than men agree that it's hardly fair to bring a child into the world.

Perhaps most notable of all is the widespread belief that public officials are not really interested in the problems of the average man. Nearly two-thirds or more of each age group holds this view, and it has persisted over the term of the survey. Persons age 55-84 express this sense most frequently, and women differ little from men at any age.

Happiness and Excitement in Life. Feelings of happiness are said to differ from life satisfaction because the former refer to "now" whereas the latter represent a more generalized evaluation of one's life situation. (Schulz, 1985, p. 539) The General Social Survey has included a question on happiness alone that has appeared every year since 1972. The results have remained quite stable over the period, with about one-third reporting being very happy, over half being pretty happy, and close to 13 percent not too happy. The youngest respondents express the lowest rate of happiness - only 27 percent say they are very happy. The ratios reporting being very happy increase with age until 65-74, when there's a peak at almost 39 percent. After that they decline even though they still remain high relative to the youngest age group.

From 18-24 through 55-64 higher ratios of women than men report being very happy. After 55-64 the men take the lead, with the most striking change at 65-74, when the difference is nearly 7 percent.

The figures on excitement in life show the highest rates in the earliest years of life followed by a steady decline. At every age a greater proportion of men than women report an exciting life. Few of either sex find that life is dull at any age, but the proportions of the oldest age groups who say they find life dull has increased over the term of the survey.

G1.1

Q172Q. In how many organizations do you hold membership? (1)

			1974 - 1986				
	No membership 1	One 2	Two 3	Three 4	Four or more 5	NA 6	N's
All Ages	28.7	26.1	17.6	11.6	15.8	0.2	=11992
18-24 Combined	38.4	25.7	14.8	9.1	11.7	0.2	= 1515
Males	32.6	28.0	17.0	9.3	12.9	0.3	= 690
Females	43.3	23.9	13.0	9.0	10.8	0.1	= 825
25-34 Combined	30.4	25.4	17.3	11.3	15.4	0.2	= 2923
Males	25.7	26.3	18.6	13.3	16.0	0.2	= 1245
Females	33.8	24.7	16.4	9.9	15.0	0.2	= 1678
35-44 Combined	23.6	22.2	17.9	14.4	21.8	0.2	= 2179
Males	20.2	24.4	17.0	14.4	23.9	---	= 994
Females	26.4	20.3	18.6	14.3	20.0	0.3	= 1185
45-54 Combined	25.3	23.9	19.4	13.3	17.9	0.2	= 1696
Males	20.9	23.2	20.4	15.3	20.2	---	= 766
Females	28.9	24.4	18.6	11.7	16.0	0.3	= 930
55-64 Combined	25.3	29.3	17.9	11.4	15.7	0.5	= 1620
Males	17.5	27.7	19.6	14.7	19.9	0.6	= 714
Females	31.5	30.5	16.6	8.7	12.4	0.4	= 906
65-74 Combined	30.4	30.2	17.6	10.1	11.7	0.1	= 1356
Males	26.3	29.2	20.9	10.8	12.9	---	= 575
Females	33.4	30.9	15.2	9.6	10.8	0.1	= 781
75-84 Combined	27.9	31.9	19.1	9.2	11.7	0.2	= 596
Males	23.7	28.4	19.5	10.7	17.7	---	= 215
Females	30.2	33.9	18.9	8.4	8.4	0.3	= 381
85 + Combined	37.4	29.0	15.0	9.3	9.3	---	= 107
Males	38.2	20.6	14.7	8.8	17.6	---	= 34
Females	37.0	32.9	15.1	9.6	5.5	---	= 73

(1) See appendix A

G1.2

Q170A. Would you use this card and tell me which answer comes
closest to how often you do the following thing:
Spend a social evening with relatives. (1) (2)

	1974 - 1986					
	At least weekly	Monthly	Yearly	Never	DK-NA	N's
	1	2	3	4	5	
All Ages	36.1	34.3	25.0	4.3	0.3	=12087
18-24 Combined	46.1	29.2	22.1	2.6	0.1	= 1449
Males	41.6	28.8	26.8	2.7	0.2	= 664
Females	49.9	29.6	18.1	2.4	---	= 785
25-34 Combined	37.9	37.6	22.2	2.0	0.3	= 2987
Males	36.6	38.9	22.6	1.6	0.3	= 1310
Females	38.9	36.5	21.9	2.4	0.2	= 1677
35-44 Combined	30.1	36.5	29.3	3.9	0.2	= 2172
Males	27.9	37.9	31.1	3.0	0.2	= 972
Females	31.9	35.4	27.8	4.7	0.2	= 1200
45-54 Combined	34.3	34.0	27.0	4.4	0.2	= 1713
Males	28.5	33.7	33.0	4.8	---	= 793
Females	39.3	34.3	21.8	4.1	0.3	= 920
55-64 Combined	36.9	34.0	24.1	4.6	0.4	= 1663
Males	33.2	35.6	25.9	5.1	0.3	= 731
Females	39.8	32.7	22.7	4.3	0.4	= 932
65-74 Combined	35.2	32.1	24.4	8.0	0.4	= 1365
Males	30.7	34.0	26.4	8.3	0.5	= 579
Females	38.4	30.7	22.9	7.8	0.3	= 786
75-84 Combined	30.5	32.0	26.8	9.6	1.0	= 622
Males	27.6	31.6	27.2	12.3	1.3	= 228
Females	32.2	32.2	26.6	8.1	0.8	= 394
85 + Combined	34.5	14.7	34.5	15.5	0.9	= 116
Males	35.9	17.9	25.6	20.5	---	= 39
Females	33.8	13.0	39.0	13.0	1.3	= 77

(1) See appendix A
(2) See appendix B

G1.3

Q170B. Would you use this card and tell me which answer comes
closest to how often you do the following thing:
Spend a social evening with someone who lives in your
neighborhood. (1) (2)

	1974 - 1986					
	At least weekly 1	Monthly 2	Yearly 3	Never 4	DK-NA 5	N's
All Ages	27.2	27.1	21.1	24.2	0.4	=12087
18-24 Combined	41.9	26.6	13.8	17.5	0.2	= 1449
Males	46.4	27.9	11.4	14.2	0.2	= 664
Females	38.1	25.6	15.8	20.3	0.3	= 785
25-34 Combined	28.6	29.0	19.7	22.4	0.3	= 2987
Males	29.5	27.9	20.5	21.6	0.5	= 1310
Females	27.8	29.9	19.1	23.0	0.2	= 1677
35-44 Combined	21.9	29.9	26.0	21.9	0.3	= 2172
Males	21.9	31.3	27.7	18.8	0.3	= 972
Females	21.9	28.8	24.6	24.4	0.3	= 1200
45-54 Combined	21.7	28.6	25.0	24.2	0.5	= 1713
Males	22.3	28.0	26.5	22.7	0.5	= 793
Females	21.2	29.1	23.8	25.4	0.4	= 920
55-64 Combined	22.1	26.5	23.8	27.2	0.4	= 1663
Males	18.3	28.2	27.4	25.6	0.5	= 731
Females	25.1	25.1	20.9	28.5	0.3	= 932
65-74 Combined	30.1	21.8	17.4	30.3	0.4	= 1365
Males	27.3	21.9	21.1	29.2	0.5	= 579
Females	32.2	21.8	14.6	31.0	0.4	= 786
75-84 Combined	26.8	20.7	19.8	32.0	0.6	= 622
Males	21.5	21.5	27.2	28.9	0.9	= 228
Females	29.9	20.3	15.5	33.8	0.5	= 394
85 + Combined	27.6	15.5	14.7	41.4	0.9	= 116
Males	35.9	23.1	7.7	33.3	---	= 39
Females	23.4	11.7	18.2	45.5	1.3	= 77

(1) See appendix A
(2) See appendix B

G1.4

Q170C. Would you use this card and tell me which answer comes
closest to how often you do the following thing:
Spend a social evening with friends who live outside
the neighborhood. (1) (2)

	1974 - 1986					
	At least weekly	Monthly	Yearly	Never	DK-NA	N's
	1	2	3	4	5	
All Ages	21.6	40.9	26.4	10.7	0.3	=12087
18-24 Combined	42.2	41.5	12.1	4.1	0.1	= 1449
Males	45.8	40.4	11.4	2.3	0.2	= 664
Females	39.1	42.4	12.6	5.7	0.1	= 785
25-34 Combined	26.5	48.8	19.2	5.2	0.2	= 2987
Males	29.1	48.9	18.0	3.8	0.2	= 1310
Females	24.6	48.8	20.1	6.3	0.2	= 1677
35-44 Combined	19.4	43.9	29.7	6.8	0.3	= 2172
Males	18.3	43.9	31.5	6.1	0.2	= 972
Females	20.3	43.8	28.2	7.3	0.3	= 1200
45-54 Combined	16.6	38.6	34.3	10.3	0.2	= 1713
Males	18.4	34.8	38.0	8.8	---	= 793
Females	15.0	41.8	31.2	11.5	0.4	= 920
55-64 Combined	13.7	38.9	34.7	12.4	0.3	= 1663
Males	12.0	40.9	35.8	10.9	0.3	= 731
Females	15.0	37.3	33.8	13.5	0.3	= 932
65-74 Combined	13.7	33.1	29.5	23.4	0.3	= 1365
Males	11.2	35.6	32.1	20.6	0.5	= 579
Females	15.5	31.3	27.5	25.6	0.1	= 786
75-84 Combined	11.6	23.5	33.1	30.4	1.4	= 622
Males	11.8	24.1	34.6	27.6	1.8	= 228
Females	11.4	23.1	32.2	32.0	1.3	= 394
85 + Combined	10.3	25.0	23.3	38.8	2.6	= 116
Males	7.7	33.3	20.5	38.5	---	= 39
Females	11.7	20.8	24.7	39.0	3.9	= 77

(1) See appendix A
(2) See appendix B

G1.5

Q170F. Would you use this card and tell me which answer comes
closest to how often you do the following thing:
Spend a social evening with a brother or sister. (2)

			1978 - 1986			
	At least weekly	Monthly	Yearly	Never	DK-NA	N's
	1	2	3	4	5	
All Ages	19.8	28.1	40.9	10.5	0.6	= 6874
18-24 Combined	40.5	30.8	24.1	4.3	0.4	= 790
Males	38.8	29.6	25.0	5.7	0.9	= 348
Females	41.9	31.7	23.3	3.2	---	= 442
25-34 Combined	23.2	34.0	36.9	5.6	0.3	= 1899
Males	20.0	34.1	40.8	4.7	0.4	= 848
Females	25.7	34.0	33.8	6.4	0.2	= 1051
35-44 Combined	13.9	30.3	45.9	9.4	0.5	= 1262
Males	11.4	29.5	49.7	8.9	0.5	= 563
Females	16.0	30.9	42.8	9.9	0.4	= 699
45-54 Combined	13.1	24.0	49.6	12.7	0.6	= 895
Males	12.0	19.3	54.5	13.9	0.2	= 409
Females	14.0	28.0	45.5	11.7	0.8	= 486
55-64 Combined	13.8	24.9	46.6	13.9	0.9	= 916
Males	10.0	23.9	52.7	12.9	0.5	= 389
Females	16.5	25.6	42.1	14.6	1.1	= 527
65-74 Combined	17.8	22.3	42.1	16.7	1.1	= 718
Males	12.5	24.4	44.6	18.1	0.3	= 287
Females	21.3	20.9	40.4	15.8	1.6	= 431
75-84 Combined	12.6	15.8	44.3	25.6	1.7	= 348
Males	7.7	14.5	48.7	26.5	2.6	= 117
Females	15.2	16.5	42.0	25.1	1.3	= 231
85 + Combined	21.7	8.7	32.6	32.6	4.3	= 46
Males	29.4	17.6	29.4	23.5	---	= 17
Females	17.2	3.4	34.5	37.9	6.9	= 29

(2) See appendix B

G2.1

Q161D. For each area of life I am going to name, tell me how much
satisfaction you get from that area.
Your friendships. (1) (2)

| | 1973 - 1986 | | | | | |
	A great deal 1	A fair amount 2	Some or little 3	None 4	DK-NA 5	N's
All Ages	69.6	24.6	4.8	0.6	0.5	=16479
18-24 Combined	68.3	25.9	5.3	0.3	0.2	= 2111
Males	68.0	27.0	4.8	0.1	0.1	= 978
Females	68.6	24.9	5.7	0.4	0.4	= 1133
25-34 Combined	68.0	25.9	5.1	0.7	0.3	= 3965
Males	65.6	28.0	5.1	0.9	0.5	= 1716
Females	69.9	24.2	5.2	0.6	0.1	= 2249
35-44 Combined	67.9	26.9	4.6	0.3	0.2	= 2930
Males	63.4	31.6	4.4	0.4	0.2	= 1322
Females	71.6	23.0	4.9	0.2	0.2	= 1608
45-54 Combined	70.2	24.8	4.0	0.6	0.5	= 2351
Males	66.6	27.7	4.4	0.7	0.7	= 1051
Females	73.1	22.5	3.6	0.5	0.3	= 1300
55-64 Combined	72.3	22.2	3.9	0.9	0.7	= 2302
Males	67.5	25.8	5.0	1.1	0.6	= 1010
Females	76.1	19.4	3.0	0.8	0.7	= 1292
65-74 Combined	72.1	21.4	4.8	0.8	0.9	= 1851
Males	70.0	22.1	5.9	1.0	1.0	= 807
Females	73.8	20.9	3.9	0.7	0.8	= 1044
75-84 Combined	71.0	21.6	5.6	1.0	0.9	= 816
Males	67.4	24.5	5.4	1.3	1.3	= 298
Females	73.0	19.9	5.8	0.8	0.6	= 518
85 + Combined	68.0	17.6	9.2	1.3	3.9	= 153
Males	70.4	20.4	9.3	---	---	= 54
Females	66.7	16.2	9.1	2.0	6.1	= 99

(1) See appendix A
(2) See appendix B

G3.1.1

Q153A. Now I want to read you some things some people
have told us they have felt from time to time.
Do you tend to feel or not.....
The people running the country don't
really care what happens to you.

		1978		
	Yes, feel 1	No, not feel 2	DK-NA 3	N's
All Ages	50.8	44.3	4.9	= 1525
18-24 Combined	51.5	43.6	4.9	= 204
Males	55.1	41.0	3.8	= 78
Females	49.2	45.2	5.6	= 126
25-34 Combined	51.3	45.5	3.3	= 398
Males	49.7	46.8	3.5	= 173
Females	52.4	44.4	3.1	= 225
35-44 Combined	49.4	48.3	2.2	= 271
Males	48.4	48.4	3.2	= 126
Females	50.3	48.3	1.4	= 145
45-54 Combined	51.5	42.4	6.1	= 198
Males	58.1	37.6	4.3	= 93
Females	45.7	46.7	7.6	= 105
55-64 Combined	49.0	46.0	5.0	= 200
Males	47.4	48.7	3.9	= 76
Females	50.0	44.4	5.6	= 124
65-74 Combined	55.1	35.3	9.6	= 156
Males	54.7	35.9	9.4	= 64
Females	55.4	34.8	9.8	= 92
75-84 Combined	45.8	45.8	8.4	= 83
Males	41.4	48.3	10.3	= 29
Females	48.1	44.4	7.4	= 54
85 + Combined	53.3	33.3	13.3	= 15
Males	66.7	33.3	---	= 3
Females	50.0	33.3	16.7	= 12

G3.1.2

Q153B. Now I want to read you some things some people
have told us they have felt from time to time.
Do you tend to feel or not.....
The rich get richer and the poor get
poorer.

	1978				
	Yes, feel 1	No, not feel 2	DK-NA 3		N's
All Ages	73.0	23.3	3.7	=	1525
18-24 Combined	73.0	24.0	2.9	=	204
Males	69.2	28.2	2.6	=	78
Females	75.4	21.4	3.2	=	126
25-34 Combined	80.4	17.1	2.5	=	398
Males	82.7	16.2	1.2	=	173
Females	78.7	17.8	3.6	=	225
35-44 Combined	75.6	21.8	2.6	=	271
Males	73.8	23.0	3.2	=	126
Females	77.2	20.7	2.1	=	145
45-54 Combined	63.6	30.8	5.6	=	198
Males	67.7	28.0	4.3	=	93
Females	60.0	33.3	6.7	=	105
55-64 Combined	65.5	30.5	4.0	=	200
Males	60.5	38.2	1.3	=	76
Females	68.5	25.8	5.6	=	124
65-74 Combined	75.6	18.6	5.8	=	156
Males	78.1	17.2	4.7	=	64
Females	73.9	19.6	6.5	=	92
75-84 Combined	66.3	26.5	7.2	=	83
Males	86.2	13.8	---	=	29
Females	55.6	33.3	11.1	=	54
85 + Combined	60.0	40.0	---	=	15
Males	33.3	66.7	---	=	3
Females	66.7	33.3	---	=	12

G3.1.3

Q153C. Now I want to read you some things some people
have told us they have felt from time to time.
Do you tend to feel or not.....
    What you think doesn't count very much
    anymore.

	1978			
	Yes, feel 1	No, not feel 2	DK-NA 3	N's
All Ages	54.5	38.9	6.6	= 1525
18-24 Combined	48.5	48.5	2.9	= 204
Males	47.4	51.3	1.3	= 78
Females	49.2	46.8	4.0	= 126
25-34 Combined	53.5	41.0	5.5	= 398
Males	57.2	37.6	5.2	= 173
Females	50.7	43.6	5.8	= 225
35-44 Combined	53.1	41.7	5.2	= 271
Males	50.8	45.2	4.0	= 126
Females	55.2	38.6	6.2	= 145
45-54 Combined	51.5	39.9	8.6	= 198
Males	51.6	38.7	9.7	= 93
Females	51.4	41.0	7.6	= 105
55-64 Combined	57.5	36.5	6.0	= 200
Males	56.6	38.2	5.3	= 76
Females	58.1	35.5	6.5	= 124
65-74 Combined	65.4	23.7	10.9	= 156
Males	67.2	26.6	6.3	= 64
Females	64.1	21.7	14.1	= 92
75-84 Combined	56.6	31.3	12.0	= 83
Males	48.3	37.9	13.8	= 29
Females	61.1	27.8	11.1	= 54
85 + Combined	60.0	20.0	20.0	= 15
Males	66.7	----	33.3	= 3
Females	58.3	25.0	16.7	= 12

G3.1.4

Q153D. Now I want to read you some things some people
        have told us they have felt from time to time.
        Do you tend to feel or not.....
            You're left out of things going on around
            you.

| | 1978 | | | |
	Yes, feel 1	No, not feel 2	DK-NA 3	N's
All Ages	28.0	68.3	3.7	= 1525
18-24 Combined	33.3	63.7	2.9	= 204
Males	28.2	67.9	3.8	= 78
Females	36.5	61.1	2.4	= 126
25-34 Combined	26.9	69.1	4.0	= 398
Males	26.0	71.1	2.9	= 173
Females	27.6	67.6	4.9	= 225
35-44 Combined	28.4	68.6	3.0	= 271
Males	25.4	71.4	3.2	= 126
Females	31.0	66.2	2.8	= 145
45-54 Combined	22.7	73.7	3.5	= 198
Males	34.4	63.4	2.2	= 93
Females	12.4	82.9	4.8	= 105
55-64 Combined	26.0	69.5	4.5	= 200
Males	30.3	67.1	2.6	= 76
Females	23.4	71.0	5.6	= 124
65-74 Combined	34.6	62.2	3.2	= 156
Males	31.3	65.6	3.1	= 64
Females	37.0	59.8	3.3	= 92
75-84 Combined	26.5	69.9	3.6	= 83
Males	34.5	58.6	6.9	= 29
Females	22.2	75.9	1.9	= 54
85 + Combined	13.3	73.3	13.3	= 15
Males	----	66.7	33.3	= 3
Females	16.7	75.0	8.3	= 12

G3.1.5

Q158. Would you say that most of the time people try to
        be helpful, or that they are mostly just looking
        out for themselves? (1)

	1972 - 1986				
	Helpful	Lookout for self	Depends	DK-NA	
	1	2	3	4	N's
All Ages	51.7	42.6	5.0	0.7	=13592
18-24 Combined	40.4	54.6	4.3	0.7	= 1738
Males	37.1	58.6	3.7	0.6	= 811
Females	43.4	51.1	4.7	0.8	= 927
25-34 Combined	49.0	45.4	5.0	0.6	= 3272
Males	44.6	49.7	5.0	0.8	= 1445
Females	52.5	42.0	5.1	0.4	= 1827
35-44 Combined	55.3	40.1	4.1	0.4	= 2389
Males	50.1	45.0	4.4	0.5	= 1089
Females	59.6	36.1	3.9	0.4	= 1300
45-54 Combined	56.3	37.6	5.3	0.9	= 1994
Males	52.4	41.4	5.4	0.8	= 904
Females	59.4	34.4	5.2	0.9	= 1090
55-64 Combined	53.0	41.4	4.8	0.8	= 1898
Males	48.9	44.9	5.3	0.8	= 848
Females	56.2	38.6	4.5	0.8	= 1050
65-74 Combined	53.7	39.7	5.6	1.1	= 1494
Males	48.9	44.9	5.4	0.8	= 646
Females	57.3	35.7	5.7	1.3	= 848
75-84 Combined	58.5	33.2	7.7	0.6	= 687
Males	54.5	37.6	7.4	0.4	= 242
Females	60.7	30.8	7.9	0.7	= 445
85 + Combined	58.3	32.5	5.8	3.3	= 120
Males	50.0	40.9	4.5	4.5	= 44
Females	63.2	27.6	6.6	2.6	= 76

(1) See appendix A

157

G3.1.6

Q159. Do you think most people would try to take
advantage of you if they got a chance, or
would they try to be fair? (1)

	1972 - 1986				
	Take advantage 1	Fair 2	Depends 3	DK-NA 4	N's
All Ages	33.8	60.5	4.8	0.9	=13592
18-24 Combined	47.4	47.5	4.5	0.5	= 1738
Males	48.1	47.0	4.3	0.6	= 811
Females	46.8	48.0	4.7	0.4	= 927
25-34 Combined	37.5	57.0	4.7	0.8	= 3272
Males	39.5	55.0	4.6	0.9	= 1445
Females	35.9	58.6	4.8	0.8	= 1827
35-44 Combined	31.9	62.8	4.5	0.8	= 2389
Males	34.3	60.3	4.4	1.0	= 1089
Females	29.9	64.9	4.5	0.6	= 1300
45-54 Combined	29.5	65.2	4.4	0.9	= 1994
Males	33.6	61.5	3.9	1.0	= 904
Females	26.1	68.3	4.8	0.8	= 1090
55-64 Combined	29.9	63.8	5.3	1.1	= 1898
Males	32.3	61.2	5.3	1.2	= 848
Females	27.9	65.8	5.3	1.0	= 1050
65-74 Combined	29.8	64.3	5.1	0.9	= 1494
Males	33.6	59.4	6.0	0.9	= 646
Females	26.9	67.9	4.4	0.8	= 848
75-84 Combined	22.6	70.0	6.1	1.3	= 687
Males	27.7	67.4	3.3	1.7	= 242
Females	19.8	71.5	7.6	1.1	= 445
85 + Combined	23.3	65.8	5.8	5.0	= 120
Males	29.5	63.6	2.3	4.5	= 44
Females	19.7	67.1	7.9	5.3	= 76

(1) See appendix A

G3.1.7

Q160A. Generally speaking, would you say that most
people can be trusted or that you can't be
too careful in dealing with people? (1)

	1972 - 1986				
	Can trust 1	Cannot trust 2	Depends 3	DK-NA 4	N's
All Ages	42.7	53.3	3.5	0.5	=12799
18-24 Combined	32.7	62.8	4.1	0.4	= 1644
Males	35.2	60.8	3.8	0.3	= 768
Females	30.6	64.6	4.3	0.5	= 876
25-34 Combined	40.1	56.0	3.5	0.4	= 3051
Males	42.8	53.6	3.3	0.3	= 1405
Females	37.7	58.1	3.6	0.5	= 1646
35-44 Combined	48.0	48.6	3.0	0.4	= 2254
Males	49.9	46.7	3.2	0.2	= 1052
Females	46.3	50.2	2.8	0.7	= 1202
45-54 Combined	49.6	46.8	3.3	0.4	= 1895
Males	51.1	44.8	3.9	0.2	= 882
Females	48.2	48.5	2.9	0.5	= 1013
55-64 Combined	44.8	50.8	3.8	0.6	= 1782
Males	49.4	46.6	3.7	0.4	= 820
Females	41.0	54.4	3.8	0.8	= 962
65-74 Combined	39.7	56.4	3.2	0.6	= 1405
Males	43.8	52.1	3.8	0.3	= 624
Females	36.5	59.9	2.7	0.9	= 781
75-84 Combined	43.3	51.8	3.7	1.2	= 651
Males	45.7	49.1	3.4	1.7	= 234
Females	42.0	53.2	3.8	1.0	= 417
85 + Combined	39.3	54.7	3.4	2.6	= 117
Males	37.2	58.1	---	4.7	= 43
Females	40.5	52.7	5.4	1.4	= 74

(1) See appendix A

159

G3.2.1

Q175A. Now I'm going to read you several statements.
Some people agree with a statement, others
disagree. As I read each one, tell me whether
you more or less agree with it, or more or
less disagree?
Next to health, money is the most important
thing in life.

	1973, 1974, 1976			
	Agree 1	Disagree 2	DK-NA 3	N's
All Ages	31.6	67.8	0.5	= 4471
18-24 Combined	22.1	77.7	0.2	= 619
Males	23.5	76.5	---	= 311
Females	20.8	78.9	0.3	= 308
25-34 Combined	23.5	76.2	0.3	= 980
Males	21.3	78.2	0.5	= 422
Females	25.1	74.7	0.2	= 558
35-44 Combined	27.3	72.3	0.4	= 769
Males	23.5	76.5	---	= 332
Females	30.2	69.1	0.7	= 437
45-54 Combined	35.4	63.9	0.7	= 711
Males	32.9	66.5	0.6	= 319
Females	37.5	61.7	0.8	= 392
55-64 Combined	36.7	62.8	0.5	= 656
Males	39.9	60.1	---	= 313
Females	33.8	65.3	0.9	= 343
65-74 Combined	45.2	54.0	0.8	= 502
Males	44.7	54.1	1.2	= 257
Females	45.7	53.9	0.4	= 245
75-84 Combined	49.5	48.5	2.0	= 196
Males	56.5	41.2	2.4	= 85
Females	44.1	54.1	1.8	= 111
85 + Combined	55.3	42.1	2.6	= 38
Males	66.7	33.3	---	= 18
Females	45.0	50.0	5.0	= 20

G3.2.2

Q175B. Now I'm going to read you several statements.
Some people agree with a statement, others
disagree. As I read each one, tell me whether
you more or less agree with it, or more or
less disagree?
You sometimes can't help wondering whether
anything is worthwhile any more.

		1973, 1974, 1976		
	Agree 1	Disagree 2	DK-NA 3	N's
All Ages	41.0	57.9	1.1	= 4471
18-24 Combined	47.5	52.2	0.3	= 619
Males	43.7	55.9	0.3	= 311
Females	51.3	48.4	0.3	= 308
25-34 Combined	38.9	60.4	0.7	= 980
Males	37.7	61.6	0.7	= 422
Females	39.8	59.5	0.7	= 558
35-44 Combined	36.4	62.0	1.6	= 769
Males	35.5	63.0	1.5	= 332
Females	37.1	61.3	1.6	= 437
45-54 Combined	42.2	57.1	0.7	= 711
Males	39.8	59.6	0.6	= 319
Females	44.1	55.1	0.8	= 392
55-64 Combined	40.5	58.1	1.4	= 656
Males	40.9	57.8	1.3	= 313
Females	40.2	58.3	1.5	= 343
65-74 Combined	41.4	56.6	2.0	= 502
Males	35.0	63.0	1.9	= 257
Females	48.2	49.8	2.0	= 245
75-84 Combined	45.9	51.0	3.1	= 196
Males	38.8	57.6	3.5	= 85
Females	51.4	45.9	2.7	= 111
85 + Combined	31.6	68.4	---	= 38
Males	33.3	66.7	---	= 18
Females	30.0	70.0	---	= 20

161

G3.2.3

Q175C. Now I'm going to read you several statements.
Some people agree with a statement, others
disagree. As I read each one, tell me whether
you more or less agree with it, or more or
less disagree?
To make money, there are no right and wrong
ways any more, only easy and hard ways.

	1973, 1974, 1976			
	Agree 1	Disagree 2	DK-NA 3	N's
All Ages	24.1	73.4	2.5	= 4471
18-24 Combined	28.1	70.3	1.6	= 619
Males	34.1	65.3	0.6	= 311
Females	22.1	75.3	2.6	= 308
25-34 Combined	24.6	74.3	1.1	= 980
Males	24.4	74.4	1.2	= 422
Females	24.7	74.2	1.1	= 558
35-44 Combined	19.2	78.8	2.0	= 769
Males	19.6	79.8	0.6	= 332
Females	19.0	78.0	3.0	= 437
45-54 Combined	23.3	74.1	2.5	= 711
Males	24.1	74.9	0.9	= 319
Females	22.7	73.5	3.8	= 392
55-64 Combined	23.5	73.2	3.4	= 656
Males	26.2	71.6	2.2	= 313
Females	21.0	74.6	4.4	= 343
65-74 Combined	26.7	68.7	4.6	= 502
Males	25.7	70.4	3.9	= 257
Females	27.8	66.9	5.3	= 245
75-84 Combined	29.6	65.8	4.6	= 196
Males	30.6	68.2	1.2	= 85
Females	28.8	64.0	7.2	= 111
85 + Combined	10.5	84.2	5.3	= 38
Males	11.1	83.3	5.6	= 18
Females	10.0	85.0	5.0	= 20

G3.2.4

Q176A. Now I'd like your opinions on a number of
        different things.
        Nowadays, a person has to live pretty much
        for today and let tomorrow take care of
        itself. Do you more or less agree with that,
        or more or less disagree?

	1973, 1974, 1976			
	Agree 1	Disagree 2	DK-NA 3	N's
All Ages	44.4	54.8	0.8	= 4471
18-24 Combined	46.2	53.3	0.5	= 619
Males	44.1	55.0	1.0	= 311
Females	48.4	51.6	---	= 308
25-34 Combined	43.1	56.2	0.7	= 980
Males	37.9	61.6	0.5	= 422
Females	47.0	52.2	0.9	= 558
35-44 Combined	39.8	59.9	0.3	= 769
Males	31.9	68.1	---	= 332
Females	45.8	53.8	0.5	= 437
45-54 Combined	41.4	57.9	0.7	= 711
Males	35.7	63.3	0.9	= 319
Females	45.9	53.6	0.5	= 392
55-64 Combined	45.0	53.5	1.5	= 656
Males	41.9	56.9	1.3	= 313
Females	47.8	50.4	1.7	= 343
65-74 Combined	52.6	46.2	1.2	= 502
Males	52.1	46.3	1.6	= 257
Females	53.1	46.1	0.8	= 245
75-84 Combined	51.0	48.0	1.0	= 196
Males	51.8	48.2	---	= 85
Females	50.5	47.7	1.8	= 111
85 + Combined	52.6	44.7	2.6	= 38
Males	50.0	50.0	---	= 18
Females	55.0	40.0	5.0	= 20

G3.2.5

Q176B. Now I'd like your opinions on a number of
different things.
In spite of what some people say, the lot
(situation/condition) of the average man
is getting worse, not better.

		1973 - 1985		
	Agree 1	Disagree 2	DK-NA 3	N's
All Ages	57.5	39.1	3.4	=11941
18-24 Combined	60.0	37.5	2.5	= 1549
Males	56.9	40.2	2.9	= 736
Females	62.7	35.1	2.2	= 813
25-34 Combined	59.5	38.5	2.1	= 2775
Males	56.1	42.1	1.8	= 1203
Females	62.0	35.7	2.3	= 1572
35-44 Combined	58.2	39.7	2.1	= 2101
Males	56.1	42.7	1.2	= 935
Females	59.9	37.3	2.8	= 1166
45-54 Combined	56.6	40.4	3.0	= 1731
Males	52.3	45.6	2.1	= 794
Females	60.3	36.0	3.7	= 937
55-64 Combined	56.1	40.1	3.8	= 1737
Males	53.9	43.3	2.8	= 785
Females	57.9	37.5	4.6	= 952
65-74 Combined	55.2	38.7	6.1	= 1345
Males	56.3	38.6	5.1	= 593
Females	54.3	38.8	6.9	= 752
75-84 Combined	51.5	38.9	9.6	= 584
Males	52.4	40.0	7.6	= 210
Females	51.1	38.2	10.7	= 374
85 + Combined	54.6	34.5	10.9	= 119
Males	54.2	35.4	10.4	= 48
Females	54.9	33.8	11.3	= 71

G3.2.6

Q176C. Now I'd like your opinions on a number of
different things.
It's hardly fair to bring a child into
the world with the way things look for
the future.

	1973 - 1985			
	Agree 1	Disagree 2	DK-NA 3	N's
All Ages	37.9	59.1	3.0	=11941
18-24 Combined	38.6	59.4	2.0	= 1549
Males	36.5	61.4	2.0	= 736
Females	40.5	57.6	2.0	= 813
25-34 Combined	35.9	62.2	1.8	= 2775
Males	34.2	64.2	1.6	= 1203
Females	37.2	60.8	2.0	= 1572
35-44 Combined	35.5	62.2	2.3	= 2101
Males	35.4	62.8	1.8	= 935
Females	35.5	61.7	2.7	= 1166
45-54 Combined	37.4	60.4	2.2	= 1731
Males	34.9	63.0	2.1	= 794
Females	39.6	58.2	2.2	= 937
55-64 Combined	38.4	58.0	3.6	= 1737
Males	35.4	61.5	3.1	= 785
Females	40.9	55.0	4.1	= 952
65-74 Combined	43.0	52.3	4.7	= 1345
Males	44.7	51.4	3.9	= 593
Females	41.8	52.9	5.3	= 752
75-84 Combined	41.1	50.2	8.7	= 584
Males	38.1	53.8	8.1	= 210
Females	42.8	48.1	9.1	= 374
85 + Combined	41.2	44.5	14.3	= 119
Males	39.6	45.8	14.6	= 48
Females	42.3	43.7	14.1	= 71

G3.2.7

Q177A. Now I'm going to read you a statement.
Most public officials (people in public
office) are not really interested in the
problems of the average man.

		1973 - 1985		
	Agree 1	Disagree 2	DK-NA 3	N's
All Ages	64.5	32.4	3.1	=11941
18-24 Combined	62.4	34.8	2.8	= 1549
Males	62.5	34.6	2.9	= 736
Females	62.4	34.9	2.7	= 813
25-34 Combined	63.9	33.4	2.7	= 2775
Males	64.3	33.7	2.0	= 1203
Females	63.5	33.3	3.2	= 1572
35-44 Combined	65.2	32.6	2.2	= 2101
Males	66.0	33.2	0.9	= 935
Females	64.6	32.2	3.3	= 1166
45-54 Combined	63.0	34.5	2.4	= 1731
Males	63.2	35.1	1.6	= 794
Females	62.9	34.0	3.1	= 937
55-64 Combined	65.6	31.3	3.1	= 1737
Males	66.1	32.0	1.9	= 785
Females	65.2	30.8	4.0	= 952
65-74 Combined	67.4	27.8	4.8	= 1345
Males	69.1	28.3	2.5	= 593
Females	66.0	27.4	6.6	= 752
75-84 Combined	65.6	28.8	5.7	= 584
Males	67.1	31.4	1.4	= 210
Females	64.7	27.3	8.0	= 374
85 + Combined	60.5	26.9	12.6	= 119
Males	58.3	33.3	8.3	= 48
Females	62.0	22.5	15.5	= 71

G3.2.8

Q177B. Now I'm going to read you a statement.
        These days a person doesn't really
        know whom he can count on.

	1973, 1974, 1976			
	Agree 1	Disagree 2	DK-NA 3	N's
All Ages	71.3	27.6	1.1	= 4471
18-24 Combined	71.7	28.1	0.2	= 619
Males	66.9	33.1	---	= 311
Females	76.6	23.1	0.3	= 308
25-34 Combined	68.2	31.1	0.7	= 980
Males	65.9	33.6	0.5	= 422
Females	69.9	29.2	0.9	= 558
35-44 Combined	69.2	29.5	1.3	= 769
Males	66.6	32.8	0.6	= 332
Females	71.2	27.0	1.8	= 437
45-54 Combined	70.9	27.8	1.3	= 711
Males	67.4	31.0	1.6	= 319
Females	73.7	25.3	1.0	= 392
55-64 Combined	75.0	23.9	1.1	= 656
Males	73.5	25.6	1.0	= 313
Females	76.4	22.4	1.2	= 343
65-74 Combined	74.7	23.1	2.2	= 502
Males	73.5	23.3	3.1	= 257
Females	75.9	22.9	1.2	= 245
75-84 Combined	74.0	24.5	1.5	= 196
Males	71.8	28.2	---	= 85
Females	75.7	21.6	2.7	= 111
85 + Combined	73.7	23.7	2.6	= 38
Males	61.1	38.9	---	= 18
Females	85.0	10.0	5.0	= 20

G3.2.9

Q177C. Now I'm going to read you a statement.
Most people don't really care what
happens to the next fellow.

	1973, 1974, 1976			
	Agree 1	Disagree 2	DK-NA 3	N's
All Ages	54.8	43.8	1.4	= 4471
18-24 Combined	58.3	39.9	1.8	= 619
Males	56.9	41.2	1.9	= 311
Females	59.7	38.6	1.6	= 308
25-34 Combined	54.4	44.6	1.0	= 980
Males	54.5	45.0	0.5	= 422
Females	54.3	44.3	1.4	= 558
35-44 Combined	50.7	48.1	1.2	= 769
Males	53.3	45.5	1.2	= 332
Females	48.7	50.1	1.1	= 437
45-54 Combined	52.0	46.7	1.3	= 711
Males	51.7	47.0	1.3	= 319
Females	52.3	46.4	1.3	= 392
55-64 Combined	56.9	41.6	1.5	= 656
Males	57.5	41.9	0.6	= 313
Females	56.3	41.4	2.3	= 343
65-74 Combined	59.0	39.2	1.8	= 502
Males	62.3	35.8	1.9	= 257
Females	55.5	42.9	1.6	= 245
75-84 Combined	55.1	43.9	1.0	= 196
Males	57.6	42.4	---	= 85
Females	53.2	45.0	1.8	= 111
85 + Combined	52.6	42.1	5.3	= 38
Males	50.0	44.4	5.6	= 18
Females	55.0	40.0	5.0	= 20

G3.3.1

Q154. Taken altogether, how would you say things are
these days -- would you say that you are very
happy, pretty happy, or not too happy?

	1972 - 1986				
	Very happy 1	Pretty happy 2	Not too happy 3	DK-NA 4	N's
All Ages	33.1	53.7	12.6	0.6	=19614
18-24 Combined	27.3	57.3	14.7	0.8	= 2468
Males	24.0	59.6	15.6	0.8	= 1162
Females	30.2	55.1	13.9	0.8	= 1306
25-34 Combined	31.2	57.6	10.7	0.6	= 4696
Males	27.2	61.0	10.9	0.8	= 2070
Females	34.2	54.9	10.5	0.4	= 2626
35-44 Combined	32.5	55.5	11.5	0.4	= 3451
Males	30.5	57.0	12.0	0.4	= 1552
Females	34.2	54.3	11.1	0.4	= 1899
45-54 Combined	34.8	51.4	13.3	0.6	= 2877
Males	33.1	52.3	14.1	0.5	= 1330
Females	36.2	50.7	12.5	0.6	= 1547
55-64 Combined	35.2	50.7	13.4	0.6	= 2775
Males	34.7	50.2	14.4	0.7	= 1245
Females	35.7	51.0	12.7	0.6	= 1530
65-74 Combined	38.6	47.4	13.2	0.9	= 2181
Males	42.2	45.1	12.3	0.4	= 946
Females	35.8	49.1	13.8	1.2	= 1235
75-84 Combined	36.5	49.5	13.4	0.6	= 984
Males	37.6	49.2	12.7	0.6	= 354
Females	35.9	49.7	13.8	0.6	= 630
85 + Combined	33.5	50.0	15.4	1.1	= 182
Males	35.3	50.0	14.7	---	= 68
Females	32.5	50.0	15.8	1.8	= 114

G3.3.2

Q157. In general, do you find life exciting, pretty
       routine, or dull? (1)

	1973 - 1985				
	Exciting 1	Routine 2	Dull 3	DK-NA 4	N's
All Ages	44.9	48.4	5.3	1.4	=11941
18-24 Combined	52.2	42.3	4.8	0.6	= 1549
Males	53.9	41.8	3.8	0.4	= 736
Females	50.7	42.7	5.8	0.9	= 813
25-34 Combined	49.1	46.4	3.0	1.5	= 2775
Males	53.2	42.7	2.4	1.7	= 1203
Females	46.0	49.2	3.4	1.4	= 1572
35-44 Combined	47.6	47.4	3.9	1.1	= 2101
Males	50.9	45.1	3.2	0.7	= 935
Females	44.9	49.1	4.5	1.5	= 1166
45-54 Combined	42.8	50.7	5.0	1.4	= 1731
Males	45.3	48.2	4.8	1.6	= 794
Females	40.7	52.8	5.2	1.3	= 937
55-64 Combined	40.0	52.4	6.2	1.4	= 1737
Males	43.9	48.9	6.2	0.9	= 785
Females	36.7	55.4	6.1	1.9	= 952
65-74 Combined	38.4	51.0	8.9	1.6	= 1345
Males	42.5	47.9	7.9	1.7	= 593
Females	35.2	53.5	9.7	1.6	= 752
75-84 Combined	33.9	51.9	11.5	2.7	= 584
Males	34.3	50.5	11.0	4.3	= 210
Females	33.7	52.7	11.8	1.9	= 374
85 + Combined	34.5	49.6	13.4	2.5	= 119
Males	43.8	37.5	16.7	2.1	= 48
Females	28.2	57.7	11.3	2.8	= 71

(1) See appendix A

SOCIAL CONTROL

Responses to questions about social control show considerable difference between women and men and young and old. Women at every age show far higher rates of fear about walking alone than men. Men are more likely to own weapons, and to have been hit, threatened, and mugged. The great majority of both sexes feel safe at home at night, even though between five and ten percent report an illegal entry to their homes in the past year. Younger men and women are more likely than old to have been subjected to some form of violence, yet the young express fear of crime less frequently than the old.

High proportions of all groups favor police permits for guns, and also think that the treatment of criminals is not harsh enough. Proportionately more women than men feel strongly on both issues. Although two-thirds or more of both sexes favor the death penalty, higher proportions of women oppose it. A majority of all but the youngest males opposes the legalization of marijuana. Women and the older age groups are most opposed. The majority favors more spending on crime control, with little difference among the groups.

H1.1

Q238. Do you happen to have in your home (IF HOUSE: or garage)
       any guns or revolvers?

	1973 - 1985				
	Yes 1	No 2	Refused 3	DK-NA 4	N's
All Ages	46.6	52.2	0.7	0.5	=11941
18-24 Combined	42.0	57.2	0.2	0.6	= 1549
Males	47.6	51.8	0.4	0.3	= 736
Females	37.0	62.1	---	0.9	= 813
25-34 Combined	45.2	54.0	0.5	0.3	= 2775
Males	50.9	48.1	0.8	0.2	= 1203
Females	40.9	58.5	0.2	0.4	= 1572
35-44 Combined	51.6	47.2	0.9	0.3	= 2101
Males	56.4	41.9	1.3	0.4	= 935
Females	47.9	51.4	0.6	0.2	= 1166
45-54 Combined	52.6	45.7	1.2	0.5	= 1731
Males	56.3	42.1	1.1	0.5	= 794
Females	49.4	48.8	1.3	0.5	= 937
55-64 Combined	50.4	48.6	0.5	0.5	= 1737
Males	56.4	42.7	0.5	0.4	= 785
Females	45.4	53.5	0.5	0.6	= 952
65-74 Combined	42.7	55.8	0.7	0.8	= 1345
Males	54.5	44.0	0.8	0.7	= 593
Females	33.4	65.2	0.5	0.9	= 752
75-84 Combined	31.3	67.5	0.5	0.7	= 584
Males	50.0	48.1	1.4	0.5	= 210
Females	20.9	78.3	---	0.8	= 374
85 + Combined	29.4	68.1	1.7	0.8	= 119
Males	52.1	47.9	---	---	= 48
Females	14.1	81.7	2.8	1.4	= 71

173

H2.1

Q230. Have you ever been punched or beaten by
       another person? (1)

| | 1973 - 1986 | | | |
	Yes 1	No 2	DK-NA 3	N's
All Ages	34.8	65.1	0.1	=11984
18-24 Combined	46.6	53.4	---	= 1538
Males	64.8	35.2	---	= 698
Females	31.5	68.5	---	= 840
25-34 Combined	44.2	55.7	0.1	= 2914
Males	64.1	35.9	---	= 1263
Females	28.9	70.9	0.2	= 1651
35-44 Combined	39.6	60.3	0.1	= 2149
Males	60.9	39.0	0.1	= 981
Females	21.7	78.2	0.2	= 1168
45-54 Combined	31.8	68.2	---	= 1678
Males	51.2	48.8	---	= 735
Females	16.8	83.2	---	= 943
55-64 Combined	25.8	74.2	0.1	= 1646
Males	43.1	56.9	---	= 722
Females	12.2	87.7	0.1	= 924
65-74 Combined	19.3	80.5	0.1	= 1336
Males	32.2	67.7	0.2	= 572
Females	9.7	90.2	0.1	= 764
75-84 Combined	15.0	85.0	---	= 612
Males	30.4	69.6	---	= 214
Females	6.8	93.2	---	= 398
85 + Combined	10.8	88.3	0.9	= 111
Males	15.4	84.6	---	= 39
Females	8.3	90.3	1.4	= 72

(1) See appendix A

H2.2

Q231. Have you ever been threatened with a gun,
        or shot at?

		1973 - 1986		
	Yes 1	No 2	DK-NA 3	N's
All Ages	19.1	80.8	0.2	=11984
18-24 Combined	19.5	80.5	---	= 1538
Males	28.8	71.2	---	= 698
Females	11.8	88.2	---	= 840
25-34 Combined	22.0	77.8	0.2	= 2914
Males	35.2	64.6	0.2	= 1263
Females	12.0	87.9	0.1	= 1651
35-44 Combined	22.7	77.2	0.1	= 2149
Males	36.4	63.4	0.2	= 981
Females	11.1	88.9	---	= 1168
45-54 Combined	20.4	79.4	0.2	= 1678
Males	34.4	65.3	0.3	= 735
Females	9.5	90.3	0.1	= 943
55-64 Combined	17.8	82.1	0.1	= 1646
Males	33.0	67.0	---	= 722
Females	6.0	93.8	0.2	= 924
65-74 Combined	12.0	87.6	0.4	= 1336
Males	22.7	76.6	0.7	= 572
Females	3.9	95.8	0.3	= 764
75-84 Combined	8.3	91.5	0.2	= 612
Males	18.7	80.8	0.5	= 214
Females	2.8	97.2	---	= 398
85 + Combined	7.2	91.0	1.8	= 111
Males	17.9	82.1	---	= 39
Females	1.4	95.8	2.8	= 72

H2.3

Q236. During the last year -- that is, between March
and now -- did anyone break into or somehow
illegally get into your (apartment/home)?

	1973 - 1985			
	Yes 1	No 2	DK-NA 3	N's
All Ages	7.3	92.6	0.2	=11941
18-24 Combined	10.0	89.9	0.1	= 1549
Males	9.0	91.0	---	= 736
Females	10.9	88.9	0.1	= 813
25-34 Combined	9.2	90.6	0.2	= 2775
Males	6.8	93.2	---	= 1203
Females	11.0	88.7	0.3	= 1572
35-44 Combined	7.4	92.6	---	= 2101
Males	7.2	92.8	---	= 935
Females	7.6	92.4	---	= 1166
45-54 Combined	6.6	93.1	0.3	= 1731
Males	8.7	90.9	0.4	= 794
Females	4.8	94.9	0.3	= 937
55-64 Combined	5.2	94.6	0.2	= 1737
Males	5.1	94.8	0.1	= 785
Females	5.4	94.4	0.2	= 952
65-74 Combined	4.7	95.1	0.2	= 1345
Males	4.6	95.3	0.2	= 593
Females	4.8	94.9	0.3	= 752
75-84 Combined	4.6	95.2	0.2	= 584
Males	3.8	96.2	---	= 210
Females	5.1	94.7	0.3	= 374
85 + Combined	7.6	92.4	---	= 119
Males	10.4	89.6	---	= 48
Females	5.6	94.4	---	= 71

H2.4

Q237. During the last year, did anyone take
       something directly from you by using
       force -- such as a stickup, mugging,
       or threat?

		1973 - 1985		
	Yes 1	No 2	DK-NA 3	N's
All Ages	2.1	97.6	0.3	=11941
18-24 Combined	3.6	96.4	0.1	= 1549
Males	4.3	95.5	0.1	= 736
Females	2.8	97.2	---	= 813
25-34 Combined	2.5	97.1	0.4	= 2775
Males	2.1	97.5	0.4	= 1203
Females	2.9	96.8	0.4	= 1572
35-44 Combined	2.0	97.9	0.1	= 2101
Males	2.0	97.9	0.1	= 935
Females	1.9	97.9	0.2	= 1166
45-54 Combined	1.4	98.3	0.3	= 1731
Males	1.8	97.6	0.6	= 794
Females	1.1	98.8	0.1	= 937
55-64 Combined	1.6	98.0	0.4	= 1737
Males	1.8	98.0	0.3	= 785
Females	1.4	98.1	0.5	= 952
65-74 Combined	1.6	97.9	0.4	= 1345
Males	1.2	98.3	0.5	= 593
Females	2.0	97.6	0.4	= 752
75-84 Combined	1.2	98.6	0.2	= 584
Males	0.5	99.5	---	= 210
Females	1.6	98.1	0.3	= 374
85 + Combined	2.5	97.5	---	= 119
Males	4.2	95.8	---	= 48
Females	1.4	98.6	---	= 71

H3.1

Q234. Is there any area right around here--that is,
within a mile -- where you would be afraid to
walk alone at night? (1)

	1973 - 1985			
	Yes 1	No 2	DK-NA 3	N's
All Ages	43.1	56.1	0.8	=11941
18-24 Combined	39.2	60.2	0.6	= 1549
Males	17.9	81.9	0.1	= 736
Females	58.4	40.5	1.1	= 813
25-34 Combined	41.6	57.8	0.6	= 2775
Males	18.9	80.6	0.5	= 1203
Females	59.0	40.3	0.7	= 1572
35-44 Combined	38.6	60.8	0.6	= 2101
Males	19.5	80.2	0.3	= 935
Females	53.9	45.3	0.8	= 1166
45-54 Combined	40.7	58.9	0.4	= 1731
Males	20.8	78.8	0.4	= 794
Females	57.6	41.9	0.4	= 937
55-64 Combined	45.2	54.0	0.8	= 1737
Males	25.4	74.4	0.3	= 785
Females	61.6	37.2	1.3	= 952
65-74 Combined	49.5	48.7	1.8	= 1345
Males	31.2	67.8	1.0	= 593
Females	64.0	33.6	2.4	= 752
75-84 Combined	58.7	39.6	1.7	= 584
Males	36.2	63.3	0.5	= 210
Females	71.4	26.2	2.4	= 374
85 + Combined	58.0	39.5	2.5	= 119
Males	39.6	60.4	---	= 48
Females	70.4	25.4	4.2	= 71

(1) See appendix A

H3.2

Q235. How about at home at night -- do you feel
        safe and secure, or not?

		1982			
		Yes 1	No 2	DK-NA 3	N's
All Ages		85.5	13.4	1.1	= 1494
18-24	Combined	83.8	15.6	0.6	= 179
	Males	91.5	8.5	---	= 82
	Females	77.3	21.6	1.0	= 97
25-34	Combined	87.1	12.6	0.3	= 389
	Males	93.2	6.8	---	= 176
	Females	82.2	17.4	0.5	= 213
35-44	Combined	88.9	9.8	1.2	= 244
	Males	93.5	5.6	0.9	= 107
	Females	85.4	13.1	1.5	= 137
45-54	Combined	83.6	14.8	1.6	= 183
	Males	87.3	8.9	3.8	= 79
	Females	80.8	19.2	---	= 104
55-64	Combined	86.0	12.6	1.4	= 222
	Males	89.3	8.3	2.4	= 84
	Females	84.1	15.2	0.7	= 138
65-74	Combined	84.9	13.4	1.7	= 172
	Males	83.1	14.1	2.8	= 71
	Females	86.1	12.9	1.0	= 101
75-84	Combined	76.5	22.4	1.2	= 85
	Males	75.9	24.1	---	= 29
	Females	76.8	21.4	1.8	= 56
85 +	Combined	80.0	10.0	10.0	= 20
	Males	71.4	14.3	14.3	= 7
	Females	84.6	7.7	7.7	= 13

H4.1

Q88. Would you favor or oppose a law which would
require a person to obtain a police permit
before he or she could buy a gun?

	1972 - 1985			
	Favor 1	Oppose 2	DK-NA 3	N's
All Ages	71.8	26.0	2.2	=15034
18-24 Combined	73.7	25.2	1.1	= 1964
Males	66.3	32.3	1.4	= 945
Females	80.5	18.6	0.9	= 1019
25-34 Combined	74.7	23.7	1.5	= 3470
Males	66.8	32.0	1.2	= 1532
Females	81.0	17.2	1.8	= 1938
35-44 Combined	69.7	28.3	2.0	= 2591
Males	60.7	37.7	1.5	= 1164
Females	77.0	20.7	2.3	= 1427
45-54 Combined	68.8	29.3	1.9	= 2283
Males	60.8	37.9	1.2	= 1065
Females	75.7	21.8	2.5	= 1218
55-64 Combined	69.6	27.8	2.6	= 2185
Males	63.4	34.8	1.8	= 1000
Females	74.9	21.9	3.3	= 1185
65-74 Combined	73.3	23.2	3.5	= 1674
Males	67.5	30.9	1.6	= 744
Females	78.0	17.1	4.9	= 930
75-84 Combined	73.6	21.3	5.1	= 727
Males	67.8	28.9	3.3	= 270
Females	77.0	16.8	6.1	= 457
85 + Combined	67.9	27.9	4.3	= 140
Males	67.8	30.5	1.7	= 59
Females	67.9	25.9	6.2	= 81

H5.1

Q90. In general, do you think the courts in this area deal
       too harshly or not harshly enough with criminals? (1)

	Too harsh	Not harsh enough	About right	DK-NA	
	1972 - 1986				
	1	2	3	4	N's
All Ages	3.7	80.4	9.6	6.3	=18131
18-24 Combined	8.9	69.4	13.2	8.5	= 2258
Males	10.5	66.6	15.2	7.8	= 1068
Females	7.5	71.9	11.3	9.2	= 1190
25-34 Combined	4.4	78.6	10.1	6.9	= 4329
Males	5.0	77.7	10.5	6.7	= 1931
Females	3.9	79.3	9.8	7.0	= 2398
35-44 Combined	3.4	82.1	8.6	5.9	= 3194
Males	3.4	80.7	9.5	6.4	= 1462
Females	3.5	83.2	7.9	5.4	= 1732
45-54 Combined	2.9	82.4	9.1	5.6	= 2671
Males	3.0	84.5	7.8	4.7	= 1255
Females	2.8	80.5	10.3	6.4	= 1416
55-64 Combined	2.0	85.2	8.4	4.4	= 2562
Males	2.1	85.1	9.4	3.3	= 1169
Females	1.9	85.2	7.6	5.3	= 1393
65-74 Combined	1.7	84.8	8.2	5.3	= 2029
Males	1.8	87.6	7.3	3.3	= 885
Females	1.6	82.6	8.9	6.9	= 1144
75-84 Combined	1.1	82.4	9.2	7.3	= 919
Males	0.6	85.3	9.9	4.2	= 333
Females	1.4	80.7	8.9	9.0	= 586
85 + Combined	1.2	72.8	11.2	14.8	= 169
Males	---	77.4	11.3	11.3	= 62
Females	1.9	70.1	11.2	16.8	= 107

(1) See appendix A

H6.1

Q86. Do you favor or oppose the death penalty for
persons convicted of murder? (1)

	1974 - 1985			
	Favor 1	Oppose 2	DK-NA 3	N's
All Ages	68.3	25.8	5.9	=16506
18-24 Combined	63.4	32.2	4.4	= 2054
Males	68.9	26.6	4.5	= 940
Females	58.8	36.9	4.3	= 1114
25-34 Combined	68.3	26.4	5.3	= 4033
Males	74.2	22.0	3.8	= 1752
Females	63.7	29.9	6.4	= 2281
35-44 Combined	69.9	24.9	5.2	= 2936
Males	75.7	20.7	3.6	= 1322
Females	65.1	28.4	6.5	= 1614
45-54 Combined	69.7	24.8	5.5	= 2303
Males	76.0	20.4	3.6	= 1049
Females	64.4	28.5	7.1	= 1254
55-64 Combined	71.3	22.9	5.8	= 2292
Males	77.7	18.7	3.7	= 1007
Females	66.3	26.3	7.4	= 1285
65-74 Combined	67.9	24.0	8.1	= 1855
Males	77.2	17.6	5.2	= 786
Females	61.1	28.7	10.2	= 1069
75-84 Combined	66.3	24.4	9.3	= 863
Males	75.0	19.1	5.9	= 304
Females	61.5	27.4	11.1	= 559
85 + Combined	60.0	27.6	12.4	= 170
Males	78.7	9.8	11.5	= 61
Females	49.5	37.6	12.8	= 109

(1) See appendix A

H7.1

Q95. Do you think the use of marijuana should
       be made legal or not? (1)

	1973 - 1986			
	Legal 1	Not Legal 2	DK-NA 3	N's
All Ages	22.6	73.8	3.6	=11984
18-24 Combined	40.6	55.8	3.6	= 1538
Males	47.3	48.3	4.4	= 698
Females	35.1	62.0	2.9	= 840
25-34 Combined	32.7	63.8	3.5	= 2914
Males	40.4	55.3	4.4	= 1263
Females	26.8	70.4	2.8	= 1651
35-44 Combined	21.1	75.9	3.0	= 2149
Males	25.3	72.5	2.2	= 981
Females	17.6	78.9	3.6	= 1168
45-54 Combined	15.5	81.3	3.2	= 1678
Males	16.6	79.7	3.7	= 735
Females	14.6	82.5	2.9	= 943
55-64 Combined	13.2	83.3	3.5	= 1646
Males	14.0	83.0	3.0	= 722
Females	12.7	83.5	3.8	= 924
65-74 Combined	11.3	84.7	4.0	= 1336
Males	15.4	79.9	4.7	= 572
Females	8.2	88.4	3.4	= 764
75-84 Combined	7.7	86.8	5.6	= 612
Males	10.3	81.8	7.9	= 214
Females	6.3	89.4	4.3	= 398
85 + Combined	7.2	84.7	8.1	= 111
Males	7.7	87.2	5.1	= 39
Females	6.9	83.3	9.7	= 72

(1) See appendix A

183

H8.1

Q69E. We are faced with many problems in this country, none of
which can be solved easily or inexpensively. I'm going
to name some of these problems, and for each one I'd
like you to tell me whether you think we're spending too
much money on it, too little money, or about the right
amount.
Halting the rising crime rate.

	1973 - 1986				
	Too little 1	About right 2	Too much 3	DK-NA 4	N's
All Ages	64.7	24.5	5.5	5.3	=18006
18-24 Combined	64.9	27.4	4.2	3.4	= 2268
Males	62.6	29.4	5.1	3.0	= 1049
Females	66.9	25.8	3.5	3.8	= 1219
25-34 Combined	65.4	26.2	4.8	3.6	= 4338
Males	61.7	29.5	5.8	3.1	= 1888
Females	68.4	23.6	4.1	3.9	= 2450
35-44 Combined	63.7	27.3	4.8	4.2	= 3211
Males	62.5	27.6	6.4	3.4	= 1444
Females	64.6	26.9	3.5	4.9	= 1767
45-54 Combined	66.1	21.9	6.6	5.3	= 2561
Males	64.4	24.0	7.8	3.8	= 1161
Females	67.6	20.2	5.6	6.6	= 1400
55-64 Combined	66.7	20.4	6.1	6.8	= 2523
Males	66.4	20.1	7.3	6.2	= 1119
Females	67.0	20.6	5.1	7.3	= 1404
65-74 Combined	63.2	22.8	6.6	7.3	= 2023
Males	61.1	25.0	8.9	4.9	= 872
Females	64.8	21.2	4.9	9.1	= 1151
75-84 Combined	59.5	22.3	7.2	11.0	= 909
Males	59.8	23.3	9.2	7.7	= 326
Females	59.3	21.8	6.0	12.9	= 583
85 + Combined	54.3	23.1	6.9	15.6	= 173
Males	52.4	30.2	7.9	9.5	= 63
Females	55.5	19.1	6.4	19.1	= 110

H8.2

Q69F. We are faced with many problems in this country, none of which can be solved easily or inexpensively. I'm going to name some of these problems, and for each one I'd like you to tell me whether you think we're spending too much money on it, too little money, or about the right amount.
Dealing with drug addiction.

	1973 - 1986				
	Too little 1	About right 2	Too much 3	DK-NA 4	N's
All Ages	57.8	28.2	7.3	6.7	=18006
18-24 Combined	56.0	34.8	5.8	3.4	= 2268
Males	55.9	34.7	6.5	3.0	= 1049
Females	56.1	34.9	5.2	3.8	= 1219
25-34 Combined	58.4	31.1	6.6	3.9	= 4338
Males	57.2	30.2	9.1	3.5	= 1888
Females	59.3	31.8	4.7	4.2	= 2450
35-44 Combined	60.0	28.4	7.2	4.4	= 3211
Males	59.3	28.0	9.3	3.4	= 1444
Females	60.4	28.8	5.5	5.3	= 1767
45-54 Combined	58.3	26.8	7.7	7.2	= 2561
Males	59.5	24.8	10.0	5.7	= 1161
Females	57.3	28.4	5.9	8.4	= 1400
55-64 Combined	57.5	24.8	8.4	9.3	= 2523
Males	58.8	23.2	10.1	7.9	= 1119
Females	56.4	26.0	7.1	10.5	= 1404
65-74 Combined	56.5	23.8	8.3	11.5	= 2023
Males	56.2	24.8	9.3	9.7	= 872
Females	56.7	23.0	7.5	12.8	= 1151
75-84 Combined	55.3	22.4	8.5	13.8	= 909
Males	52.5	27.6	8.9	11.0	= 326
Females	56.9	19.6	8.2	15.3	= 583
85 + Combined	53.2	16.8	6.9	23.1	= 173
Males	54.0	19.0	4.8	22.2	= 63
Females	52.7	15.5	8.2	23.6	= 110

HEALTH, SUICIDE, AND EUTHANASIA

The younger age groups report higher levels of family hospitalization than the older groups, and women from 18 to 64 report higher levels of family hospitalization than men. Personal hospitalization increases with age and varies for the sexes, though older men cite more frequent hospitalization than women. Self-rated health is positive (excellent or good) for all ages, but slightly less so for women than for men. Over the term of the survey a drop has occurred in the proportions who claim good to excellent health, while satisfaction with health has not. Rates of satisfaction differ by age and sex.

In general, the younger age groups are more likely than the older to accept the idea of a right to suicide. Over 50 percent of the youngest age cluster accepts the idea of suicide under conditions of incurable disease, but less than half of the other ages accept the idea for this reason. Conditions of incurable disease, however, is the only justification for suicide that receives any substantial endorsement. The rate of acceptance shows considerable difference between the sexes, with men more willing to approve than women. The difference shown here is consistent with actual suicide pattern in America - depending on their age group, men are from four to ten times more likely to commit suicide than women. (Bureau of the Census, 1986, p. 79)

In the GSS euthanasia is defined as a physician's painless termination of one's life following a request by the patient and family in the presence of an incurable disease. (Davis and Smith, 1986, p. 240) The rate of approval for this idea falls from over 70 percent among the 18-24 year olds to 53 percent among the 65-74 year olds. After that age approval drops below 50 percent. For the 75-84 year olds 43 percent are opposed, but 8 percent don't know or didn't answer. The 85+ group expresses the greatest opposition, which raises an interesting question of whether those who survive longest might be the most tenacious of life. Women and men differ somewhat on the issue, with men more favorable to euthanasia than women.

The majority of each age group, excepting the oldest, feels that too little is being spent on the nation's health.

187

I1.1

Q272. Hospitalization and disability during last five years. (1)

		1978 - 1986				
	None 1	Prior 4 years 2	Last year 3	Both periods 4	NA 5	N's
All Ages	58.3	20.4	7.4	12.6	1.3	= 7506
18-24 Combined	61.3	19.5	8.5	10.0	0.7	= 906
Males	57.8	20.7	10.1	10.9	0.5	= 396
Females	63.9	18.6	7.3	9.4	0.8	= 510
25-34 Combined	65.3	18.3	6.8	8.4	1.1	= 1924
Males	69.5	17.7	5.1	6.6	1.1	= 821
Females	62.1	18.9	8.1	9.8	1.2	= 1103
35-44 Combined	62.0	21.7	5.6	9.6	1.1	= 1392
Males	64.6	20.7	5.5	8.1	1.1	= 639
Females	59.8	22.6	5.7	10.8	1.2	= 753
45-54 Combined	56.2	20.4	7.2	14.5	1.6	= 970
Males	61.6	17.8	7.7	11.5	1.4	= 427
Females	51.9	22.5	6.8	16.9	1.8	= 543
55-64 Combined	53.9	19.5	7.1	17.8	1.7	= 990
Males	52.7	19.7	6.2	20.0	1.4	= 421
Females	54.8	19.3	7.7	16.2	1.9	= 569
65-74 Combined	49.5	22.0	10.2	16.4	1.9	= 842
Males	48.2	21.9	10.8	17.1	2.1	= 334
Females	50.4	22.0	9.8	15.9	1.8	= 508
75-84 Combined	42.8	25.4	9.5	20.5	1.7	= 409
Males	37.5	26.6	11.7	22.7	1.6	= 128
Females	45.2	24.9	8.5	19.6	1.8	= 281
85 + Combined	38.4	26.0	9.6	24.7	1.4	= 73
Males	25.0	40.0	10.0	25.0	---	= 20
Females	43.4	20.8	9.4	24.5	1.9	= 53

(1) See appendix A

I1.2

Q273A. Number of relatives hospitalized/disabled
        last year. (1)

| | 1978 - 1984 | | | |
	None 1	One 2	2 - 6 3	N's
All Ages	60.2	30.1	9.7	= 6043
18-24 Combined	65.8	27.3	6.9	= 770
Males	70.2	24.8	5.0	= 339
Females	62.4	29.2	8.4	= 431
25-34 Combined	57.9	30.5	11.6	= 1545
Males	57.4	30.8	11.8	= 643
Females	58.3	30.3	11.4	= 902
35-44 Combined	58.8	31.3	9.8	= 1091
Males	60.7	30.3	9.0	= 509
Females	57.2	32.3	10.5	= 582
45-54 Combined	56.1	30.9	12.9	= 782
Males	60.6	29.7	9.6	= 343
Females	52.6	31.9	15.5	= 439
55-64 Combined	59.2	31.0	9.8	= 816
Males	64.2	27.2	8.7	= 346
Females	55.5	33.8	10.6	= 470
65-74 Combined	63.6	28.6	7.8	= 665
Males	60.8	31.0	8.2	= 268
Females	65.5	27.0	7.6	= 397
75-84 Combined	65.2	30.7	4.1	= 316
Males	61.0	35.0	4.0	= 100
Females	67.1	28.7	4.2	= 216
85 + Combined	77.6	19.0	3.4	= 58
Males	73.7	21.1	5.3	= 19
Females	79.5	17.9	2.6	= 39

(1) See appendix A

I1.3

Q273B. Number of relatives hospitalized/disabled
during previous four years. (1)

	1978 - 1984			
	None 1	One 2	2 - 7 3	N's
All Ages	46.0	34.1	19.9	= 6043
18-24 Combined	51.3	34.3	14.4	= 770
Males	54.9	31.9	13.3	= 339
Females	48.5	36.2	15.3	= 431
25-34 Combined	45.4	32.8	21.8	= 1545
Males	46.2	34.1	19.8	= 643
Females	44.8	31.9	23.3	= 902
35-44 Combined	42.1	33.9	24.0	= 1091
Males	46.2	30.8	23.0	= 509
Females	38.5	36.6	24.9	= 582
45-54 Combined	39.3	33.5	27.2	= 782
Males	42.6	32.1	25.4	= 343
Females	36.7	34.6	28.7	= 439
55-64 Combined	43.8	37.4	18.9	= 816
Males	45.1	37.0	17.9	= 346
Females	42.8	37.7	19.6	= 470
65-74 Combined	52.2	33.8	14.0	= 665
Males	50.0	35.4	14.6	= 268
Females	53.7	32.7	13.6	= 397
75-84 Combined	54.7	36.1	9.2	= 316
Males	55.0	30.0	15.0	= 100
Females	54.6	38.9	6.5	= 216
85 + Combined	72.4	20.7	6.9	= 58
Males	63.2	31.6	5.3	= 19
Females	76.9	15.4	7.7	= 39

(1) See appendix A

I2.1

Q156. Would you say that your own health, in general, is
excellent, good, fair, or poor? (1)

			1972 - 1985			
	Excellent 1	Good 2	Fair 3	Poor 4	DK-NA 5	N's
All Ages	31.7	42.0	19.7	6.3	0.2	=15034
18-24 Combined	39.7	45.6	13.7	1.0	---	= 1964
Males	42.2	45.0	11.9	1.0	---	= 945
Females	37.4	46.1	15.5	1.0	---	= 1019
25-34 Combined	41.1	45.0	11.6	2.2	0.2	= 3470
Males	44.3	44.3	9.6	1.6	0.3	= 1532
Females	38.5	45.5	13.1	2.7	0.1	= 1938
35-44 Combined	38.0	43.4	15.6	2.8	0.2	= 2591
Males	42.6	42.0	13.1	2.2	0.1	= 1164
Females	34.2	44.5	17.7	3.3	0.3	= 1427
45-54 Combined	29.8	42.0	21.7	6.3	0.2	= 2283
Males	30.5	42.7	20.3	6.3	0.2	= 1065
Females	29.1	41.5	22.9	6.2	0.2	= 1218
55-64 Combined	22.0	39.1	26.6	11.9	0.3	= 2185
Males	22.6	40.6	24.5	12.1	0.2	= 1000
Females	21.5	37.9	28.4	11.7	0.4	= 1185
65-74 Combined	16.5	36.3	32.0	14.8	0.4	= 1674
Males	17.7	37.1	30.6	14.2	0.3	= 744
Females	15.6	35.7	33.0	15.3	0.4	= 930
75-84 Combined	16.0	36.7	32.3	14.7	0.3	= 727
Males	20.7	37.4	28.5	13.0	0.4	= 270
Females	13.1	36.3	34.6	15.8	0.2	= 457
85 + Combined	17.1	31.4	32.1	19.3	---	= 140
Males	18.6	35.6	27.1	18.6	---	= 59
Females	16.0	28.4	35.8	19.8	---	= 81

(1) See appendix A

I3.1

Q161E. For each area of life I am going to name, tell me the number
that shows how much satisfaction you get from that area.
Your health and physical condition. (2)

	A great deal 1	A fair amount 2	Some or little 3	None 4	DK-NA 5	N's
	1973 - 1986					
All Ages	59.9	29.1	8.3	2.1	0.5	=16479
18-24 Combined	67.1	26.8	5.3	0.6	0.2	= 2111
Males	70.0	24.8	4.6	0.3	0.2	= 978
Females	64.5	28.4	5.9	0.9	0.3	= 1133
25-34 Combined	67.5	25.9	5.4	0.8	0.4	= 3965
Males	69.2	24.3	5.2	0.6	0.6	= 1716
Females	66.1	27.2	5.6	0.9	0.2	= 2249
35-44 Combined	63.7	28.4	6.7	1.0	0.2	= 2930
Males	65.7	26.5	6.5	1.0	0.3	= 1322
Females	62.1	30.0	6.9	0.9	0.1	= 1608
45-54 Combined	59.0	29.3	8.4	2.8	0.5	= 2351
Males	61.1	27.4	8.4	2.4	0.8	= 1051
Females	57.3	30.9	8.4	3.2	0.2	= 1300
55-64 Combined	54.2	30.2	11.0	3.8	0.8	= 2302
Males	56.4	28.1	9.8	4.8	0.9	= 1010
Females	52.5	31.8	11.9	3.1	0.7	= 1292
65-74 Combined	48.2	34.6	12.6	4.0	0.6	= 1851
Males	50.7	31.6	13.0	4.1	0.6	= 807
Females	46.3	36.9	12.4	3.9	0.6	= 1044
75-84 Combined	40.6	36.8	16.5	5.4	0.7	= 816
Males	48.3	31.5	14.4	5.0	0.7	= 298
Females	36.1	39.8	17.8	5.6	0.8	= 518
85 + Combined	38.6	32.7	19.0	5.9	3.9	= 153
Males	38.9	38.9	20.4	---	1.9	= 54
Females	38.4	29.3	18.2	9.1	5.1	= 99

(2) See appendix B

I4.1

Q228A. Do you think a person has the right to
end his or her own life if this person ...
Has an incurable disease? (1)

	1977 - 1986			
	Yes 1	No 2	DK-NA 3	N's
All Ages	44.1	52.1	3.8	= 9124
18-24 Combined	56.3	40.4	3.3	= 1032
Males	60.5	36.9	2.6	= 463
Females	52.9	43.2	3.9	= 569
25-34 Combined	55.0	42.3	2.8	= 2323
Males	56.5	41.7	1.8	= 1036
Females	53.8	42.7	3.5	= 1287
35-44 Combined	47.1	49.3	3.6	= 1660
Males	53.1	43.4	3.5	= 740
Females	42.3	54.0	3.7	= 920
45-54 Combined	40.0	56.8	3.2	= 1238
Males	45.3	51.6	3.1	= 578
Females	35.3	61.4	3.3	= 660
55-64 Combined	33.4	62.5	4.1	= 1271
Males	39.7	57.5	2.8	= 541
Females	28.6	66.3	5.1	= 730
65-74 Combined	30.9	64.1	4.9	= 1015
Males	36.7	57.6	5.7	= 406
Females	27.1	68.5	4.4	= 609
75-84 Combined	26.6	65.7	7.7	= 493
Males	40.0	50.9	9.1	= 165
Females	19.8	73.2	7.0	= 328
85 + Combined	17.4	72.8	9.8	= 92
Males	17.9	67.9	14.3	= 28
Females	17.2	75.0	7.8	= 64

(1) See appendix A

I4.2

Q228B. Do you think a person has the right to
        end his or her own life if this person...
        Has gone bankrupt?

	1977 - 1986			
	Yes 1	No 2	DK-NA 3	N's
All Ages	6.9	91.7	1.4	= 9124
18-24 Combined	7.2	92.0	0.9	= 1032
Males	9.3	89.8	0.9	= 463
Females	5.4	93.7	0.9	= 569
25-34 Combined	8.3	90.4	1.3	= 2323
Males	8.9	90.2	1.0	= 1036
Females	7.8	90.7	1.6	= 1287
35-44 Combined	8.2	90.9	0.9	= 1660
Males	10.1	89.2	0.7	= 740
Females	6.6	92.3	1.1	= 920
45-54 Combined	6.9	91.9	1.2	= 1238
Males	7.6	90.8	1.6	= 578
Females	6.2	92.9	0.9	= 660
55-64 Combined	5.4	93.2	1.4	= 1271
Males	4.6	94.3	1.1	= 541
Females	6.0	92.3	1.6	= 730
65-74 Combined	4.3	93.1	2.6	= 1015
Males	5.4	92.4	2.2	= 406
Females	3.6	93.6	2.8	= 609
75-84 Combined	5.1	92.5	2.4	= 493
Males	9.1	89.1	1.8	= 165
Females	3.0	94.2	2.7	= 328
85 + Combined	5.4	89.1	5.4	= 92
Males	3.6	92.9	3.6	= 28
Females	6.3	87.5	6.3	= 64

I4.3

Q228C. Do you think a person has the right to
end his or her own life if this person...
Has dishonored his or her family?

	1977 - 1986			
	Yes 1	No 2	DK-NA 3	N's
All Ages	7.1	91.2	1.7	= 9124
18-24 Combined	7.7	91.5	0.9	= 1032
Males	9.7	89.4	0.9	= 463
Females	6.0	93.1	0.9	= 569
25-34 Combined	8.9	89.9	1.2	= 2323
Males	9.7	89.2	1.2	= 1036
Females	8.3	90.4	1.2	= 1287
35-44 Combined	8.3	90.6	1.1	= 1660
Males	10.4	88.4	1.2	= 740
Females	6.5	92.4	1.1	= 920
45-54 Combined	7.0	91.4	1.5	= 1238
Males	7.6	90.7	1.7	= 578
Females	6.5	92.1	1.4	= 660
55-64 Combined	4.8	93.5	1.7	= 1271
Males	4.6	94.1	1.3	= 541
Females	4.9	93.2	1.9	= 730
65-74 Combined	4.3	92.3	3.3	= 1015
Males	6.2	90.4	3.4	= 406
Females	3.1	93.6	3.3	= 609
75-84 Combined	5.9	90.3	3.9	= 493
Males	7.9	87.3	4.8	= 165
Females	4.9	91.8	3.4	= 328
85 + Combined	3.3	91.3	5.4	= 92
Males	---	92.9	7.1	= 28
Females	4.7	90.6	4.7	= 64

I4.4

Q228D. Do you think a person has the right to end
         his or her own life if this person...
              Is tired of living and ready to die?

	1977 - 1986			
	Yes 1	No 2	DK-NA 3	N's
All Ages	13.5	84.1	2.4	= 9124
18-24 Combined	15.7	82.7	1.6	= 1032
Males	18.6	79.7	1.7	= 463
Females	13.4	85.1	1.6	= 569
25-34 Combined	15.2	82.8	2.1	= 2323
Males	17.1	81.5	1.4	= 1036
Females	13.6	83.8	2.6	= 1287
35-44 Combined	14.2	83.9	1.9	= 1660
Males	16.6	81.6	1.8	= 740
Females	12.3	85.7	2.1	= 920
45-54 Combined	12.0	86.0	1.9	= 1238
Males	13.0	84.9	2.1	= 578
Females	11.2	87.0	1.8	= 660
55-64 Combined	10.9	86.5	2.7	= 1271
Males	13.1	84.8	2.0	= 541
Females	9.2	87.7	3.2	= 730
65-74 Combined	11.9	85.3	2.8	= 1015
Males	16.7	81.0	2.2	= 406
Females	8.7	88.2	3.1	= 609
75-84 Combined	12.8	82.2	5.1	= 493
Males	18.8	76.4	4.8	= 165
Females	9.8	85.1	5.2	= 328
85 + Combined	14.1	77.2	8.7	= 92
Males	10.7	75.0	14.3	= 28
Females	15.6	78.1	6.3	= 64

196

I5.1

Q227. When a person has a disease that cannot be
cured, do you think doctors should be allowed
to end the patient's life by some painless means
if the patient and his family request it? (1)

	1977 - 1985			
	Yes 1	No 2	DK-NA 3	N's
All Ages	61.7	34.1	4.2	= 9124
18-24 Combined	70.9	25.9	3.2	= 1032
Males	74.7	22.7	2.6	= 463
Females	67.8	28.5	3.7	= 569
25-34 Combined	69.6	27.0	3.4	= 2323
Males	71.1	25.4	3.5	= 1036
Females	68.3	28.3	3.4	= 1287
35-44 Combined	64.0	33.2	2.8	= 1660
Males	69.9	28.1	2.0	= 740
Females	59.2	37.3	3.5	= 920
45-54 Combined	56.3	39.5	4.2	= 1238
Males	62.3	33.7	4.0	= 578
Females	51.1	44.5	4.4	= 660
55-64 Combined	55.6	39.1	5.3	= 1271
Males	61.7	34.4	3.9	= 541
Females	51.1	42.6	6.3	= 730
65-74 Combined	53.4	40.8	5.8	= 1015
Males	58.6	36.7	4.7	= 406
Females	49.9	43.5	6.6	= 609
75-84 Combined	48.5	43.4	8.1	= 493
Males	57.0	33.9	9.1	= 165
Females	44.2	48.2	7.6	= 328
85 + Combined	39.1	53.3	7.6	= 92
Males	46.4	50.0	3.6	= 28
Females	35.9	54.7	9.4	= 64

(1) See appendix A

I6.1

Q69C. We are faced with many problems in this country, none of
which can be solved easily or inexpensively. I'm going to
name some of these problems, and for each one I'd like you
to tell me whether you think we're spending too much money
on it, too little money, or about the right amount.
Improving and protecting the nation's health.

	1973 - 1986				
	Too little 1	About right 2	Too much 3	DK-NA 4	N's
All Ages	58.0	31.8	6.0	4.2	=18006
18-24 Combined	55.9	37.3	3.7	3.1	= 2268
Males	53.7	39.9	3.6	2.8	= 1049
Females	57.8	35.1	3.7	3.4	= 1219
25-34 Combined	63.0	29.9	4.5	2.7	= 4338
Males	62.0	30.0	5.5	2.5	= 1888
Females	63.7	29.8	3.7	2.7	= 2450
35-44 Combined	61.2	28.7	6.7	3.4	= 3211
Males	59.9	29.1	8.5	2.5	= 1444
Females	62.2	28.4	5.3	4.2	= 1767
45-54 Combined	60.1	29.9	6.2	3.9	= 2561
Males	59.6	30.1	7.3	3.0	= 1161
Females	60.4	29.7	5.3	4.6	= 1400
55-64 Combined	56.4	32.0	7.0	4.6	= 2523
Males	56.7	30.9	8.5	3.9	= 1119
Females	56.1	32.8	5.8	5.2	= 1404
65-74 Combined	51.0	34.0	8.0	7.0	= 2023
Males	51.1	33.4	10.2	5.3	= 872
Females	50.9	34.5	6.3	8.3	= 1151
75-84 Combined	46.4	36.2	8.3	9.1	= 909
Males	48.5	33.1	12.0	6.4	= 326
Females	45.3	37.9	6.2	10.6	= 583
85 + Combined	41.6	38.2	5.8	14.5	= 173
Males	47.6	39.7	3.2	9.5	= 63
Females	38.2	37.3	7.3	17.3	= 110

LEISURE ACTIVITY AND PERSONAL HABITS

A majority of all age groups expresses satisfaction with hobbies, with little change over the term of the survey except among the oldest group, which shows a decline of 15 percent. At younger ages men express more satisfaction with hobbies than women, but in most older age segments women report more satisfaction than men.

The older age clusters indicate more frequent newspaper reading (daily) than the young, an as do greater proportions of men than women. TV watching hours differ little by age, but women report slightly more time watching than men do. Hours spent listening to a radio decrease with age.

Proportions of persons who say they smoke, use alcohol, and sometimes drink to excess drop markedly with age. Larger proportions of women than men say they abstain.

J1.1

Q161B. For each area of life I am going to name, tell me how much
        satisfaction you get from that area.
            Your non-working activities -- hobbies and so on. (1) (2)

| | 1973 - 1986 | | | | | |
	A great deal 1	A fair amount 2	Some or little 3	None 4	DK-NA 5	N's
All Ages	55.6	30.3	9.7	3.6	0.8	=16479
18-24 Combined	54.2	32.0	11.0	2.5	0.3	= 2111
Males	59.3	30.1	8.9	1.6	0.1	= 978
Females	49.8	33.6	12.9	3.3	0.4	= 1133
25-34 Combined	56.5	31.0	9.9	2.2	0.4	= 3965
Males	62.8	27.3	8.3	1.3	0.3	= 1716
Females	51.7	33.8	11.1	2.9	0.4	= 2249
35-44 Combined	55.5	32.3	9.4	2.4	0.4	= 2930
Males	57.6	30.8	9.4	1.9	0.4	= 1322
Females	53.9	33.5	9.5	2.9	0.4	= 1608
45-54 Combined	55.9	29.6	9.7	3.8	0.9	= 2351
Males	58.4	27.6	10.0	3.1	0.9	= 1051
Females	53.9	31.3	9.5	4.3	0.9	= 1300
55-64 Combined	57.0	28.9	9.3	3.8	1.0	= 2302
Males	55.9	29.9	9.1	4.3	0.8	= 1010
Females	57.8	28.1	9.4	3.4	1.2	= 1292
65-74 Combined	55.8	28.4	7.9	6.1	1.8	= 1851
Males	53.5	28.7	10.0	5.8	1.9	= 807
Females	57.6	28.2	6.3	6.2	1.7	= 1044
75-84 Combined	51.6	27.2	10.3	8.6	2.3	= 816
Males	46.3	30.5	13.1	7.4	2.7	= 298
Females	54.6	25.3	8.7	9.3	2.1	= 518
85 + Combined	45.1	21.6	11.1	17.0	5.2	= 153
Males	37.0	25.9	14.8	16.7	5.6	= 54
Females	49.5	19.2	9.1	17.2	5.1	= 99

(1) See appendix A
(2) See appendix B

J2.1

Q241. How often do you read the newspaper--every day, a few times a week,
once a week, less than once a week, or never? (1)

		1972 - 1986					
	Everyday	Few times a week	Once a week	> once a week	Never	DK-NA	
	1	2	3	4	5	6	N's
All Ages	58.7	18.9	10.5	6.7	5.1	0.2	=12217
18-24 Combined	33.9	32.0	14.1	14.2	5.6	0.1	= 1447
Males	40.9	30.5	11.8	11.0	5.8	---	= 672
Females	27.9	33.3	16.1	17.0	5.4	0.3	= 775
25-34 Combined	46.0	25.3	14.8	9.7	4.0	0.1	= 3018
Males	49.3	24.8	12.8	9.0	4.0	0.1	= 1365
Females	43.3	25.8	16.4	10.3	4.1	0.1	= 1653
35-44 Combined	60.7	19.7	10.0	5.2	4.3	---	= 2150
Males	65.1	16.3	8.5	4.6	5.5	---	= 969
Females	57.2	22.5	11.3	5.7	3.3	---	= 1181
45-54 Combined	69.9	14.6	7.6	4.1	3.5	0.2	= 1790
Males	70.6	14.1	7.5	3.7	4.0	0.1	= 849
Females	69.3	15.1	7.7	4.6	3.1	0.3	= 941
55-64 Combined	73.1	11.7	7.2	3.2	4.5	0.3	= 1719
Males	75.4	11.4	6.1	2.4	4.6	0.1	= 756
Females	71.3	11.9	8.0	3.8	4.5	0.4	= 963
65-74 Combined	72.1	10.4	7.4	3.6	6.3	0.1	= 1344
Males	75.2	10.2	5.4	2.7	6.3	0.2	= 557
Females	69.9	10.5	8.9	4.3	6.2	0.1	= 787
75-84 Combined	71.1	6.9	7.1	3.0	11.6	0.3	= 636
Males	76.4	6.2	5.3	2.7	8.9	0.4	= 225
Females	68.1	7.3	8.0	3.2	13.1	0.2	= 411
85 + Combined	49.6	7.1	8.8	8.0	25.7	0.9	= 113
Males	53.8	5.1	2.6	10.3	25.6	2.6	= 39
Females	47.3	8.1	12.2	6.8	25.7	---	= 74

(1) See appendix A

J3.1

Q242. On the average day, about how many hours do you personally
watch television?

	1975 - 1986						
	00 Hrs. 1	One Hr. 2	2 - 4 Hrs 3	5 - 6 Hrs 4	7 - 24 Hrs 5	NA 6	N's
All Ages	5.1	18.9	58.8	11.6	5.2	0.4	=12068
18-24 Combined	4.8	16.7	54.8	15.1	8.4	0.2	= 1441
Males	5.0	20.5	57.8	12.1	4.6	---	= 635
Females	4.6	13.8	52.5	17.4	11.4	0.4	= 806
25-34 Combined	6.1	18.7	58.5	11.3	5.0	0.4	= 3010
Males	7.1	18.5	61.3	9.8	3.1	0.3	= 1343
Females	5.3	18.9	56.3	12.5	6.5	0.4	= 1667
35-44 Combined	6.0	23.5	60.2	7.5	2.6	0.2	= 2149
Males	5.1	26.2	60.6	6.3	1.6	0.1	= 978
Females	6.7	21.2	59.8	8.5	3.4	0.3	= 1171
45-54 Combined	5.5	22.5	60.3	7.6	3.6	0.5	= 1674
Males	5.7	24.7	60.5	6.5	2.5	0.1	= 770
Females	5.3	20.6	60.1	8.6	4.6	0.8	= 904
55-64 Combined	3.2	18.8	61.1	11.5	4.7	0.7	= 1675
Males	3.2	21.9	60.7	8.7	5.0	0.6	= 726
Females	3.3	16.4	61.4	13.6	4.5	0.7	= 949
65-74 Combined	3.7	11.9	58.3	17.7	7.9	0.5	= 1366
Males	3.6	15.7	59.5	14.8	6.1	0.4	= 555
Females	3.7	9.4	57.5	19.7	9.1	0.6	= 811
75-84 Combined	4.3	14.2	57.3	16.6	7.4	0.2	= 632
Males	4.1	15.1	61.9	11.9	6.4	0.5	= 218
Females	4.3	13.8	54.8	19.1	8.0	---	= 414
85 + Combined	9.9	19.0	51.2	13.2	3.3	3.3	= 121
Males	9.3	11.6	65.1	9.3	---	4.7	= 43
Females	10.3	23.1	43.6	15.4	5.1	2.6	= 78

J4.1

Q243A. Do you ever listen to the radio?
IF YES: On the average, about how many hours a day do you usually listen to the radio?

				1978 - 1983				
	00 Hrs.	One Hr.	2 - 4 Hrs	5 - 6 Hrs	7 - 24 Hrs	NA		N's
	1	2	3	4	5	6		
All Ages	0.5	37.2	38.2	9.0	14.7	0.5	=	4186
18-24 Combined	0.4	25.1	40.7	11.4	22.0	0.4	=	518
Males	0.9	19.7	44.4	12.0	23.1	---	=	234
Females	---	29.6	37.7	10.9	21.1	0.7	=	284
25-34 Combined	0.5	32.4	40.4	10.7	15.8	0.2	=	1181
Males	0.8	34.6	38.7	12.5	13.5	---	=	520
Females	0.3	30.7	41.8	9.2	17.7	0.3	=	661
35-44 Combined	0.5	42.9	36.0	6.5	13.9	0.1	=	755
Males	0.6	45.5	38.2	3.8	12.0	---	=	343
Females	0.5	40.8	34.2	8.7	15.5	0.2	=	412
45-54 Combined	0.2	41.1	36.2	9.8	12.1	0.8	=	531
Males	---	49.2	34.9	8.8	6.7	0.4	=	238
Females	0.3	34.5	37.2	10.6	16.4	1.0	=	293
55-64 Combined	0.4	40.3	36.2	8.9	13.6	0.7	=	553
Males	---	49.5	30.0	9.5	10.5	0.5	=	220
Females	0.6	34.2	40.2	8.4	15.6	0.9	=	333
65-74 Combined	0.7	41.2	36.5	7.0	12.9	1.7	=	417
Males	---	50.3	34.6	5.6	8.9	0.6	=	179
Females	1.3	34.5	37.8	8.0	16.0	2.5	=	238
75-84 Combined	1.0	45.4	40.7	5.2	7.2	0.5	=	194
Males	2.9	51.4	37.1	2.9	5.7	---	=	70
Females	---	41.9	42.7	6.5	8.1	0.8	=	124
85 + Combined	---	48.6	37.8	2.7	5.4	5.4	=	37
Males	---	36.4	45.5	---	---	18.2	=	11
Females	---	53.8	34.6	3.8	7.7	---	=	26

204

J5.1

Q173. Do you ever have occasion to use any
alcoholic beverages such as liquor, wine
or beer, or are you a total abstainer?

		1977 - 1986		
	Yes 1	No 2	DK-NA 3	N's
All Ages	71.9	27.8	0.2	= 9029
18-24 Combined	79.0	20.9	0.1	= 1098
Males	84.3	15.7	---	= 489
Females	74.7	25.1	0.2	= 609
25-34 Combined	81.9	18.0	0.2	= 2259
Males	87.4	12.4	0.2	= 971
Females	77.6	22.2	0.2	= 1288
35-44 Combined	77.3	22.5	0.2	= 1667
Males	81.6	18.2	0.1	= 762
Females	73.6	26.1	0.3	= 905
45-54 Combined	71.8	28.1	0.1	= 1221
Males	78.2	21.8	---	= 551
Females	66.6	33.3	0.1	= 670
55-64 Combined	66.3	33.1	0.6	= 1228
Males	73.7	25.8	0.6	= 524
Females	60.8	38.6	0.6	= 704
65-74 Combined	56.3	43.5	0.2	= 1006
Males	66.2	33.3	0.5	= 402
Females	49.7	50.3	---	= 604
75-84 Combined	44.3	55.2	0.4	= 467
Males	57.9	40.8	1.3	= 152
Females	37.8	62.2	---	= 315
85 + Combined	31.3	68.7	---	= 83
Males	47.8	52.2	---	= 23
Females	25.0	75.0	---	= 60

J5.2

Q173A. Do you sometimes drink more than you
        think you should?

	1977 - 1986			
	Yes 1	No 2	DK-NA 3	N's
All Ages	37.4	61.3	1.3	= 6515
18-24 Combined	51.2	47.9	0.9	= 868
Males	60.4	39.1	0.5	= 412
Females	42.8	55.9	1.3	= 456
25-34 Combined	44.1	54.8	1.1	= 1853
Males	52.6	45.8	1.5	= 851
Females	36.8	62.5	0.7	= 1002
35-44 Combined	40.6	58.1	1.2	= 1292
Males	51.7	47.8	0.5	= 623
Females	30.3	67.7	1.9	= 669
45-54 Combined	37.1	61.7	1.1	= 878
Males	45.7	53.1	1.2	= 431
Females	28.9	70.0	1.1	= 447
55-64 Combined	24.5	73.0	2.6	= 821
Males	33.7	63.5	2.8	= 389
Females	16.2	81.5	2.3	= 432
65-74 Combined	18.3	80.6	1.1	= 568
Males	27.2	71.3	1.5	= 268
Females	10.3	89.0	0.7	= 300
75-84 Combined	9.1	89.0	1.9	= 209
Males	15.6	80.0	4.4	= 90
Females	4.2	95.8	---	= 119
85 + Combined	3.8	96.2	---	= 26
Males	9.1	90.9	---	= 11
Females	----	100.0	---	= 15

J6.1

Q174. Do you smoke? (1)

		1977 - 1984		
	Yes 1	No 2	DK-NA 3	N's
All Ages	38.2	61.5	0.2	= 9029
18-24 Combined	41.4	58.6	---	= 1098
Males	44.0	56.0	---	= 489
Females	39.4	60.6	---	= 609
25-34 Combined	40.5	59.5	0.1	= 2259
Males	43.6	56.4	---	= 971
Females	38.1	61.7	0.2	= 1288
35-44 Combined	44.6	55.2	0.2	= 1667
Males	51.7	48.3	---	= 762
Females	38.6	61.1	0.3	= 905
45-54 Combined	44.2	55.6	0.2	= 1221
Males	53.0	47.0	---	= 551
Females	37.0	62.7	0.3	= 670
55-64 Combined	37.5	61.9	0.7	= 1228
Males	42.0	57.3	0.8	= 524
Females	34.1	65.3	0.6	= 704
65-74 Combined	26.4	73.4	0.2	= 1006
Males	35.6	63.9	0.5	= 402
Females	20.4	79.6	---	= 604
75-84 Combined	15.2	84.4	0.4	= 467
Males	31.6	67.1	1.3	= 152
Females	7.3	92.7	---	= 315
85 + Combined	4.8	95.2	---	= 83
Males	17.4	82.6	---	= 23
Females	----	100.0	---	= 60

(1) See appendix A

PERFORMANCE

The younger age groups perform better on the GSS word test than the old, most likely reflecting differences in amount of education rather than declining intelligence with age. Women perform slightly better than men.

The interviewers rate the respondents' understanding of the GSS questions. (Davis and Smith, 1986, p. 252) They have felt that younger groups understand the questions better than the older ones, but they apply the term "poor" to the understanding of the elderly only rarely. Moreover, over the term of the survey they have assigned the most favorable rating (good) to larger proportions of the elderly. The very large majority of the respondents have been rated as friendly or cooperative. Though only small percentages have been rated as "restless' during the interview, this rating increases with age.

K1.1

Q326K. Total number of correct words.

	1974 - 1984					
	None correct 1	1 - 4 correct 2	5 - 7 correct 3	8 -10 correct 4	NA 5	N's
All Ages	0.8	22.4	49.2	23.8	3.8	= 7457
18-24 Combined	0.8	29.7	53.4	14.4	1.7	= 996
Males	0.9	32.7	52.0	13.3	1.1	= 465
Females	0.8	27.1	54.6	15.3	2.3	= 531
25-34 Combined	0.4	19.6	55.2	23.1	1.6	= 1810
Males	---	22.7	52.8	23.0	1.6	= 758
Females	0.8	17.4	57.0	23.2	1.6	= 1052
35-44 Combined	0.6	18.4	49.8	29.4	1.8	= 1302
Males	0.9	20.1	48.0	28.8	2.3	= 577
Females	0.4	17.1	51.2	29.9	1.4	= 725
45-54 Combined	0.5	20.1	49.9	25.2	4.3	= 1010
Males	0.4	20.6	49.2	25.7	4.0	= 451
Females	0.5	19.7	50.4	24.9	4.5	= 559
55-64 Combined	1.3	20.0	47.2	27.3	4.1	= 1039
Males	0.5	20.6	46.5	27.7	4.8	= 441
Females	2.0	19.6	47.7	27.1	3.7	= 598
65-74 Combined	1.2	26.4	39.8	25.1	7.5	= 817
Males	1.4	29.8	38.0	23.5	7.4	= 366
Females	1.1	23.7	41.2	26.4	7.5	= 451
75-84 Combined	0.8	30.3	36.8	20.3	11.8	= 399
Males	0.7	34.0	34.7	18.1	12.5	= 144
Females	0.8	28.2	38.0	21.6	11.4	= 255
85 + Combined	1.2	33.3	31.0	7.1	27.4	= 84
Males	---	46.4	28.6	----	25.0	= 28
Females	1.8	26.8	32.1	10.7	28.6	= 56

K2.1

Q247. Was respondent's understanding of the questions: (1)

	1972 - 1986				
	Good 1	Fair 2	Poor 3	NA 4	N's
All Ages	78.4	17.2	3.1	1.1	=19614
18-24 Combined	82.1	15.0	1.8	1.1	= 2468
Males	81.7	15.7	1.6	0.9	= 1162
Females	82.4	14.4	1.9	1.3	= 1306
25-34 Combined	85.5	11.4	1.7	1.4	= 4696
Males	86.7	9.9	1.7	1.7	= 2070
Females	84.5	12.7	1.7	1.1	= 2626
35-44 Combined	83.9	12.7	1.9	1.5	= 3451
Males	84.0	12.5	2.2	1.4	= 1552
Females	83.9	12.8	1.7	1.6	= 1899
45-54 Combined	79.9	15.7	3.1	1.3	= 2877
Males	81.4	15.0	2.3	1.2	= 1330
Females	78.6	16.3	3.8	1.3	= 1547
55-64 Combined	74.6	20.0	4.1	1.3	= 2775
Males	78.2	17.3	3.5	1.0	= 1245
Females	71.7	22.2	4.6	1.5	= 1530
65-74 Combined	65.6	28.2	5.2	1.0	= 2181
Males	67.8	27.6	3.6	1.1	= 946
Females	64.0	28.7	6.4	0.9	= 1235
75-84 Combined	56.1	34.9	7.8	1.2	= 984
Males	61.3	30.8	7.1	0.8	= 354
Females	53.2	37.1	8.3	1.4	= 630
85 + Combined	44.5	37.9	16.5	1.1	= 182
Males	42.6	38.2	16.2	2.9	= 68
Females	45.6	37.7	16.7	---	= 114

(1) See appendix A

K3.1

Q246. In general, what was the respondent's attitude toward
        the interview?

		1973 - 1986			
	Friendly 1	Cooperative 2	Restless 3	Hostile 4	N's
All Ages	80.9	14.9	2.9	1.2	=18006
18-24 Combined	79.2	17.9	2.1	0.8	= 2268
Males	75.7	21.1	2.5	0.8	= 1049
Females	82.2	15.1	1.8	0.9	= 1219
25-34 Combined	83.4	13.4	2.0	1.2	= 4338
Males	82.0	14.7	1.7	1.5	= 1888
Females	84.5	12.4	2.2	0.9	= 2450
35-44 Combined	82.2	13.9	2.6	1.3	= 3211
Males	79.7	16.3	2.8	1.2	= 1444
Females	84.3	11.9	2.4	1.4	= 1767
45-54 Combined	81.1	14.6	2.9	1.5	= 2561
Males	79.6	15.3	3.7	1.4	= 1161
Females	82.3	14.0	2.1	1.6	= 1400
55-64 Combined	80.7	14.3	3.5	1.5	= 2523
Males	80.7	14.3	3.8	1.2	= 1119
Females	80.7	14.3	3.3	1.7	= 1404
65-74 Combined	78.6	16.0	4.1	1.3	= 2023
Males	77.4	17.7	3.7	1.3	= 872
Females	79.5	14.8	4.4	1.3	= 1151
75-84 Combined	75.0	18.5	5.4	1.1	= 909
Males	79.4	16.3	3.7	0.6	= 326
Females	72.6	19.7	6.3	1.4	= 583
85 + Combined	72.3	18.5	8.7	0.6	= 173
Males	73.0	17.5	9.5	---	= 63
Females	71.8	19.1	8.2	0.9	= 110

BIBLIOGRAPHY

Abercrombie, N., Hill, S., Turner, B. 1984 _Dictionary of Sociology. Hammondsworth, England: Penguin._

Davis, J. A., Smith, T. W. 1986 _General Social Survey, 1972-1986: Cumulative Codebook._ Chicago: National Opinion Research Center.

Holmes, T. H., Rahe, R. 1967 "The Social Readjustment Scale" _Journal of Psychosomatic Research_ 11:213-218.

Janda, K., Berry, J. M., Goldman, J. 1987 _The Challenge of Democracy._ Boston: Houghton Mifflin.

Merton, P. 1968 _Social Theory and Social Structure._ New York: Free Press.

        1987 "From a Sociologist's Notebooks." In Vol. 13 _Annual Review of Sociology._ pp. 1-28.

Robertson, I. 1981 _Sociology._ 2nd Edition. New York: Worth Publishers.

Schulz, R. 1985 In Birren, J. E., Schaie, K. W. _Handbook of the Psychology of Aging._ New York: Van Nostrand Reinhold Co.. Pp. 532-543.

U.S. Bureau of the Census. 1986 _Statistical Abstract of the United States, 1987,_ 107th Edition. Washington, D.C.: U.S. Government Printing Office.

Appendix A

Footnote 1. These tables include at least one category where there was a change of 5 percent or more between the 1972-76 period and the 1982-86 period. For example, table C2.11 shows a drop of 8 percent in the proportion of 18-24 year olds who report having seen an X-rated movie in 1982-86 as compared with 1972-76.

Sets of tables which show such changes from 1972-76, 1977-81, and 1982-86 can be obtained from the authors at cost at:

108 Main St. North

Bethlehem, Ct. 06751

APPENDIX B

Footnote 2 General Social Survey questions include several response choices. For some questions the response choices in this volume have been combined to simplify presentation of the data. In most cases the way they have been combined is obvious, but in other cases researchers may want to know which of the response choices were grouped together. The relevant information appears below.

IN ALL CASES CHOICES OF DK (DON'T KNOW) AND NA (NO ANSWER) ARE COMBINED INTO A SINGLE CHOICE

Variable Number in This Volume	Variable number in GSS Codebook	Mnemonic
A1.1	52	XNORCSIZ

    Choice 01 = 1
      New Name: City GT 250K
    Choice 02 = 2
      New Name: City 50K-250K
    Choice 3,4 = 3
      New Name: Suburb
    Choice 5,6 = 4
      New Name: City Section
    Choice 7 = 5
      New Name: City LT 50K
    Choice 8 = 6
      New Name: Town or Village
    Choice 9,10 = 7
      New Name: Rural

A1.3	51	REGION

    Choice 1,2 = 1
      New Name: Northeast
    Choice 3,4 = 2
      New Name: Central
    Choice 5,6 = 3
      New Name: Southeast
    Choice 7-9 = 4
      New Name: West

A2.1	22	REG16

    Same modification as in A1.3

A3.1   161A   SATCITY

    Choice 1,2 = 1
     New Name: A great deal
    Choice 3,4 = 2
     New Name: A fair amount
    Choice 5,6 = 3
     New Name: Some or a little
    Choice 7 = 4
     New Name: None

B2.1   24   FAMILY16

    Choice 1 = 1
     New Name: Own parents
    Choice 2,3 = 2
     New Name: One step-parent
    Choice 4 = 3
     New Name: Father only
    Choice 5 = 4
     New Name: Mother only
    Choice 6-8 = 5
     New Name: Other relative
    Choice 7 = 7
     New Name: Other

B2.11.1   161C   SATFAM

    Same modification as B2.1

C1.3   1   WRKSTAT

    Choice 3,4 = 3
     New Name: Temp(orarily) not working

D1.1.1   2A   OCC

    Choice 0,1 = 1
     New Name: W(hite) collar professional
    Choice 2 = 2
     New Name: W(hite) collar administrative
    Choice 3 = 3
     New Name: W(hite) collar other
    Choice 4-9 = 4
     New Name: Blue Collar

217

__D1.1.3__   __2F__   __INDUSTRY__

   Choice 0 = 1
     New Name: Primary industry (term refers to Agriculture,
     Forestry, and Fisheries)
   Choice 1-3 = 2
     New Name: Manufacturing
   Choice 4 = 3
     New Name: Transp/Communic
   Choice 5,6 = 4
     New Name: Trade (wholesale and retail, etc.)
   Choice 7,8 = 5
     New Name: Service (finance, insurance, real estate,
     business and repair srvices, entertainment)
   Choice 9 = 6
     New Name: Government

__D1.2.1__   __5A__   __SPOCC__
__D1.2.3__   __5C__   __SPIND__

   Same modification as D1.1.3

__D2.1.1__   __12__   __EDUC__

   Choice 00-08 = 1
     New Name: 8th grade or less
   Choice 9-11 = 2
     New Name: Some HS
   Choice 12 = 3
     New Name: HS grad
   Choice 13-15 = 4
     New Name: Some college
   Choice 16 = 5
     New Name: College grad
   Choice 17-20 = 6
     New Name: Post college

__D3.7__   __187A__   __SATFIN__

   Same modification as D2.1.1

D5.1.1   55   DWELLING

    Choice 01 = 1
      New Name: Trailer
    Choice 02 = 2
      New Name: Detached 1-fam. H.
    Choice 03,04 = 3
      New Name: 2 units
    Choice 05 = 4
      New Name: 3-4 fam. house
    Choice 06 = 5
      New Name: Row house
    Choice 07-09 = 6
      New Name: Apartment
    Choice 10 = 7
      New Name: Other

E1.2.1   28   PARBORN

    Choice 0 = 1
      New Name: Both in U.S.
    Choice 1,2 = 2
      New Name: One in U.S.
    Choice 3-7 = 3
      New Name: DK, one or both
    Choice 8 = 4
      New Name: Neither

E1.2.2   30   ETHNIC

    Choice 01 = 4
      New Name: Africa
    Choice 02, 06-15, 19, 21, 23-27, 32-36 = 3
      New Name: Europe
    Choice 03, 04, 30, 97 = 1
      New Name: North America
    Choice 17, 22, 28, 29 = 2
      New Name: South America
    Choice 05, 16, 20, 31 = 5
      New Name: Asia
    Choice 29, 37 = 6
      New Name: Other

E4.1   105   ATTEND

    Choice 0 = 1
      New Name: Never
    Choice 1,2 = 2
      New Name: Yearly
    Choice 3,4 = 3
      New Name: Monthly
    Choice 5,6 = 4
      New Name: Weekly
    Choice 7,8 = 5
      New Name: More than weekly

F2.1   61   PARTYID

    Choice 0-2 = 1
      New Name: Democrat
    Choice 3 = 2
      New Name: Independent
    Choice 4-6 = 3
      New Name: Republican
    Choice 7 = 4
      New Name: Other

F2.2   67   POLVIEWS

    Choice 1-3 = 1
      New Name: Liberal
    Choice 4 = 2
      New Name: Moderate
    Choice 5-7 = 3
      New Name: Conservative

G1.2   170A   SOCREL

    Choice 1,2 = 1
      New Name: At least weekly
    Choice 3,4 = 2
      New Name: Monthly
    Choice 5,6 = 3
      New Name: Yearly
    Choice 7 = 4
      New Name: Never

G1.3   170B   SOCFREND
G1.4   170C   SOCOMMUN
G1.5   170F   SOCSIBS

    Same modification as 170A

G2.1	161D	SATFRND
I3n	161E	SATHEALT
J1.1	161B	SATHOBBY

Same modification as A3.1

F1.8	65	VOTE80

With the one exception of the polls for the 1980 election GSS polls have closely approximated the national election results. For a technical paper on the reasons the 1980 poll gave the election to Carter rather than to Reagan, write Prof. Tom Smith at the National Opinion Research Center, University of Chicago.

225

```
Nixon, R.                                 POLITICAL

OCCUPATION                                LABOR FORCE
    Respondent          D1.1.1      82      STATUS, OCCUPA-
    Spouse              D1.2.1      85      TIONAL
                                            PRESTIGE,
                                            WORK

OCCUPATIONAL PRESTIGE                     also OCCUPATION
    Respondent          D1.1.2      83
    Spouse              D1.2.2      86

Old people                                AGED

Organizations                             MEMBERSHIPS

Party identification                      POLITICAL

PEOPLE                                    also ANOMIA
    Fair                G3.1.6      157
    Helpful             G3.1.5      156
    Trust               G3.1.7      158

POLITICAL
    Liberal/conser-
      vative            F2.2        135
    Preference          F2.1        134
    Vote 68             F1.1,       124
                        F1.2        125
    Vote 72             F1.3,       126
                        F1.4        127
    Vote 76             F1.5,       128
                        F1.6        129
    Vote 80             F1.7,       130
                        F1.8        131
    Vote 84             F1.9,       132
                        F1.10       133

Poor                                      INCOME

Pornography                               SEX

Press                                     NEWSPAPER

Prestige                                  OCCUPATIONAL
                                          PRESTIGE

Problems                                  UNITED STATES

RACE                    E5.1        118   also ETHNICITY

RADIO                   J4.1        203

REGION                                    also GEOGRAPHIC
    Age 16              A2.2        7       MOBILITY
    Time of interview   A1.3        5

Relatives                                 SIBLINGS, SOCIA-
                                          BILITY, TRAUMA
```

RELIGION
  Respondent
    Life after death   E4.3   117
    Preference   E3.1   113
    Raised in   E2.1   111
    Religious service
     attendance   E4.1   115
    Strength of   E4.2   116
  Spouse
    Preference   E3.2   114
    Raised in   E2.2   112

Republicans   POLITICAL

RESIDENCE   SATISFACTION,
  Age 16   A2.1   6   DWELLING
  At time of   A1.1,   3
   interview   A1.2   4
  Fear neighborhood H3.1   177
  Fear at home   H3.2   178

ROBBERY   H2.4   176   also BURGLARY

SATISFACTION (with)   also INCOME,
  City   A3.1   9   HAPPINESS
  Family   B2.11 31
  Friends   G2.1   151
  Finances   D3.7   97
  Health   I3.1   191
  Leisure   J1.1   200

Schools   EDUCATION

SEX
  Actual gender   C1.1   55
  Attitudes
   Extra-marital   C2.3   62
   Homosexual   C2.4   63
   Pornography   C2.5- 64
             C2.8, 67
             C2.10, 69
             C2.11 70
  Laws   C2.12 71
  Pre-marital   C2.2   61
  Teen-sex   C2.1   60
  X-rated movie   C2.9   68

SIBLINGS   B2.7   27

Sisters   SIBLINGS

SIZE OF PLACE OF
  INTERVIEW
  Actual   A1.2   4
  NORC place size A1.1.   3

SMOKING   J6.1   206

SOCIABILITY
  Friends   G1.4   149

228

UNITED STATES
    In world affairs   F5.1   140
    Problems:
     Big city   A4.2   11
     Black persons   E5.2   119
     Crime   H8.1   183
     Drugs   H8.2   184
     Education   D2.2   90
     Environment   A4.1   10
     Foreign aid   F4.2   138
     Health   I6.1   197
     Military   F4.1   137
     Welfare   D3.8   98

VETERAN STATUS   C1.5   59

VIOLENCE   also GUN
    Experienced
     being hit   H2.1   173
     Spanking   B2.10   30

VOCABULARY TEST   K1.1   208

Voting   POLITICAL

Wealth   INCOME

Welfare   INCOME, UNITED
                                  STATES

Wordsum   VOCABULARY TEST

WORK   LABOR FORCE
    Attitudes   D4.2   100
    Unemployment   C1.2   56